REVISED VERSION

Wind & STEEL

BY
LEE KOHN

WORKBOOK PRESS LLC
187 E Warm Springs Rd,
Suite B285 Las Vegas NV 89119 USA

Website: https://workbookpress.com/
Hotline: 1-888-818-4856
Email: admin@workbookpress.com

Ordering Information:
Quantity sales. Special discounts are available on quantity purchases by corporations, associations, and others. For details, contact the publisher at the address above.

ISBN-13:   978-1-963718-60-7 Paperback Version
              978-1-963718-62-1 Hardback Version
              978-1-963718-61-4 Digital Version

REV. DATE: 04/23/2024

Wind and *Steel*

Revised Version

By

Lee Kohn

From the original screenplay by: Lee Kohn

Date: 06/06/03

Lonemonkey56@gmail.com

Dedication and Acknowledgments

I dedicate this book to Danny Clancy; a very good friend of mine who spent many years teaching me to work on Harleys and never charged me a dime. One of the best Harley mechanics and friends a man could ask for. And last, but not least; I dedicate it to the American people who still ride the American machines, keeping our American heritage alive and the Harley Davidson people who keep that dream going.

*When this dedication was written, Danny Clancy was in good health, but sadly he passed away from cancer and he will be missed dearly and will not be replaced anytime soon. I will miss his friendship. **I would also like to thank Lance Boggan for the beautiful cover. The man is a creative genius. Also to my brother Dale who I miss every day.***

Prologue

June 2014

In the afternoon on a hot sweltering sunny day in Southern New Mexico, a young beautiful woman and her eight-year-old son sits on a wooden bench in the town square. In the center rest a large bronze statue of a man standing next to large bronze motorcycle mounted on a six-foot concrete pedestal.

She slowly turned to her son with great apprehension and said, "You're getting old enough now, and I think it's about time I tell you the story of your father. He was a very good-looking young man and very well built much like you. He was the love of my life and that's the very reason I never got married. He was the greatest horseman and motorcycle rider anyone had ever seen. Now this story isn't just about a great man, it's also about an awesome, big, maroon and chrome hunk of steel that went by the name 'Elvira.' She was a quite a lady. Beautiful, tender to the touch, yet strong and made from American iron. She and Josh are still spoken of in Sun Valley today and her story has been heard as far as Flagstaff and some say as far as Billings, Montana."

The young boy with his big brown eyes gleaning in the sunlight glances up at the statue and asks, "So is that my daddy?"

Jill, "It sure is."

"Wow, is Uncle Bubba in the story?"

"Yes, I couldn't even tell this story without mentioning fat Bubba. Now sit back sweetie and relax….it all started on a bright sunny morning like today."

But before she could start telling the story, Uncle Bubba shows up in his old pickup truck clunking as if ever lose bolt was about to fall out. The overweigh bubba with a long gray beard parks and steps from the truck with that big smile of his.

He walks over and takes a seat next to Josh Jr and looks over at Jill, "What's my two favorite people talking about?"

"I was just about to tell Josh the story behind that statue."

"Let me tell him about it sugar. Nobody can tell it better that me."

Josh Jr, "Uncle Bubba, I see rain clouds coming from across the mountains way over yonder."

"Yea, yea, yea, we won't get a drop of that rain, so stop interrupting old Bubba here and let me tell you about an adventure of a lifetime."

"But Uncle Bubba; you told me that if the clouds came from that way and the wind blew over the mountains that way, that, that meant…"

The young lad is interrupted again by Bubba as he scans the far distance mountain range to the southwest, "I know what I said. You misunderstood me. It just looks that way little buddy, but you see, your old Uncle Bubba here is a bit of a weather expert and that storm's gonna pass to the north of us. Now let me tell you this story. Now where was I? You made me lose my place. Let me see here…Oh yeah, living on a ranch just south of Sun Valley, was a young, strong and a good-looking man much like your Uncle Bubba who…"

Jill laughs, "You tell him Bubba, I'm gonna go home and start supper. Drop him off when your through, I'll save you, Martha and Josh some chicken and a big piece of apple pie."

Bubba, "Will do sweetie. He turns to Josh Jr, "Again where was I? Oh yea it all started many years before you were born.….

July 1990

A man in his early seventies with long, brown, stringy hair and a slight bend in his back from years of hard work, stood casually on the front porch of his old ranch house having a very unfriendly conversation with a short, heavy-set man known as Walter McNally.

Walter throws his haft smoked cigar on the old, worn, wooden porch planks and with a frustrated expression on his face, "Look you old Billy goat, I'm offering you twice what this land is worth. Take the money and get out while you can."

"I've said it a thousand times Walter, it's not for sale."

"You stubborn old bastard. I need that access to those damn mountains."

"What for?"

"I have my own reasons."

"You know that the gold in those mountains has been fished out for over a hundred years."

"There are some things worth more than gold."

"You own the entire mountain range for two miles. That's not counting all the land around it. My few hundred acres won't make a difference. You have Bertha's Pass."

"That's over ten miles from here and it's snowed in six months of the year, besides I'll have to gain permission from the feds to go through that damn God forsaken Indian land. It would take years to get the paperwork through all that government red tape. If you won't sale your ranch to me at least let me buy a right-of-way into the foothills."

"I have a lot of horses on that prime grazing land and I'm not fencing it off so you can wreck it with heavy equipment. During the summer my horses will be without water if you cut me off from Deer Lake."

"Okay Willie, if you won't sale, I'll take it from you." McNally angrily turns and walks to his white Ford F-350, gives the old man another menacing glance and then rips out down the long driveway kicking up dust and rock in all directions.

Minutes later Josh walks from the barn wearing new denim jeans and a nice brown long sleeve shirt covered with a denim jacket. He steps up on the porch and takes a seat next to Willie on the old wooden swing.

"Boy, you sure pissed him off this time."

"He'll get over it. You sure are dressed to kill."

"I bought these new jeans at lunch. I wanna look good for Susan. Tonight's the night I'm gonna pop the question."

"What might that be, hmmm, 'can I have a BJ?'"

"No, we're past that already. I'm gonna ask her to marry me."

"Why buy the cow, when you're getting the milk for free?"

"I'm in love with that cow. I wanna settle down and build my own horse ranch."

"Are you taking fat Bubba out with ya?"

"It's kind of a double date. We're gonna take the girls up to Deer Lake and then Susan and I are going to get off to ourselves and then I'm gonna pop the question."

"Who's Bubba taking?"

"Susan's cousin, Charlotte."

"Now that's one ugly girl. The livestock runs away when she shows up."

"Bubba doesn't care. He's just grateful he's not staying home with a tube of KY jelly."

"Didn't his mama catch him out back of the station doing a loaf of bread a week ago?"

"That's not the first time he's been caught humping food. That boy can wreak a melon patch. Enough about all that…I need to borrow that jug of moonshine you have stashed in the grain bin."

"Sure, are you planning on staying out late?"

"Yeah…But I'll still be ready for work at sunrise."

"I'm not worried about that; I just feel funny about being alone tonight. My hip is acting up again and that means there's trouble on the horizon."

"I'll try to cut it short." Josh leans toward Willie, "How do I smell?"

"Like one of Mabel's whores."

"You're kidding me? This is a man's cologne. I paid almost ten dollars for it at Lou's Grab a Bag. It covers the odor of horse shit pretty good."

"Why are you asking me, I'm not the one you're gonna propose too anyway."

"Gotta go old man. Make sure you lockup before turning in."

"I haven't locked my doors in thirty years."

"I know that, but I feel better telling you to do it."

"Before you go, I wanna show you something." Willie stands and walks inside then returns a few seconds later carrying a large cowboy boot box.

"Wow! New boots I could use a new pair."

"It's not boots."

"Then what may it be old man, please do tell?"

"Something I've been saving for a long time." He opens the box and to Josh's surprise it's full of money, a pistol and a piece of paper.

"Holy cow! You rob a bank? And why is your old 45 Colt pistol in here?"

"I've been putting a little cash back every time I sale a horse. It's yours. It will buy that Harley you always wanted. I wanted you to have my old pistol. Hell, you carry it more than I ever did."

"I can't take that, it's your retirement money."

"I don't have much need for money anymore, and I know how much you want that motor scooter."

"I can't, you…"

Willie interrupts, "Just take it and here's something else." He takes a folded piece of paper from under the money and gun and unfolds it.

Josh asks, "What's that?"

"It's the deed to this ranch. I want you to sign at the bottom on the dotted line so if anything happens to me the ranch will be yours."

"Don't you have kin somewhere who you can leave it to?"

"I have a rich brother in New York, but I would rather see that asshole McNally have it then let him get his greedy hands on it. No, I want you to have it. You have always been closer than a son to me."

"Nothing's gonna happen to you, old man, not as long as I'm still breathing."

"Look Josh; I want you to take this box and hide it up in the hayloft, in that footlocker of yours for safe keeping."

Josh reluctantly takes the box from Willie's hand, "I'll put it in the barn and lock it up for you. Now, you gonna let me borrow the pickup or not?"

Willie reaches in his pocket and takes out a set of keys, "You be careful and don't get all tanked up on that moonshine. I wouldn't have a reason to live if you had a wreck and got seriously hurt."

"I'll be careful." Josh pats him on the shoulder and starts for the barn.

Willie yells out across the yard, "Little Bit called here looking for you!"

He stops, turns and yells back, "You didn't tell her anything did ya!!?"

"Tell her what? I just found out myself not more than five minutes ago!"

"Forget it; if she calls back, tell her I'm with Bubba on a hunting trip!"

"She's just gonna be on horseback in those mountains looking for you!"

"Tell her we went east into the foothills. That should keep her busy for a while!" He disappears into the barn. A few minutes later, he leaves in the old pickup as Willie stares off into the distance watching the taillights of his truck disappear into the night.

Three hours later, Willie turns the TV off and walks to the kitchen to fix himself a warm glass of milk and then walks out on the back porch. Suddenly two dark shadowy figures, one tall and the other short, appear in the night. Willie is startled and yells out, "Who goes there!!?"

In a deep voice one answers, "You should have sold the ranch Willie."

"Ya'll some of Walter's boys?"

"Never mind that; I need you to sign this deed over to Walter."

"Where did you get that?"

"The same place we got this gun and lots of money. Thank you for that. Now sign it over to Walter."

"You two step in the light; I wanna see your faces."

The figures step forward into the light that shines through the kitchen window. Willie steps back, "What the hell!?"

"You gonna sign it or do we have to kill you right here?"

"I'll give you two nothing."

"Have it your way old man." The sound of a gun being cocked then a muzzle flash brightens up the back porch. The loud gunshot sound echoes off the walls of the canyons scattered near the base of the mountains as the blast cuts through the cool night air.....

A month later in a large courtroom, "The prosecutor gives his last statement to the jury, "Josh Harley James fingerprints were found on the gun and the money and the deed to the ranch was the motive."

Two hours later the jury returns and takes their seat. The Judge, "Has the jury reached a decision?"

The jury foreman stands, "Yes your honor, we find the defendant guilty of 1st murder."

An hour later the Judge, "Will the defendant please rise. Joshua Harley James, you have been found guilty by your peers and you are here by sentence to twenty years in the state of New Mexico Penitentiary for murder in the first degree. You will be up for parole in five years. This court is no longer in session."

TABLE OF CONTENTS

CHAPTER 1

July of 2006, New Mexico State Penitentiary Corrections Facility, 58 miles west of Albuquerque.

Josh is out in the yard pumping iron when a prison guard walks over, "Hey Josh, they're ready to see you now."

"Thanks Rufus, can I shower first?"

"No problem, I wouldn't take more than ten. You know how those assholes are about us bringing you late."

"Thanks, I appreciate that."

The sound of shoes tapping out a steady rhythm on the freshly waxed floors can be heard echoing throughout the hallways as three men, two in uniform and one in orange prison coveralls, slowly make their way down several deserted corridors. The three cast shadows on the cold gray floors as they walk under the glowing fluorescent lights. The man in the center sporting a three-inch scar under his right eye is none other than Josh. Imagine a muscular built, handsome man of 38 standing 6 feet 220lbs, sporting an unassuming smile. As they turn another corner, the guard on the left glances over with genuine kindness, "I sure hope it goes through this time Josh. Lord knows you deserve it more than anyone."

Josh remarks in a soft voice, "Let's not count those chicks before the eggs hatch gentlemen, if history has any say so, you'll still be losing at cards every Saturday night."

Carl laughs, "Yeah, I guess you're right, but if it goes through, I'll be stuck losing to Ernie here."

The guard on the right frowns, "Face it Carl, when it comes to poker, you suck." He turns to Josh, "Still, if things do go your way, it won't be the same without you. Man...just can't imagine this place without you."

They stroll past a small glass booth occupied by another guard casually reading a newspaper. They stop and give him a thumbs-up. He strikes a large red knob on the wall to open a set of metal doors and yells, "Good luck Josh!" The three men slowly, but surely continue their journey as they make a turn down yet another long hallway. The strong odor of lemon disinfectant fills the air and is so overpowering it can clear a man's sinuses out.

Ernie glances past Josh and asks Carl, "Why in the hell does the parole boardroom have to be so damn far from the holding cells? The man who designed this place must have been a village idiot."

Carl, jokingly responds, "You say that every time. I think it's to keep us guys on A-block from getting fat like the boys on C-block."

"We don't need exercise; the food around here runs through a man's insides like shit through a goose; nothing personal Josh."

Josh gives him a serious look, "It's not my cooking Ernie; it's the lard I have to use."

They finally come to a stop in front of a pair of large double oak doors with fancy polished brass door handles. Josh, taking a few steps forward, slowly turns to Carl and Ernie and asks, "Well guys, how do I look? You think my scar will scare the hell out of 'em?"

Carl turns to Ernie, "What do you think Ernie?"

"I think it gives him character."

"I agree. No! Wait a minute, something's missing." Ernie wets his index finger and sticks it in Josh's ear. Carl laughs as Josh slaps his hand. Carl with a grin, "He does now. Hell, any better and I would bypass the entire parole process and let him out the front gate myself."

Ernie snaps back, "Too far to walk; just give him the keys so he can let himself out."

Josh holds his hand out to shake Carl's hand and with a grin, "You boys wish me luck."

Carl smiles back. "Good luck Josh and don't forget to give them that pretty-boy smile of yours."

Ernie reaches out and shakes Josh's hand, "Yeah, me too and I have a good feeling this time."

"Why is that?" Josh asks as he tilts his head in puzzlement.

Ernie lets out a chuckle, "There are three women and two men on that board this time and a sharp looking dude like you will dazzle the shit out of 'em. Crap, those women will think Rudolph Valentino on steroids has been resurrected. Just flex your muscles every chance you get."

Carl spits in his hand and rubs Josh's head, "I can't let you just walk in there with a cowlick sticking up there like a horn growing out of the back of your head."

Josh lightly punches Carl in the mid-section, gives a wink, then opens the door and nervously enters the room. There sitting across the room at a long rectangle table in front of a large plate-glass window is three women and two men just as Ernie had said there would be. The sunlight from the large window streaks across the floor of a room that is void of all other furniture giving it the appearance of a very large cellblock. There are two guards standing against the walls opposite each other. One gives Josh a smile and a nod. Josh hesitates then continued to make the short journey across the hardwood floors to the far side of the room. The short walk felt like a mile, but he finally finds himself standing next to a lonely chair on the opposite side of the table across from the five board members, who are staring at him as if he were naked.

Mr. Riley, a thin man in his late fifties with premature gray hair and dark rim glasses glances at Josh's hands and then his feet with a menacing stare, then turns to the guard on the right, "You're late, why is this man not in handcuffs or shackles?"

The guard, with a puzzled look, "This is Josh; he doesn't need any."

Mr. Riley, with an angry glare, "Rules and regulations of the New Mexico Prison Commission specifically states all prisoners must be handcuffed and shackled upon leaving their cellblock regardless of who they are. We go over this every time his hearing comes up."

Mr. Stinson, a potbellied man in his early forties sitting to the right of Mr. Riley says, "The guard is right, he doesn't need to be shackled. He works in the kitchen and is one of the most well-mannered trustees we have here."

Mr. Riley, with a hostile look on his face, stands, grits his teeth and yells for another guard. "I don't care where he works; will someone bring the shackles and handcuffs!!" He then turns and stares severely at Josh but directs his statement to the board. "He is still a prisoner of the State of New Mexico and will be treated as such, until we vote otherwise, which I doubt will ever happen as long as I'm on this panel. I never even heard of a man serving time for murder working as a trustee and I don't approve of it." Carl steps inside the door as Mr. Riley yells out again across the room, "This prisoner has no handcuffs or shackles!"

Carl gives him a funny look as if he didn't understand and yells back across the room, "They've never had to put handcuffs or shackles on Josh!"

Riley yells again, "Is there any reason why no one can hear the words I'm saying!?"

Carl shakes his head, "It was the warden's idea to remove the shackles and handcuffs in the first place and he makes the rules here."

Riley fires back, "I'm also in charge of finances and that includes payroll, so I say put 'em on this prisoner, now!"

Josh smiles and says in a soft voice, "You can have them put handcuffs and shackles on me if you want. I don't mind, but you'll never get anyplace in life if you yell at everyone in that tone of voice. You ever heard the saying, 'you can always get more with honey than you can with shit'?"

One of the females lets out a short chuckle. Mr. Riley quickly snaps his head around toward Josh and with an intense evil glare, "I don't need any lessons in manners from a cold-blooded killer."

Josh smiles, "I never killed anyone in my life and yes, you could use a few lessons in kindness. I will pray for you."

Riley, with his face turning from a light blush red to a deep dark shade of purple says, "That brings up another matter; you've never admitted to the crime of murder in the first degree; we shouldn't even be having this conversation." He turns back to Carl, "Remove this prisoner."

Carl hesitates and then strolls over to Josh, "Let's go, seems like you're up against a stacked deck anyway."

Mr. Stinson interrupts the commotion, "There are four other members on this Board of Paroles who have a say, and we would like to finish this hearing if Mr. Riley here will be so kind as to shut his overbearing piehole and sit down."

Mr. Riley, burning with anger, takes his seat at last. Mr. Stinson turns to Josh, "Mr. James, please take a seat, we would like to ask you some questions."

Josh glances at Carl and then takes a seat. The kind gentleman gives him a gentle smile, "I was here at your last hearing, but in case you don't remember me, I'm Mr. Edward Stinson. May I call you Josh?"

Josh nods, "Yes sir, I do remember you and please excuse me for speaking without permission, but rudeness has always clouded my better judgment."

Mr. Stinson glances down at the paperwork and then back at him. "Josh, it says here that you've worked in the kitchen for the past few years and the warden says you're a model inmate. How's the treatment for your cancer going?"

Josh responds, "Yes sir, I have and that's very nice of Mike to say those things about me. I stop taking the treatments a year ago."

Mr. Stinson, "Why would you do that Josh?"

"The prison doctor informed me that I only had a year maybe less before I die with or without it."

Mr. Riley interrupts, "You will address the warden as warden and not by his first name."

Mr. Stinson quickly turns and gives Mr. Riley a daunting frown, "If you're through interrupting me, I would like to hear the man out." He turns to Josh, "Please continue."

Josh glances up at the large window and continues, "I had a rocky start at first as you can see by the scar on my cheek, but the warden has been very kind to me over the past few years and I've adapted well to my life here."

The beautiful, petite brunette sitting to the far left gives Josh a smile, "You have a girlfriend waiting for you on the outside, Josh?"

Mr. Riley gives her a look, "What the hell does that have to do with this hearing?"

The woman gives him an angry stare and fires back, "I wasn't asking for myself, I wanted to know something about his future plans before we vote you dirty-minded ornery old hack."

"No, I do not; all I have is my Mama." Josh replies, after being satisfied with the way she had scolded Mr. Riley for insinuating alternative motives for her asking the question.

Mr. Stinson leans back in the creaky leather chair, "You've served sixteen years of a twenty-year sentence, do you think you're ready for the outside world?"

Josh, staring out the window behind the group of well-dressed people takes in the rocky mountain range that the morning haze had turned a purplish gray and answers, "Yes sir I do."

Mr. Stinson then asks, "What about your inoperable brain tumor? Even if you have decided to stop the treatments, you might change your mind when it gets worst. You do know that once you leave this institution, the State of New Mexico will no longer be responsible for the expensive treatments and medicine?"

Josh glances out the window again and takes another look at the far-reaching mountain range and with a big smile replies, "If I die after one day out there: it's better than living another year in here. I would still like to spend my remaining time taking care of my mama and I sure can't do that from inside these prison walls."

Mr. Riley, noticing Josh's keen interest in something outside the window asks, "Mr. James, is there something outside that window that keeps drawing your attention from this board? You seem a little distracted at the questions we're asking you."

"Yes, sir there is," Josh replies. "I don't get to see the mountains from my cellblock or from the exercise yard. They're the most beautiful sight to the human eyes. Don't you agree?"

Mr. Riley snaps back, "It's just giant piles of dirt to me and if it's left up to my vote, you'll only be able to view them from this boardroom once a year."

An hour later, back in his small, cold, damp cell, Josh lies on his worn and stain cot staring up at the concrete ceiling with its cracked paint, day-dreaming of the blue and amber-colored mountains as the sun rises and strikes the east face of the Rockies. He then turns his attention to a small picture taped to the wall next to the bunk of him sitting on the leather seat of an old black 65 Pan-Head Harley Davidson. He and his father had put it together from scattered parts they'd collected over a long period of time.

Of course, his contribution to the assembling process was more in the line of watching and handing his father tools from time to time. Being only four, his father had to stand behind the bike and prop him up for the photograph. It's been over twenty-eight years since his father was struck down by a group of drunken teenagers. It was the worst rainstorm in years when the old Harley motorcycle he was riding stalled in the middle of a slick, dark and lonely highway. The old distributor models didn't take too well to moisture. He was just a few feet from being safely off the road, but it's not easy to push eight hundred pounds of American steel off the highway on slippery asphalt and in a blinding, wind driven downpour.

Josh is so caught up in his trip down memory lane that he didn't hear Carl calling out his name at first. Carl yells again, "Josh; the warden wants to see you!"

Josh sits up and wipes his eyes, "That was quick, I guess the verdict's in."

Carl frowns, "Yeah, they didn't take very long. I guess that arrogant bastard Riley got his way again. Jackass had the gall to threaten us with our payroll. Nothing from nothing is still nothing."

Josh stands with the opening of the cell door, places his hand on Carl's shoulder and with a grin, "Don't get so angry; I can think of worse things than spending what's left of my life with my friends in here. I still would have like to spend some time with my Mama."

Josh hesitates at the dark mahogany door of the warden's office and then lightly taps several times. He hears a loud voice from the opposite side, "Come in!"

Josh steps through the door and closes it behind him. The warden, with a rough textured face, full head of thick brown hair with a touch of gray and wearing a white shirt and black tie just sat there with a depressed look in his eyes that were starting to tear up.

"Come and have a seat Josh."

Josh slides the heavy wooden chair out as the warden continues by asking, "How're the headaches?"

"Some days they go easy on me and some days they don't."

"How regular are the blackouts?"

"I had one yesterday morning, but as usual I got through it." Josh could tell that there was something else eating at the warden. He had never seen him this depressed. "They have rejected my parole many times over the last sixteen years Mike, but I've never seen you take the news this hard before."

Mike slowly tilts his head up and responds, "Your parole went through Josh."

Josh, with a stunned and blank expression on his face, "You're kidding me?"

Mike slides a sheet of paper across the desk in front of him. "You should have seen ole man Riley's face. The vote was four to one in your favor. He was thoroughly pissed and stomped from the room like a seven-year-old that had his G.I. Joe taken from him. I think he may even go home and shoot himself in the head. No matter: the sun will rise tomorrow either way."

Josh takes the piece of paper in hand, reads it and with a smile on his face, "I know you like my company for my cooking and poker skills, but I haven't been so valuable that the news wouldn't bring a smile to your face."

Mike stands and walks over to the liquor cabinet as Josh follows with his eyes, trying to figure out why the sad look on the well-dressed man's face. He takes two glasses from a liquor cabinet and pours from an old bottle of scotch, filling them both to the top, then hands one to Josh and downs the other. Josh takes a sip of his drink as Mike sits back down, opens a small rosewood humidor and takes out two large Dominican stogies before handing one to him.

Josh smiles, "Looks can be misleading. You must be a little happy for me since you just poured me a glass of twenty-five-year-old Scotch whiskey and gave me a twenty-dollar cigar."

Mike holds out a chrome lighter, lights Josh's cigar then his own, leans back in the chair and rubs the inside corners of his eyes with his index and thumb, "I'm very happy for you. I can't think of anyone in this institution who deserves it more."

Josh, still not understanding Mike's attitude, "The expression on your face looks like your dog took a dump in your oatmeal this morning. Why the long face; wife treating you bad?"

Mike leans forward, hesitates for a second and then answers, "Yes she still treats me bad from time to time, but she has her good side." He hesitates for a second, "I don't quite know how to say this." He pours his empty glass full again and downs the whole glass with one big swig, takes a deep breath and continues in a broken voice, "Your mother passed away this morning. I couldn't get the message to you because of your parole hearing, and I thought it would be best if I was the one that gave you the news."

Josh's cigar falls from his mouth and hits the floor as he just sat there with a blank, silent expression on his face. The shocking and unexpected news caused his eyes to become glassy, and a tear ran down his cheek across his scar as the message cut his heart to the core. With a lump in his throat and staggered words he asks, "Did you just say my Mama's … gone?"

Mike stands, walks around the desk and places his hand on Josh's shoulder, "She's had pancreatic cancer for some time now. She never even tried to get treatment. As a matter of fact, she never went back to the doctor after receiving word."

Josh, barely able to hold his emotions in, repeats, "My Mama's gone?"

Mike gets choked up, "There's not a soul in this institution that's not feeling your pain. Even the other incarcerated are taking it hard."

Josh glances up with his glassy eyes and swallows before saying, "She never told me she had cancer. I mean I knew she had lost some weight each time she came to visit, but she never gave me a hint of being sick. I thought it was because of her nerves."

Mike shakes his head, "She must have wanted to spare you the worry. The burial is tomorrow at 9 a.m. If I rush up the paperwork, you can make the afternoon bus to Albuquerque. Your mother's padre should be at the grave site when you get there."

Josh turns to him and with a stuttering of words says, "I…I'm alone now…I have nobody left."

"I'm really sorry; even my wife and kids took the news hard."

Josh tries to swallow, takes a deep breath, stands and walks to the window, "I have nowhere to go. My Mama was my last living relative." He slowly turns to Mike and asks, "Why can't I stay here? I have no reason to leave now."

Mike reluctantly shakes his head back and forth, "I wish you could," and with a grunt continues, "Uh, it's a little ironic, you've been hoping for sixteen years to get out of here and now you wanna stay. I'm sorry, but there's just no way; you're a free man and thanks to Mr. Stinson there's only a short probation. Why don't you come and stay with me and my family? I'll pay you to cook and I have a few chores you can help me with. I'm raising a little beef now. I know for a fact you know your way around livestock, and no one can handle a horse like you can."

Josh stands straight, sliding the chair back with his calves of his legs, "I'm not going to be a burden to anyone Mike. When I go, I want to go fast and on my own terms. I'll be alright."

"You can still live in your Mama's home."

"My Mama lost her place years ago. She stayed in a rest home."

Mike stands and walks over to a file cabinet and takes out a small brown fluff out paper bag. He hands it to Josh and with a smile, "This is from all the guards on A, B and C block. It's not much, but it will last a few months."

He takes the bag and glances inside, finding a few plastic containers of pain medicine. He gives the sad warden a look, "This stuff must have cost a fortune."

"Not really, it came up missing from the pharmacy this morning." With a reserved grin, he continues, "Some bastards stole it. I'm running a full investigation though. You can't just leave shit like that lying around a prison full of convicts and drug addicts."

"Investigation?"

"You don't really think for one minute that there's not going to be an investigation with that much medicine missing, do ya? I have my best man on it, old blind Travis."

They both let out a chuckle when Josh walks back over to the desk, "Thanks; thanks for everything. Tell the boys I'm gonna miss 'em and I'll miss you and your family more than any."

"Feel free to come visit from time to time." Mike reaches out for a handshake, "I'm gonna miss you too Josh. You be careful out there; things have changed over the last sixteen years and if you ever need anything, anything at all, just give me a call."

Josh shakes his hand, "You know I will." He starts to walk off when suddenly he stops and turns, "When my time comes, will you make the funeral arrangements and have me buried next to my mother and father?"

Mike, with a tear running down his face, takes another big drink and a hard swallow before saying, "It will be an honor."

Josh, with a grin, "I want you, Carl, Ernie, Scott, Raven, Travis and Jim to be my pallbearers. Nothing would make me feel better than knowing one of you boys got a hernia carrying me. Make sure Travis is in the center."

Mike chugs down the last swallow of whiskey from the glass, "A thousand wild horses couldn't keep us away. Maybe it won't come to that. They're making new advances in medicine every day. Now get out of here before you turn me into a sobbing, raging alcoholic and don't forget to stop by the cafeteria; all the boys are having a going away party for you… wait a minute, that didn't come out right."

Josh shakes his head, "I know what you meant; you take care of yourself and give my regards to your wife and kids." With that he walks out the door......

CHAPTER 2

A short, gray-haired padre in his late sixties, dressed in black, sporting a white collar opens a black leather covered bible, hesitates for a few seconds and then slowly closes it, and gently placing it under his armpit. He slowly turns to Josh who is just standing there with a solemn look on his face, and watches as he stares with cold emptiness in his eyes down at the wooden stained colored casket lying across the dark green lowering straps. The padre then slowly turns back facing the grave and in a soft voice says a few brief words of comfort, making the sign of the cross over the casket. Grief is such a personal journey and he thought about that very thing as he was trying to decide just what words to say for Josh. He is thoughtful and allows him to stand there in silence for a few more minutes. Anyone who has ever lost a close relative always seems to go through those various stages of shock, denial, depression and then finally acceptance. He knew for sure what was running through Josh's mind at this very moment. Not even a padre can ease the pain of someone grieving over the mother who brought him into this world. He can pray that God will be merciful and allow his grief to be a brief experience.

He says to Josh, "Let's pray now. 'Lord God our Father in Heaven, we are gathered here to pay our last respects and say our good-byes to a wonderful, God-fearing, loving woman, and a caring mother. She endured a great deal of pain, physically and emotionally, over the last few years and now that pain is gone, and she is at rest with our Lord Jesus Christ. She leaves behind a strong, fine, devoted son to carry on her memory. May she rest in peace forever and forever, Amen'." The old man walks around the open grave, stops just behind Josh and gently places his hand on his shoulder. The old padre and Josh stood alone as two grave diggers watched at a distance waiting to lower the casket and then shovel from the red dirt that's piled up next to the grave. Josh leans over and places a small potted cactus rose with a white bloom at the head of the grave. Still staring at the casket containing his last known relative, he says, "She loved those cactus roses."

The padre, feeling Josh's agony, "I'll see to it that she gets a marker and I'll make sure the cactus rose is planted between her and your father. There wasn't a day passed by, that your name didn't flow from between her lips. She just sat in that rest home at the same table every day thinking of you; sometimes staring out a window for hours on end."

They both walk over to an old green wooden bench and take a seat. The padre looks out across the rows and rows of headstones, "It seems like only yesterday we buried your father. They loved each other very much and now they're together after all these years. You were only eleven then. She never got over his death and when they sent you off, well that was more than she could bear. She was a woman aged beyond her years. She wore that weathered look like a badge of honor."

Josh rubs his bloodshot eyes from lack of sleep and says, "They were good parents and made sure I had everything I needed. I was all my Mama had after dad was killed. I should have never moved in with Willie. She made out like it was her idea."

The padre places a hand on Josh's forearm and after taking in a deep breath of fresh air, "I told your father that motorcycle was a bad idea, he was hardheaded when it came to that bike, like someone else I won't mention."

"There's nothing wrong with motorcycles. Lots of people get killed in automobile accidents every day."

"Yeah, but for some reason, motorcycles and booze go together like a bottle of nitro and a pogo stick, a very lethal combination indeed."

"What are you talking about? My father never took a drink, and you know that."

"I wasn't talking about your father; I was talking about the teenagers. I sure miss your father a lot and I'm going to miss your mother even more. She was kneeling at that altar seven days a week praying and hoping they would find out the truth and set you free."

Josh scans the green topped out trees around the cemetery as the warm, dry air coming from the desert whipped them about, causing them to sway from side to side. They stood over the cemetery like centurions guarding the numerous grey and dull white headstones.

Josh places his hand on the padre knee and smiles, "You know something Padre, we sometimes take life for granted, thinking it will go on forever and ever. People come and go from this planet, but the trees keep growing, the clouds still float across the sky like big fluffy cotton balls, the rains fall when it wants to and out here the wind seems like it blows endlessly. I think when my time comes and I enter the gates of Heaven, I'll miss the odor the wind carries from the desert most of all."

"What odor is that?"

"The odor of moisture in the air, as it makes its way across the desert just before a big rainstorm."

"What makes you think heaven has no trees, rain, and wind to carry sweet odors?"

"I have no idea. What do you think Heaven is like?"

"Everybody has their own idea of what Heaven is like. I do know from the good book that the roads are paved with gold and there's a mansion for everyone who enters His kingdom."

Josh lets out a snicker, "I'll settle for a little cabin in the corner of a pecan orchard, where I can sit on the porch with my mama and daddy and all my friends. Just sitting there watching the birds fly overhead and the deer running in the fields and in the distant, a beautiful mountain range reaching for an endless blue sky."

The Padre stands and stretches his arms over his shoulders, "I'm like you; I'll take it any way the Lord will give it to me. Maybe when I get there, I can come over and sit on that porch with you and your folks." He starts to walk off when he suddenly stops, and remembers as he turns back to Josh, "Oh yes, your mother left something for you; it's in my car." He walks toward the vehicle as Josh follows. He reaches through an open window on the passenger's side and takes out a folded, black leather jacket and a thick leather pouch lying on the seat, hands it to him and says, "This is all she had, and it was her last order of business."

Josh asks, "What is it?"

The padre lightly rakes his hand across Josh's back and says as he walks around to the driver's side, "It's your father's old motorcycle jacket; in the pocket is his aviator glasses and a small logo plate from his old bike. It was all that was left of the thing after the collision. Your mama wanted you to have them."

"What's in the pouch?"

"It's a check for thirty thousand dollars and some old photographs. It was what she was saving for you when you got out. It was all that was left over from your father's life insurance. I can give you a ride to the First National Bank of Albuquerque if you want."

Feeling a little shocked and somber, Josh replies, "Thanks, but I think I'll hang around here for a little while. I have some things I wanna say to my folks."

The padre nods, "The bank is on Seventh Ave just off the Coronado Freeway. Good luck and whatever you do son, don't go back to Sun Valley."

As Josh places the pouch inside the leather jacket, "Why not?"

The padre answers in a loud voice before taking a seat in the car, "Because it's not there anymore and what is there is a whole pack of trouble, and you need to stay as far away from it as possible!"

CHAPTER 3

Josh steps off the bus late into the evening only to find a city that had doubled in size since he had last seen it. Traffic is racing in all different directions as if they were running some kind of European car race. He slowly strolls down the sidewalk toward the center of town with duffle bag in hand taking in all the views and many changes that have occurred over the last sixteen years. Now he asked himself, 'where to sleep'? Not being able to cash his mother's check until nine tomorrow will mean sleeping on a park bench or under a nice shade tree.

It's 8:30 a.m. now as Josh lies on an old green park bench covered with the jacket, dreaming of *riding a large Harley down a lonely highway when suddenly he feels the rain pounding on his face like wind kicking up sand on a Florida beach and lightning bolts streaking from the black clouds in every direction. He slows to a stop on the center line when out of nowhere he sees two blinding headlights approaching. Suddenly the bike stalls. He attempts to start it repeatedly, but it won't hit a lick. Closer and closer the lights overtake him, but just before they strike, he feels a stabbing pain to the ribcage.* He slowly opens one eye then the other only to discover a cool morning breeze rolling across his face and the morning sun peeking through the leaves of a large oak. There standing in front of him is a young police officer in his late twenties holding a nightstick in hand.

Then a voice is heard, "Sit up dude; I wanna see some ID."

Josh wipes his eyes with the palm of his hands, "It's in my duffle bag."

"Well take one hand and one hand only and slowly take it out."

Josh takes his right hand, eases the zipper open and slowly reaches in and takes out a small clear plastic sandwich bag with three pieces of ID inside; a Social Security card, a sixteen-year-old, expired driver's licenses and the other a New Mexico Corrections card given to him at prison check out. The officer places the nightstick under his left armpit and reads the cards.

"These licenses are sixteen years old."

"Yes sir. I'm hoping to renew them today."

"I see you're just out of prison. What were you in for?"

"Murder first."

The officer leans over and says in a low voice, "Well Joshua Harley James, we don't allow sleeping in the park."

"I'm sorry officer; I was just trying to find a place to nap until the bank opens."

"You have business at a bank?"

"Yes sir. I have a check that needs cashing."

"Which bank?"

"The First Bank of Albuquerque."

"Two blocks north of here. Where are you heading from there?"

"Sun Valley."

"Sun Valley? Never heard of it."

"It's a small-town many miles south of here."

"Nope, doesn't ring a bell. Must be one of those 'hole in the wall' places south of Platteville. Well, you can wait on the sidewalk until the bank opens. I would like you to get whatever business you have here done and get the hell outta Albuquerque."

Josh stands and stretches his arms over his head, "Yes sir. I apologize for sleeping on the bench officer. I'll leave as soon as I get my check cashed."

"See that you do." With that being said, the officer walks off placing his stick back in the loop.

An hour later, Josh steps from the large glass doors of the First National Bank of Albuquerque and places the thick brown envelope tightly in his jacket pocket. He can feel the warm, sultry air coming out of the northwest from the high desert and with his right-hand shades the bright glare from the sun's rays shining in his face. He rubs the bridge of his nose with his fingers, takes out the old pair of aviator sunglasses and places them over his eyes. He scans the main street and spots a small café just a few blocks away. Breakfast not cooked with his own hands sounds pretty good to him right about now. As he strolls across the street, he couldn't help but notice a large billboard three blocks down with large letters screaming out to him, '**Bronco Bill's Harley Davidson of Greater Albuquerque, new and used American motorcycles at the best prices in the Southwest.**'

It's been sixteen years since he's seen a new bike, so he bypasses the café, strolls down the sidewalk and steps through the front double glass doors. He's immediately mesmerized by all the shining chrome and black leather. The odor of new bikes filled the air with a sweet, spell-bounding aroma. He was amazed and astonished at how much they'd changed over the last sixteen years, but they still had that look that only an American machine could have.

Suddenly, there was a loud annoying voice screaming out from across the showroom floor, "Hotter than hell out there partner, come right on in and enjoy the air-conditioning!!" As an anxious salesman wearing cheap slacks, white, short sleeve with a loose tie quickly weaves in and out between the bikes as a snow skier sliding down the snow-covered slope of a mountain dodging ponderosa pines. When the smiling salesman finally made it across the room, he's almost out of breath and anxiously asks in an over friendly manner, "See anything you like? We just got the 2007 models in stock."

Josh hesitates, taking his time to scan the shiny reflections scattered across the showroom before answering the man; "Yes I do; everything!"

The man laughs, "I know what you mean; I own two myself. The name's Frank."

Josh, sporting a wide grin responds, "Josh is the name and I'm only looking for one."

The salesman, "Well you've come to the right place. Any specific size, color or style you have in mind?"

"I'll know when I spot it."

He slowly walks through the maze of beautiful motorcycles, running his hand over the smooth soft leather seats as he walks past each bike. There was one of every color like a perfect rainbow and then some.

The salesman, in a loud voice, "I can tell by the look on your face that you're a Tour Classic man. The kind of man who like all the accessories.

We have one with a radio, full windshield, and anything else you might need." Josh, not paying much attention to the salesman's rehearsed sales pitch, stops when a shiny, 2001 maroon Road King sitting alone in the corner away from the other bikes catches his eye. It was by far the most beautiful bike he had ever seen and brought back vivid memories of his childhood and his father.

He takes a gander around the crowed showroom of new bikes, then stops, turns to the salesman and asks, "You believe in love at first sight?"

The salesman then took acute notice of what had caught Josh's attention and with a disappointing sound in his voice replies, "Not with really old women I don't."

Josh laughs, turns to the salesman, "I want this one. I'll call her Elvira."

The salesman shakes his head, "You can call her granny for all I care. Are you sure about this? She's been sitting in this corner collecting dust and cobwebs for a few years now."

Josh runs his hand along the cool chrome rocker boxes and the beautiful silver medallion logo plate which was riveted to the side of the black six-gallon fuel tank. The deep maroon metallic paint reflected his face like an empty image in a mirror. He then stands and asks, "How does she run?"

The salesman, still shocked over Josh's choice of bike, hesitates, and thinking that with business a little slow, any sale was better than no sale at all. He answers, "Like a sweet little sewing machine, but with the sound of an F-14 Tomcat. The thundering sound that travels through those opened pipes is loud enough to rattle the teeth from your mouth. That 88 cubic inch twin cam has been stroked to 121 cubic inches, S & S G-series carburetor, headers, and I mean the real ones. Dome tops giving her 12.1 compression ratio, oversize valves, gear to gear 585 cams, and if you're not careful, too much throttle will leave your ass on the pavement. The six-gallon tank was added because there weren't any five gallon in stock at the time of repairs. Every foreign part on this bike has been replaced with new machine American parts.

Her starter has been replaced with a kick starter. Good luck with that, I can't even push it down with my foot. The engine is so strong it has compression relief valves on each cylinder to get her started." With a smirk on his face, he stares at Josh for a second and then says as he points to a new bike, "Look man, you don't want this old Road King. Right over there is a brand-new Road King with your name written all over it, or how about that green Tour Classic over there? You can start them with the push of a button."

"So, you see my name written all over that new bike uh? Well, you better wash it off, because I want this one."

"The new bike is a smooth riding 96 cubic inch. The manufacturer has removed just about all the vibration now. It's cycle technology at its best."

Josh turns to the man, "I like the vibration, lets me know I'm still alive."

"Look man, once you've ridden one of these new bikes, you'll forget all about that 2001 model."

Josh continues by asking, "If she looks this good and runs great, why hasn't anyone scooped her up yet?"

The salesman glances around to make sure no one was listening as if anyone else was in the room and answers in a low voice, "Have you ever heard the saying, 'It belonged to an old man who only rode it on Sunday to church?"

"Yep!"

"Well, this isn't the case. The old man who purchased this bike brand new in 2000 only drove it on Sunday mornings to get out of going to church. He must have been a strong man because nobody else could kick start it. Around 2003, on a beautiful Sunday morning, he was out riding the interstate going from bar to bar when he struck a piece of rubber recap left from a tractor trailer rig. We call them alligator tails. He lost control of the damn thing and was killed, which I took as an omen that his old ass should've been in church with his wife instead of out riding the interstates looking for biker whores. The bike ran off into the woods and left him lying in the middle of the highway without a scratch. Took over a year to fix and repaint her. You see, we weren't in that big of a hurry, if you get my drift."

"If he didn't have a scratch, how come he was killed?"

The salesman laughs, "His wife shot him in the back with a twelve gauge after they found a whore with a broken leg lying along the tree line near where the bike landed." The salesman slaps his knee and laughs aloud, then slowly regains control of himself and then brings his laughter to a low snicker.

Josh smiles at the salesman, "Wow! That's some story."

The salesman slaps himself on the knee again and says with a grin, "Yeah, too bad it's not all true. He was run over by a speeding dump truck before he could limp from the road, but the part about the whore was true. I just like telling people that story for a laugh or two. Big motorcycles, booze, and whores go together like lack of mental capacity, matches and gunpowder."

"So, I've heard."

"Yeah, a big Freightliner can ruin your day every time."

Josh, not laughing says, "My father was killed on a bike."

The salesman frowns as he sees the serious expression on Josh's face, "Sorry about your father, I guess the joke is wearing a little thin. Look man, nobody will buy the bike because it's considered bad luck to buy a motorcycle that someone's been killed on. Well technically the bike only took him to the location where he was run over. Save yourself the trouble and buy one of these brand-new Road Kings or Tour Classics, there's less noise."

Josh shakes his head, "I like noise even better than the vibration. I'll take this one and I want it serviced before I get back from eating my breakfast and stretching my legs."

The salesman, still holding his frown replies, "Sure." He hesitates and asks, "What's your full name for the paperwork and all?"

"Joshua Harley James and you can lose the windshield. I like the *wind* in my face when there's *steel* under my ass."

The salesman smiles, "Well Josh, I like money in my wallet and a naked drunk woman sitting on me. I'll have her serviced and the paperwork drawn up before you can cut your eggs."

"I'm having pancakes."

"Whatever 'kick-starts' your morning."

Before Josh could walk out the door, Frank yells across the showroom floor, "You want us to finance or are you using a local bank around here!?"

Josh yells back, "I'm paying cash!" As he walks out the door, the salesman smiles and says in a low mumbled voice, "That's the sweetest sound a man can hear, considering I haven't sold a bike in a week."

An hour later Josh steps from the café, throws his black leather jacket over his shoulder and walks slowly down the sidewalk allowing his breakfast to digest. As people passed him by, he was amazed at how much things had changed. Women were stopping and taking in his good look and bulging muscles. It was still early, and the New Mexico heat was sweltering. Kids were running in and out of water gushing from open fire hydrants, cooling themselves down before being run off by a store owner.

He walks by an alley and sees two men standing in the corner kissing when they stop and notice him staring. One of the men asks, "You wanna join in dude?"

Josh smiles, "I'll pass on that; it would take more than sixteen years to change the natural order of things with me. May God forgive you." With a nod he walks off.

Minutes pass and he walks back through the doors of the dealership. The salesman hears the buzzer and runs to meet Josh halfway hoping he hadn't changed his mind.

"Man, I was starting to worry whether you were ever coming back." He leads Josh into his office and offers him a chair. Josh takes a seat in an old cracked brown leather swivel chair as the grinning salesman shoves some paperwork in front of him, "Sign here, here and here." Josh takes a pen from a coffee cup filled with assorted pencils and pens and then hesitates. He quickly remembered he had forgotten to ask the price.

He gives the smiling salesman a look, "How much?"

"Since you're buying the bike with its pass history and all, I'm gonna make you deal above all deals. Ten thousand and I'll throw in a shiny new brass bell for good luck. You hang it from the frame near the bottom in front. It will keep you from having an accident or it will give the doctor something else to remove from your rectum in the E.R." He laughs as he takes a small brass bell from a desk drawer and hands it to him.

Josh holds the bell up high in his hand and stares at it for a second or two and then hands it back, "You should have given it to the original owner. You keep it, my luck is already changing. I haven't been out of prison for twenty-four hours yet and have already received an unusual kind of sex proposal from two men in an alleyway."

Frank snickers, "I believe I would keep that to myself if I was you. And the bell has already brought me luck by sending you in here to take that bad omen off my hands. I have a new Heritage Soft Tail still in the crate just waiting to be put in that corner."

Josh stands and pulls out the pouch, opens it and takes out a stack of hundred dollar bills and counts out one hundred bills one by one. Frank watches with growing anticipation like a coyote standing over a dead jackrabbit. Josh peels out the bills one after another, then stands and shakes the salesman's hand, whose smirky smile was stretched from ear to ear. "My wife will appreciate the business; she's been eyeballing a new outfit at Zingers…are you sure about the bell?"

"Yep, all I need is the key."

The man hands him the key. Josh hesitates for a second or two, "I need a few clothing accessories."

The man fires back, "You name it, I got it. What about that windshield? Should I leave it on, it will keep the rain and sand out of your eyes."

"You keep it. I need some leather chaps and a black bandana."

"Anything else?"

"Just some *wind* and eight hundred pounds of *steel*.

CHAPTER 4

As the sun peeks over the bluffs, the early morning rays of light can be seen streaking through the clouds, slowly making their journey down the eastern slopes of the Rockies until its scorching heat touches the cool sand of the desert floor. In the distance, a streak of dust and sand being kicked up by a dust devil and traveling across the hot paved and flat desert road like a rocket streaking across the sky leaving a vapor trail. An occasional tumble weed or two can be seen bouncing from one sand dune to the next. The maroon speck is moving down the lonely highway at seventy miles an hour. It wasn't even seven a.m. and it's already closing in on 90 degrees. The humid heat waves are starting to rise off the pavement like a transparent flag waving in the wind making its way in and out of the canyons. The white blistering sand is carried across the landscape like a churning sea rushing in on the beach of the Gulf coast. The sound of a rapid-fire cannon coming from the loud pipes of the big bike now known as Elvira ricocheted off the rock formations and had the muffling sound of rumbling thunder that could be heard in the far distance, echoing off the canyon walls.

The smooth rhythmic sound had a relaxing effect on the human mind. For sixteen years, Josh, wearing blue jeans and a tight black T-shirt, thought of nothing but this day. He was kicked back with his feet perched on the forward crash bar peds. His long black bandana was fastened tightly around his forehead with its tail flapping wildly in the wind. His t-shirt is pressed tightly against his ripped chest from the hot air rolling over the handlebars, passing the speedometer buried in the center of the large maroon six-gallon fuel tank. Resting on the bridge of his nose is the aviator sunglasses his father had left behind, the kind the old bomber pilots wore, flying their bomb-laden B-17s over the skies of Europe during World War II. Josh was reminded of a small diary written by an author named Bert Stiles; 'Serenade to the Big Bird'. His dad used to read it to him. Mr. Stiles, after a tour of duty completing thirty-five missions, was transferred to a fighter squadron. Just four months later he was killed in action on an escort mission to Hanover Germany. He was only twenty-four years old in 44 at the time of his death. He remembered that little book in which the airman wrote between tours and resighted to himself every day. After the crash…one of the surviving airmen mailed the diary to his folks. It was published fifteen years after the war.

With a twist of the right wrist, Josh gently throttles up and down as he lays into the curves, sometimes passing ravines several hundred feet deep. He is one with Elvira now, but he still had an unnerving respect for her, like she was only allowing him to show her the way to a destination unknown at this time even to Josh himself. Now he was reminded how it must have felt to the lonely cowboy crossing the desert on a large buckskin mare to his destination.

Josh could feel the hot air chafing his face; the sand hitting his cheeks felt like someone had turned a sand blaster on him. His mouth is so dry from the dust he felt like he could spit cotton balls. He pulls to the side of the road and grabs a black handkerchief from the saddle bag and places it over his face and ties it to the back of his neck. He jumps back on Elvira and with one kick fired her up and took off. Closing the gap between him and the mountains in the distance seemed to take forever. Maybe it's time to take a break from all the riding before night falls. He traveled east, then west, then north, but something kept pulling him south like a gigantic magnet, pulling him toward Sun Valley. The vibration traveling up through the leather seat was causing his body to go numb from the hours and hours of riding, so he starts looking for the first sign of a gas station. His parched throat could use a cold beer for sure and Elvira was getting thirsty also.

Finally, after a few more miles, he notices a large faded out red and blue billboard with the top right corner torn off from a windstorm. What's left of the sign indicated a service station a mile off the road. He quickly leans into a right turn to the west and as it turned out, the road was once the main truck route from Silver City, and from the appearance of the potholes and rain erosion, it was pretty much evident it was neglected by the New Mexico Department of Transportation.

He weaves around the small craters like he's riding through an obstacle course with clumps of busted asphalt scattered in every direction, before seeing a broken and rundown building that appears to have once been a gas station with a small house attached to the side. For some reason the shack, with its rusty gas pumps out front, appeared very familiar to him. Suddenly the memory jolts his brain, and he remembers that it's old lady Hannon's station. Man, there were a lot of fun memories in that place. It was the big hangout for teenagers bored stiff from the wind pounded desert. Twenty years ago, it looked brand new with its red coat of paint and green shutters over the windows, which is most likely why he didn't recognize the place; that and his medical condition was clouding his memory. He gears down leaving the broken pavement and pulls up to the pumps. Leaning over, he places the kickstand down in the dirt having it sink two to three inches into the hot scorching sand before striking a hard surface. After taking in his surroundings for a few minutes, he notices the place had that abandoned look about it. If anyone was still here, they would have surely heard his bike rumbling its way to the pumps. He knew he was a little more than twenty miles from Sun Valley.

He slowly swings his right leg over the black leather seat and plants his feet firmly on the sand covered concrete, grabs the pump nozzle, flips the handle and to his surprise, he hears the pump motor start humming away. He quickly unscrews the chrome gas cap from the tank, hesitates for a second and pumps a small amount of gas on the ground to make sure it was gas and not rust colored water and carefully starts filling it. As the fuel slowly made its way to its destination and before flowing over, he takes the other cap off and then fills the other side also. When finished, he places the nozzle back on the pump and yells out, "Anyone here!?" He got no reply.

He walks around to the side, takes a glance and then walks back around to the front and up the steps. There he found a screen door with a heavy weather-beaten wooden door behind it that someone had left open.

He yells through the torn screen, "Hey! Anybody home? I need to pay for my gas!" He turns around and has another look about, taking in the miles and miles of scorching desert. He turns back and opens the screen door and steps inside, noticing the kitchen to his left and living room to his right. In the kitchen on the counter was a large pitcher of water and whole lemons lying next to it as if someone was interrupted while trying to make lemonade. He slowly makes his way into the living room that is in disarray and then down a hallway stepping over the dirty clothes lying in his path. He attempts to place his feet on wooden planks that is separated by one-inch cracks, making sure the foundation was solid enough to support his weight. The place was a total wreck and void of any human activity except for the lemonade.

He says in a normal casual tone, "Hello, I'm a customer and would like to pay for the gas I pumped! Anyone here?" Still, there is no reply. He makes a few turns and checks the other rooms as he passes them by, but as he crosses the path of one bedroom, he's startled by a flock of chickens scattering in every direction. Thinking that something must be wrong, he backs out returning to the porch, scans the desert again and then steps down and walks around the side of the house with the sun beating down on his face. There sitting next to three old fifty-five-gallon oil drums is a ragged and faded out red Ford tow truck covered with rust from years gone by. The name on the door is too weathered to make out. It looked as if it hadn't run in years. As he approaches the rear, he discovers a shop built onto the back of the house and there resting nearby in a neat row were five small rice rockets. That's what people in the old days who rode American machines call Asian built bikes.

He takes a closer look, leans down, places his hand near the cylinders and could feel the intense heat radiating from the small engines. Thinking for a second that the bikes are parked in a shade so that kind of heat shouldn't be there, he stands straight and catches the faint sounds of laughter coming from a closed door at the rear, not more than ten feet away. As he steps closer, he could hear the voices of several men carrying on like they were having a celebration of some kind and as he stepped closer the voices got louder.

He knocks on the edge of the rear door, but the noises inside are way too loud and raucous, so he slowly turns the doorknob only to find it unlocked. He opens it and steps into a small storage room and in a loud voice, "Hello, I need to pay for my gas!" He was surrounded by cases of various dust covered oil cans and other things that you would expect to find at a service station. The voices and laughter got even louder, so he makes his way to yet another door and gently cracks it open. He observes three young men sitting on a work bench and two others in the center of the room striking a large overweight man in the midsection with their fist. It for sure wasn't a party for the unhappy victim on the other end of the hard striking blows to the abdomen. The large man with his pants falling off, showing the crack of his butt and a protruding belly, just took the harsh pounding as a lamb to slaughter. He could hear one smaller man who looked to be the leader, wearing a tight black leather jacket with red stripes across the front, yelling, "Damn you Bubba, this beer is hotter than lizard piss on liar's peak!" He jumps down off the bench and says to the others, "Save some of that fat ass for me boys."

All this reminded Josh of his first day in prison. If it wasn't for two guards who Josh later found out was Carl and Ernie, he'd been somebody's bitch for sure.

The young leader, the others called Pete, walks toward the big man to take his turn when Josh steps in the room and says in an easy calm voice, "I think he's had enough boys."

They all turn and see Josh standing there with his arms protruding from his black, short sleeved t-shirt like two vein-filled jackhammers.

Pete asks, "Who the hell are you?"

Josh remarks with a grin, "A concerned customer."

One of the other young men steps closer, "Well go concern yourself somewhere else asshole. What business is this of yours anyway?"

Josh takes a few steps closer, "None, just need to pay for the gas I pumped."

Pete, with a gritty look on his face, "Just give it to me unless you want an ass whipping to go with that gas."

Josh just smiles and shakes his head, "I take it the ass you guys are whipping belongs to the owner of this here establishment."

Pete takes a few steps closer himself before saying, "He will be for a few more weeks and then it belongs to me. What's that to you?"

Looking around at the spider webs and sun lithe holes in the wall, Josh says with a grin, "Hope you're not paying a lot for it. There's a good chance it won't be standing in a few months."

The large obese man being held up by two others tries to catch his breath before giving Josh an awkward stare, taking offense to the stranger downing his so-called home.

Pete glances around at his friends and then responds, "We're gonna bulldoze it down and build a poolhall anyway, again if that's any of your damn business."

Josh turns to the others then back to Pete, "You think you could spare him for a few minutes so he can tend to a small transaction?"

The two young men let the large man drop to his knees as another works his way around to Josh's side.

Pete continues, "You don't hear so good dude, just give me the money and get the hell out of here before you really piss me off."

Josh smiles and nods his head, "Let me see here, you say give you the money or piss you off, uh…uh…that's quite a dilemma." He places his thumb and index finger on his chin like he was in deep thought and then suddenly blurts out, "I'll take pissing you off for ten dollars!"

Pete laughs, "Have it your way buddy!" He takes one step forward and Josh puts his foot right in his chest sending him across the room into a stack of old crates and without hesitation or looking back, kicks backwards with the same foot, striking another in the gut so hard and fast it propelled the young man into a pile of old tires. Another attacks him but is met with a quick left fist to the jaw and a right fist to the back of the head. The other two are shocked at how easily this stranger took the three out.

Josh stares for a second and with a grin, "Should I show you more?" The two left standing help their friends to their feet.

Pete, still in pain says, "My dad will hear about this and then we'll see just how much of a smartass you are."

Josh laughs, "Let's hope he can fight better than you guys. I've seen over medicated old guys in a rest home do a better job." They all work their way out the backdoor while Josh helps the big man up from the floor; then they walk outside behind the rowdy bunch and watch them as they get on their rice rockets and fire them up. Pete guns his and does a wheelie all the way to the pavement with the others falling in behind him.

Josh in a low snicker, "He better be careful, those potholes will sure throw ya."

The large man laughs, "I hope the little bastard's break their freaking necks." He turns to Josh as dust fills the air, and with a chuckle, "I really appreciate the hand, but you just brought a whole bunch of trouble on yourself stranger. I hope you're just passing through."

Josh turns and takes a ten from his pocket and tries to give it to him, but the big man just pushes his hand to the side, "The gas is on me, my friend. Where did you learn to fight like that, and was you born with all those big muscles?"

Josh smiles, places the ten back in his pocket, stares into the man's face, "Let's just say I've spent the last sixteen years in a rough boarding school where dropping the soap can be a serious hazard, but I'm naturally clumsy, so I had to learn how to defend myself. An old Chinese man serving life for killing a man in self-defense taught me to fight. Seems a lot of that's going around."

The big man, standing there with blood on his lip couldn't help but notice Josh staring hard at him, so he asks, "Am I missing an eye or tooth, because you're looking at me like I'm not gonna make it?"

Josh steps closer and then loses all facial expression, "I have a lot of trouble with my longtime memory, but you look very much like someone I once knew a long time ago."

"Thank God, for a second or two I thought they had knocked my eye out of the socket, or I had a blood covered bugger hanging from my nose the size of a Jackrabbit."

Josh nods, "Seriously, I think I know you."

The big man steps closer, "Yeah, you definitely look like somebody I once knew. Sorry, but I didn't catch your name inside; I was too busy getting yesterday's lunch kicked out of me by Pete and his asshole buddies. They call themselves the 'Prairie Dogs from Hell'. I just call them 'Prairie Dog Shit.'"

Josh steps back and takes a glance at the entire body of the big man and says, "It can't be!"

The obese man tilts his head, "Sure it can, and I've got baby pictures to prove it!"

Josh starts laughing as the big man took a closer look and then yells out, "Well I'll be rattlesnake shit, on a funny shaped rock, if it ain't Joshua Harley James! The bandana and facial hair threw me off, not to mention that scar below your eye."

Josh, with a surprised look on his face yells, "Bubba Hannon! What a damn sight for sore eyes!"

Bubba reaches out and grabs him around the waist and gives him a big bear hug, lifting Josh's feet clear off the ground, then drops him, backs away and looks him over again and says, "Well I'll be scorpion snot; you look stronger than a mule."

Josh looks him over good and with a grin, "I smell like one too. The last time I saw you, you weren't much larger than a desert toad."

Bubba laughs and rubs his large protruding belly, "Yeah, there must be a lot of calories in desert dust, because I don't make a lot of money to buy groceries since the new road came through."

Josh, with tears of joy in his eyes, gives Bubba his rendition of a bear hug.

"I just can't believe it. What are the chances of the first person I run into being my best friend? You're as big as a Brahma bull. How in the hell do you let assholes like that rough you up?"

"I'm as big as a bull alright, but slow as a three-legged turtle with swollen hemorrhoids, which by the way, are swollen bigger than boulders as we speak thanks to Pete and his bunch knocking my guts out. Now back to the reason I let them whip on me, is because the leader of that bunch has a brother that's a deputy and a mean-ass daddy who holds the lease on this station; so, I just let them whip on me until they get tired. I make 'em think they're causing me pain, but they really hit like girls. They come around about every five or six days when they get bored and add excitement to their lives by pushing me around and drinking up my beer."

Josh just steps back and smiles, "Never take an ass whooping from anyone, even if they own the whole desert."

Bubba laughs again, "He does own the whole desert and then some or he thinks he does."

Josh shakes his head, "Damn it's good to see you, Bubba!"

They stroll back around front where Bubba takes notice of the large maroon piece of American iron parked at the pumps with the sun reflecting off the abundant amount of chrome. He shouts, "Wow, just look at the size of that hog, so you finally got that Harley you always wanted and what a beauty she is. Looks like your dad's old bike except for the color." He rubs his eyes and continues, "That sun reflecting off all that chrome will blind a bat."

Josh laughs, "She's sweet alright, and I call her Elvira, after our 'mistress of the dark', and bats are already blind."

Bubba smiles, "I can remember us sitting up all night with a hard-on watching that good looking girl host them horror flicks. That slit up that black dress and cleavage sticking out like the Grand Tetons…crap! I better stop, I'm turning myself on and I'm still a little sore from pulling on it all night. So bats are blind huh? How's your mama?"

"She passed away three days ago."

"Sorry to hear that Josh."

Josh asks, "So, how's your Mama?"

"Mama passed away seven years ago."

Josh, thinking of his own mother just passing, says in a low voice, "I'm sorry to hear that, she was a nice lady."

Bubba fires back, "Nice lady my ass; I wish I had a dime for every time she put a piece of wood across our back after catching us sneaking beer from the cooler!"

Josh tries to remember back and with a smile, "Yeah, it was amazing how she knew exactly how many beers down to the last bottle were in that damn cooler. I'm gonna miss her even if she was mean and ornery."

Bubba with a sad expression on his face hesitates a second before replying in a low voice, "Yes, she was quite a woman. She chewed that snuff up until the day she passed."

"She will be missed."

"Your mama sure was a sweet lady and could fix a mean peanut butter and jam sandwich."

Josh, "Yeah, but I guess any sandwich we didn't have to fix ourselves was great." Josh turns, takes a few steps back and looks the station over, "Good thing I got out of prison when I did. Another day and this place would have collapsed."

Bubba ponders over what Josh was saying and with a grin, "You kidding? This place is solid as a rock." He taps the corner, and a facial board falls to the ground. "I can fix that in no time. Yeah, I was going to throw some paint on it today, but Pete and his bunch had me sidetracked."

Josh changes the subject, "How come you never wrote me?"

"Because if you remember correctly, I skipped school so much I never learn to read or write and as you have already noticed, I don't have anyone around to write it for me. Yeah, those three years of school was hard on me. Thought I was never going to get out of the third grade, plus, I'm real busy around here with all the customers lined up for cold beers and gas. I did try to see you one time, but this big ugly ass prison guard said I wasn't kinfolk, so they turned me away."

"That was Skeeter."

"What was Skeeter?"

"That big ass ugly guard you mentioned."

"He didn't give me time to exchange pleasures before he threw me out the door." Bubba rubs his belly, "I bet he can't throw me very far now."

"It's okay; I couldn't bring myself to seeing anyone but my Mama anyway. So, you inherited the place uh? I guess you can drink all the beer you want now."

"I can when the cooler's working, which is about 10 % of the time and I also inherited the payments on the place. You see, before Mama passed, she took out a second mortgage from the bank, using the station and the land around it for collateral. The bank is owned by the father of the man who owns the ass you just tore a new hole in."

Josh frowns, "Sorry about that."

Bubba starts laughing, "That's okay it was well worth it to see Little Pete get an attitude adjustment."

Josh just stands there for a second trying to remember where he had heard that name, "You mean that was McNally's boy, Pete?"

"Yep, that's him and his little posse as he calls 'em. More like his little wussies than posse. Remember tongue tied Luther? He used to say posse when he tried to say p#$&%. Anyway, they just ride around on those candy-ass machines and terrorize old people....and me."

Josh shakes his head, "Boy, he sure has changed. That little dude wasn't seven or eight when I was sent off."

"Yeah, and his older brother is worse than him. Remember how we used to screw with Little Pete in school because he was so skinny, annoying as hell and always had that snot running from his camel nose?"

"Yes, I do. He would go screaming to his big brother only to get his ass whipped too."

Josh laughs, pulling thoughts from his cluttered memory bank. He then asks, "How is everyone in Sun Valley?" A silence comes over Bubba as he takes off toward the house.

Not getting an answer, Josh says as he slowly walks behind him, "Hey

Bubba, I asked you a question!"

Bubba stops, turns and answers, "There is no Sun Valley; they changed the name two years after you were sent off to the penitentiary. It's now called Platteville, as in Platteville, New Mexico."

Josh, with a stunned look on his face asks, "That explains why that officer in Albuquerque never heard of Sun Valley. How in the hell do you change the name of a town, and why would you?"

Bubba makes a hand jester for Josh to follow him inside, "I'll explain everything later, right now I have a craving for a cold beer and some three-day old fried chicken. Well, not chicken, but roadrunner tastes damn good too. Taste even better if I call it chicken. Took me two days the catch that little bastard, I felt like Wiley the coyote, but after being stung by a scorpion, almost bitten by a diamondback and falling thirty feet in a washout, I pinned him up in a boxed canyon and smashed his ugly ass head in with a rock. Felt bad about that all the way up until I threw his ass in a frying pan. Let's step inside my castle. No sense in standing in this heat when we can melt inside."

They walk inside with Bubba pulling on a string to an old squeaking ceiling fan as he made his way to the kitchen. Josh follows and takes a seat in an old worn-out chair next to a warped wooden table. Bubba takes two cold beers from the refrigerator, returns to the table and hands one to Josh, "Drink that one and I'll get you another. The icebox works fine; it's the beer cooler out back that stays broken. Of all things to malfunction out here, but I like hearing Little Pete bitch about the hot beer.

Bubba takes a drink, burps and with a big smile, "My God, that tastes great. Even better now that I have someone to drink it with." As Josh takes another sip of cold beer and savors the moment, Bubba makes a hand jester. "Let's go sit in the den and talk about the old days my friend."

Two hours and ten beers later, they stroll back out on the front porch, each carrying a bottle of brew in hand. Bubba flops down on a swing causing the porch roof to sag which in return caused the tin roof to make a popping sound. Josh takes a seat on the steps and leans his back against the porch post trying to avoid the nails protruding out of the floor joints. He looks between the large cracks in the porch and sees several chickens pecking at the ground eating whatever felled through its cracks.

"You're eating roadrunner, and you have chickens crawling everywhere?"

"You should try catching those little bastards. They won't come out from under the house, and if I could catch 'em, I wouldn't have what few eggs they lay. Hey, I did hit one with my truck once. It was like Thanksgiving around here for about five minutes, even if there was a lot of sand stuck in the meat. His little pecker put a hole through my radiator."

"Still sounds easier than trying to catch a roadrunner."

"You would think."

Josh reaches up, pulls his black bandana off, exposing an almost unnoticeable receding hair line, "Man…it is hot out here!" He stretches his head back and feels the warm breeze flowing from the distant mountains and across the Flats making its way across the porch.

Bubba takes a drink, "It can get damn cold out here at night, but it does give the desert a clean smell to it. Of course, you would already know that."

Josh takes a deep breath and turns to Bubba with a smile, "Remember all those days and nights up on Deer Lake?"

Bubba laughs, shaking his head, "I wish I had a dime for every time we puked our guts out up there. That mountain snow always had the water in that lake freezing even when it was well over 120 degrees on the Flats. My pecker would shrivel up and disappear when it hit that cold ass ice water. Looked like a girl when I came out of the water…. a real ugly girl."

"I thought your pecker always looked like that."

"Very funny; I see after sixteen years you haven't lost your sense of humor."

Josh starts laughing again, "You remember 'Lilley the licker' or was it 'Sharon the sucker'?"

Bubba, with a large grin replies, "It was 'Lilley the licker' and who could forget her? 'Sharon the sucker' was Roy's girlfriend. Yeah, I can remember one night you and 'Lilley the licker' were humping like two horny prairie dogs just around the bend near Granny's watering hole. She woke up the whole valley with that screaming of hers echoing in and out of the canyons. Everybody in the valley could hear your name being screamed out. I thought she laid her ass on a cactus the way she was carrying on."

Josh shakes his head, "Yeah, she was a screamer, whatever happened to her?"

"She finally married Gary Watson, who everybody thought was gay. They had seven kids together. She's still a whore though; goes out every Friday night and leaves him babysitting while she licks anyone who will buy her a beer and talk about anything but her kids."

A silence takes over for a few minutes and then Josh stands and walks over to the swing and sits next to Bubba causing the roof to sag even more, "So explain to me about this name changing."

"Well, after you were sent off, Willie's old place was put up for auction by the county. McNally was the only one with enough money, so he bought the ranch for little or nothing and then found platinum in the mountains above the place. What a coincidence, the only easy access to that part of the mountain range just happened to be old Willie's ranch."

Josh, with a puzzled look on his face, "I remember those fished out gold mines up there, but I don't remember anything about any platinum being there."

Bubba nods, "Nobody did. It seems that platinum wasn't worth a shit in the old days, but now it's worth more than gold and silver."

Josh stares at him for a second and then says, "Well?"

"Well, what?"

"Tell me about Susan. She stopped writing two weeks after I was sentenced."

Bubba hesitates for a second and with a sad expression on his face, shakes his head and answers. "I was wondering when you were gonna get around to her."

"I need to know."

"Well, Willie's ranch wasn't the only thing McNally bought. You weren't gone for more than two weeks and a day when she married the old bastard. Now she lives like a queen up there on that hill in that big white mansion of his. I wonder if she ever calls your name out while that old man is humping away?"

Josh, with a shocked look on his face, "Damn you say, he's thirty years older than her."

Bubba responds, "And then some......Yeah, you'll be amazed what money can buy these days. He carries enough money in his pocket to make him look like a twenty-year old Chip and Dale dancer."

"Is she still pretty as a cactus flower?"

"Still looks finger-licking good to me, but so does Martha Brown's Jersey cow when it gets dark and after about five beers."

Josh leans back in the swing, "I guess a lot of changes can happen in sixteen years."

Bubba laughs, "That's an understatement. I hardly recognized you."

Josh takes another sip of beer, scans the highway and says, "I guess I need to ride on into town and check out all the new changes."

Bubba shakes his head, "Bad idea, there's a lot of asses out there who believe you killed old Willie."

"You don't do ya?" Josh asks.

"Hell no, I never thought for one second that you did it. That old man was like a father to you, and you were like a son to him."

Josh places his hand on Bubba's knee, "Thanks old friend."

Bubba stares at the hand gently resting on his knee and then makes eye contact, "You didn't change while you were all pinned up in there did ya? I heard stories about prison sex; then on the other hand any kind of sex is better than no sex at all. I wouldn't last one day there because I'm the only person I know who takes a bath twice a month and drops the soap ten times each time I get in the tub. Slippery little bastard."

Josh quickly removes his hand, "I'm as straight as an arrow."

Bubba laughs and slaps his belly, "I was just kidding."

They both start laughing together and then Josh suddenly stops, "So, you wanna go take a shower or maybe a quick nap? I'll let you drop the soap."

Bubba stops laughing and gives him a blank look.

Josh snickers, "Just kidding also."

They both start laughing again and Bubba says in a loud voice, "I'm not just teasing you; the crack of my ass always shows like that." They both break out in uncontrollable laughter.

After the laugh ran its course, they both became silent and stared out at the unforgiving desert stretched out before them, all covered with tumble weeds and tall standing cactus.

Josh scans the horizon, "I notice the Flats haven't changed much. Still looks as harsh as ever."

"It's desert, what change were you expecting? It looked like that when you left, looked like that when you were gone and still looks like that now that you're back. It will look like that a thousand years from now too."

"Everything else has changed."

"Yep, the worst things you could have done was come back here."

Josh turns to him, "I guess I need to get going."

"Not so fast my iron riding cowboy. What's your damn hurry? You can wait till morning."

"I was just joking about the shower and nap, Bubba."

"I know that, but you see those dark clouds rising over those mountains. That's a bad storm coming in fast, and you do not wanna get caught in that shit on a bike. I would like you to stay because I really missed you and the chickens doesn't understand my jokes."

Josh nods, "Yeah, your right. It's amazing about those mountains and the weather. Sometimes you can get an all-night storm or just a brief gulley washer. You can never tell how long it will last."

Bubba, with a silly grin on his face, "I can; I've been sitting out on this porch for a long time, and you see those two highest peaks to our right in the far distance? Well, you already know that's the Dragon's teeth, the gate way to the Dragon's mouth, as we used to call 'em in the old days and when the clouds break over the top of those peaks and the wind is coming from the southeast, well that's gonna be a brief storm lasting about three or four hours. Now if the clouds come between those peaks and the wind is out of the west, well you better build a boat and gather two of every kind, because that's gonna be an all-night flashflood and a humdinger of a storm."

Josh was sitting there with a look of amazement on his face. "Wow, you had a lot of time on your hands."

"Yeah, I might have it backwards on that weather…Yep, I can even tell you how hot it's gonna be by the way the birds fly over Flat Chested Sister's Point. I'm just a damn regular meteorolog… meteorolog…"

"The word is meteorologist, but weatherman will do."

"Yeah, a weatherman, just wasting out my life pumping gas five or six times a week."

Josh takes a gander up at the sky, "Those Air Force jets still fly over every day?"

Bubba checks where the sun is located, sticks his index finger in his mouth, then holds it up in the air and then turns to him. Josh was about to say something when Bubba raises his other hand, "Listen!"

Josh listens but doesn't hear anything. "I don't hear a thing."

No sooner did those words leave his mouth, a loud thundering sound comes from the east. Josh strains his eyes and sees six Air force F-16 Fighting Falcons coming toward them at Mach one, flying 300 feet off the desert floor. They fly right over them with Josh placing his index fingers in his ears. The sound shook the whole house. Even the beer bottles shook off the swing armrests. Then as fast as they appeared, they disappeared across the Flats and over the mountains. Bubba turns and asks, "Does that answer your question?"

Josh pulls his fingers from his ears, "What?"

"I said, does that answer your question?"

"Damn that's loud!"

Bubba snickers, "Yeah, they used to be old F-4 Phantoms, now it's the new F-16s. I think they do that on purpose just to see if my station will hold together." Bubba stands and stretches as Josh does the same. The dark clouds are pouring in now at a rapid rate. The smell of rain is being carried across the dunes with the wind causing the temperature to drop fast.

Josh turns to Bubba, "You have a place I can park Elvira for the night?"

"Sure do. You can pull her around back in the workshop."

Josh nods in agreement and walks out to where the big bike was parked, then stops for a second taking in the dust covered heavy steel and shining chrome with the dark clouds rolling along in the background and lightning popping in the distance in every direction. She definitely earned the name of Elvira with this picture. It almost looked as if she was waiting with anticipation for the cool rain to wash the desert dust from her hard maroon and chrome skin.

Josh smiles and turns to Bubba, "I should leave her outside so she can enjoy the cool rain. She deserves it after riding non-stop in this heat."

Bubba yells from the porch, "I wouldn't leave her out in the weather; she a lady and deserves the warmth of my workshop! You gotta know how to treat a good woman Josh. I'm an expert on women now. I've heard a lot of, 'can I' 'no' can I' 'no'." He walks out to where Josh was taking in the scenery and says, "Hey, now you have me talking about her like she has tits."

Josh laughs and hops on the hot leather seat and with a strong bounce on the kick start fires her up shaking the pumps with her loud rumble.

Bubba yells over the loud exhaust noise, "Wow! Sounds like those jets returning!"

Josh races the motor up and yells, "Sweetest sound in the world!"

Bubba nods, "I'm getting a hard on. Just take her on in the bedroom so I can service her for you. You know, change the oil, wipe her down, shove my little monster up in her tailpipes, etc, etc, etc."

CHAPTER 5

That night, Josh, covered with an old quilt, was trying to stay warm and lay there tossing and turning trying to find a comfortable position on the left side of the iron bed with nothing more than a sheet with torn holes in between the worn-out mattress. Next to the bed was a window with a broken pane allowing the rainstorm to beat out a rhythm adding to the sound on the tin roof. The mattress had a deep hollow spot in the center causing him to roll over when he did find a position. Years of sleeping in a hard bed didn't make the tossing any easier. Bubba on the right side had stacked several yellow stained pillows between them just to make sure Josh hadn't changed over the years. He wasn't taking any chances.

Josh is snickering as they laid there listening to the rain and the old, weathered, wooden shutters banging against the wall as the wind pickup speed. He stares up at the open ceiling where a red bantam rooster is resting on a rafter when suddenly he turns his head ever so slightly to the left and asks, "Now what were the reasons I couldn't sleep in the other bedroom?"

Bubba grunts before answering, "Chicken shit!"

"What?"

"There's chicken shit everywhere. Seems they come and go as they please around here as if they owned the damn place. The room has belonged to them ever since they marked their territory with droppings."

"Yeah; I can see they pretty much come and go as they please in here too. Why don't you fix the big ass hole in the front screen door?"

"Actually, there's a good side to the whole situation." Bubba responds.

Josh shakes his head back and forth, "I can't see the good side to letting chickens' crap on the bed."

"You will when the odor of fresh eggs cooking in a frying pan fills the house with a sweet-smelling aroma in the morning. I find them all in that other bed. It reminds me of the Easter egg hunt when we were kids. Sometimes I can lift a pillow and remove breakfast like the egg fairy meant it to be."

"What about the rooster on the rafter? He doesn't lay eggs; he'll just shit on us in the middle of the night?"

"That's Gilford; to my knowledge he won't crap in the house."

"And why is that?"

Bubba, being sarcastic, "He told me so. I don't wanna sound like I've lost my marbles, but sometimes they speak to me. Yep, the desert will do that to a lonely man."

"I'm afraid to question where the bacon's coming from."

Bubba lets out a chuckle, "It only looks like bacon? It's dried Gila monster tail. I slice it real thin and then I just step back and use my imagination when I'm frying it; smart of me, huh?"

Minutes pass when suddenly drops of water start to hit the headboard and spatter down on their faces like a yard sprinkler going off wildly. Bubba reaches down and grabs a large tin pot with a broken wood handle lying on the floor next to the bed and places it on the headboard, then turns to Josh, "You take the first watch."

Josh turns his head, "Watch what?"

"It takes one hour, seven minutes and twenty seconds for the pot to fill. You empty it and then I'll take the second watch."

Josh laughs, "I have an idea, get off your big lazy butt and fix the leak. What happened to that one-hour rainstorm you predicted? It's been going on now for three hours. Any longer and I'm going to go collect two of every animal. You remember Noah, don't you?"

"Would that be the same Noah, who lost his left nut twenty years ago when his tractor rolled over on top of him?"

"Not Noah Stillwell. I haven't been here for a whole day yet and have already concluded, your weather predictions sucks?"

Bubba, with a grin, "Yeah, I forgot to tell you that I'm not right all the time with my weather predictions. It's a hit and miss situation. I definably had that prediction backwards. I forgot to take in the fact the hot air off the Flats feed it like a mama sow feeding her piglets and I would fix the damn roof, but it won't support my fat ass. The last time I tried, I started on the roof and ended up in the kitchen sink. I have a better idea, why don't you fix it tomorrow and I'll hand a bucket of tar up to you from the ground. Oh yeah, I almost forgot; if something sticks you in the ass in the middle of the night, I just want you to know it's not me. There's a bad spring on that side of the bed. They must be as tough as my truck's coil springs. I've been sleeping on this bed since I was two."

Josh laughs, "After sixteen years of sleeping on a worn-out cot, I say a spring in the ass is a compliment."

Bubba snickers, "Well the spring is the good news; the bad news is...I have gas really bad."

"I shared a cell with a three-hundred-pound fat guy from Mexico who ate beans and hot chili peppers three times a day, seven days a week and always had gas, so I can live with that too. He could burn the hair from a man's nose. I miss that guy. Two years after I got there, he told me to drop my pants and bend over."

"Oh no you didn't."

"I didn't kill the man, but I changed the sounds of his farts."

"Yeah, but my gas killed a hen and whatta ya think happened to the paint on the walls? One day I was working on my tow truck and this big ass western diamondback was coiled up next to the inside of the front tire shading his ass from the scorching sun and I cut one of my specials loose...He wouldn't even open his mouth when he struck at me. He just butted me with his nose."

"I guess your fat ass is too heavy to nail that shutter that's banging like hell on the outside wall huh?"

"No, that's just me being lazy."

Josh tilts his head over to the side, "Let me ask you something...."

Bubba interrupts, "Yes, I sleep naked."

"I was going to ask if you had a chance to do it all over again, what would you do different?"

"Let me think." He hesitates for a second and with a slight twist of his head answers, "I defiantly wouldn't have eaten those three homemade apple pies we stole from old lady Crenshaw's kitchen window. Who would think that nice old lady would put laxatives in her pies? I had the runs for five days." He hesitates for a second or two and then says, "Oh Yeah, I would have taken Carol Summers to the prom, married her and had a son who's faster than me, so he could catch those damn chickens under the house."

"Are you kidding me? Carol Summers had a face that looked a lot like a south end of a northbound jackass. Her breath alone would make a freight train take a dirt road. She had to sneak up on her lunch."

"It would have been better than nothing. They say, the uglier the woman, the better the sex."

"Whatever happened to her?"

"She married that tall skinny geek who always counted how many times he chewed his damn food and picked his nose until it bled like a stuck hog."

"Sounds like a match made in Heaven to me."

"They say she grew out of that ugly stage, ended up looking like a model in a magazine and they have sex every night of the week. Who would have known? It was a very bad decision on my part indeed."

"There's a good lesson to be learned there."

"Yeah, I know; if an ugly girl asks you to the prom…go!! It beats the hell out of staying home and using hand lotion. Oh…by the way; I figure out why they use lotion instead of soap. Soap gets in the end and stings like a pissed off scorpion."

"Every man knows that; and that's only one lesson. The other lesson is don't judge a flower until it blooms."

Bubba turns to Josh, "What about you, what would you have done different?"

"I would have never left Willie home alone that night. He felt something was wrong and asked me to stay with him, but I was taking Susan up to Deer Lake so she could pleasure me in twenty different mind-boggling ways."

Bubba snickers, "If it makes you feel any better, any dude in the county would have made the same choice." Bubba starts laughing hard.

Josh asks, "What's so funny?"

"I'm going to tell you something and I want you to promise me you won't tell a soul."

"Okay."

"You remember David Wilkins?"

"Yeah, what about him?"

"He's gay."

"Get out of here. He was the captain and quarterback for the Sun Valley High football team, and I always saw him with girls hanging around him."

"Well now we all know why he huddled so close while playing football. They did say he never missed slapping all the other players on the ass twice. Yeah, that knocked a hole in the theory about, if it quacks like a duck, walks like a duck and looks like it's a duck, it must be a freakin duck. It can also be a gander…a queer gander at that. Any way ya go, I thought that he was a lady's man too; but get this, we became friends a few years ago and we got to drinking and talking about the good old days like me and you are doing right now."

"And?"

"Well, he had too much to drink, so I let him sleep over. Sometime in the middle of the night I felt this pointed thing stabbing me in the butt. At first, I thought it was the broken spring then I suddenly remembered the spring was on the left side as you very well know, and I was laying on the right."

"Are you for real?"

"It's the truth; threw me for a loop too."

"So, did he make get any?"

"Hell no, I freaked out, jumped from the bed and drove his drunk-ass home. They just don't make water hot enough. I must have scrubbed my ass for three hours. It stayed raw for several days."

"I thought you said he didn't make penetration."

"He touched my crack, and that was way too close for comfort as far as I was concerned."

"I would have never believed that. Maybe he was dreaming about a girl and was sleep-screwing."

"I thought that too until he said, 'You sure feel warm Bubba.'"

"So that explains the pillows between us."

"Yep, that be the reason why."

"I would never try that, and you know it."

"That's what David said thirty minutes after crawling in bed. I should have made him sleep in the other room with the chicken shit. Nope! I'm not taking any chances. My ass is off limits to everyone and everything."

The room becomes silent for a few minutes when Josh rubs Bubba's foot with his toes and says, "You feel warm Bubba."

"Cut the shit Josh or go sleep with Elvira."

About this time Bubba cuts one loose. Josh wrinkles his nose, "Okay, that didn't kill a chicken, but it sure took care of some troublesome sinus problems."

"Too bad, I was hoping you wouldn't smell burnt eggs in the morning." Suddenly Bubba cuts another. "Sorry."

Josh gets another whiff and yells out, "Now that was by far the worst I have ever encountered."

Bubba laughs, "You can't say I didn't forewarn you. The second one is always the worst."

Josh clinches his nose with his thumb and index fingers, "Smells like a buzzard flew up your butt and died."

"Beats David's pecker for sure."

CHAPTER 6

The next morning, the glare of the sun penetrated the dirty glass window of the bedroom and threw the sun's rays directly in Josh's face. He awakened in a pool of sweat and Bubba was snoring away with a pillow stuck between his legs.

He's mumbling, "That's right baby, let ole Bubba take care of you. Uh, uh, don't worry, I'll be gentle…you can talk dirty if you…"

Josh interrupts by reaching over and vigorously shaking Bubba's shoulder, causing him to jump up and yell, "I wasn't doing anything wrong Mama, I swear!"

Josh laughs, "Okay, you can wake up and take your date home now before you have a little cushion in nine months."

Bubba gives him a look with half open eyes, "What are you talking about?"

"You've been having sex with that pillow for the last hour, and I think she's had enough.

"I wasn't having sex; I was having a nightmare. It was terrible. The cable people were cutting off my cable because I was two months behind on the bill."

"You have cable?"

"What part of, 'I was having a nightmare' did you not understand?"

An hour later Bubba was handing a bucket of tar up to Josh who was slowly making his way up the rickety ladder. As he gently made his way up the 45-degree slanted tin roof, placing the toes of his boots carefully on the small protruding nails, he hears Bubba yell, "A little to the right…no, too far, go back about eight inches, no, not that way, your…!"

Josh freezes for a second and yells back down, "Okay, enough with the directions; if you can do a better job, bring your fat butt up here! You know I've always had trouble with heights, so shut the up before you cause me to fall!"

Minutes later Josh is making his way down the shaky ladder when a slat breaks causing him to tumble to the ground. He quickly stands to his feet, brushes the dust from his jeans with his hands and wipes his brow with a torn dish rag stuck in his back pocket. Bubba, with a smile on his face, "You, okay?"

"Yep."

"Thanks, that roof has been leaking for a long time. I have no idea what to do with the pot now."

"I have an idea, try cooking something that doesn't run thirty miles an hour or crawls under rocks or gives you gas. That last fart you let out turned the sheets yellow."

"That's not what turned 'em yellow."

"I don't wanna know; some things are better left unsaid."

"I have a bladder problem."

"Wash the sheets Bubba with plenty of bleach."

"Good idea…again, thanks again for fixing the roof."

"Get me a hammer and some nails so I can fasten the shutters to the wall."

"Way ahead of ya." He takes a hammer with a taped-up handle and small box of bent nails from a worn-out canvas carrying bag and hands it to Josh. Josh walks over to the shutter and hammers away. Bubba snickers, "Can you cut grass?"

Josh glances around at the yard seeing nothing but sand with occasional sprigs of wild grass sticking up. He gives Bubba a look, but before he can say anything Bubba yells, "Just joking. So, whatta we do now?"

"I'm going to get a bath and take that trip into town. Fill that pot with heated water so I can get cleaned up."

I have a working hot water heater, thank you very much. Thanks for the shutters too."

Josh replies, "You're welc…" suddenly a sharp pain runs through his brain like someone drove a railroad spike through it. He places both hands on his temples and falls to his knees and then flops to the ground. His body shakes for a few minutes, and then his eyes roll back in his head.

Bubba panics, not knowing what was happening. He yells, "Josh! Josh!" And his voice fades off as Josh's body relaxes and his eye lids close shut.

Hours later, he awakens to find himself laid up in bed with a cool wet dish rag resting on his forehead and an old oscillating fan swinging from side to side in a jerking motion and making a grinding noise. A few seconds later, Bubba comes walking in the room with a glass of iced cold lemonade. He takes a seat on the edge of the bed, grabs Josh by the back of the neck and raises him up placing the glass to his lips. He takes a sip and then Bubba gently lays his head back down on the pillow. He stares into Josh's eyes and says, "You scared the shit out of me man; I thought you were a goner."

"I bet you were all upset at the thought of digging a grave." Joah with a chuckle in his voice.

"Grave? We don't need a grave this far in the desert. It takes the buzzards about twenty minutes to devour a cow, so you would last about five minutes. I plan on beating the funeral home out of all that shit."

Josh, with his speech a little slurred asks, "How long have I been out?"

"I would say about an hour and ten minutes. I was going to call a doctor, but the storm must have downed the phone lines. A very common problem this far from town. What the hell happen to you?"

"Nothing; let me rest for a few more minutes and I'll be alright."

"I bet it was a heatstroke; that's damn common this far from town also. Once I was working on my tow truck and suddenly, I became dizzy and started throwing up. Every muscle in my body started cramping."

"What happened?"

"I remembered I mixed a case of beer with a bottle of Jack the night before and then ate about ten cans of Vienna sausage."

Josh rubs his temples, "I didn't have a heatstroke. I have a condition that would take the better part of a day to explain, but if you'll get me the small bottle of green pills from my right saddlebag, I would appreciate it."

Bubba stands, "Sure thing. I just knew you had 'killed over', so I took Elvira for a ride to see if I liked her."

Josh smiles, "Well, how was she?"

"Not sure, only rode a few hundred yards before running her off into a twenty-foot gorge I throw my garbage in." Josh's smile slowly turns to a frown when Bubba starts laughing, "Just kidding; thought that would cheer you up. I would fluff that pillow for you, but I did that last night." He leaves the room as Josh takes the pillow and throws it on the floor before placing his head back down.

A while later Josh comes walking out of the bathroom and into the kitchen. Bubba was sitting at the table with a grin on his face. "Hope you feel better. You want me to bake some biscuits?"

"I'll get some breakfast in town."

"Getting a little late for breakfast, but if you insist on going, go to Jill's café on Cactus Boulevard in the center of town. She'll take care of you. Tell her you're a friend of mine and I'm sorry for the mess I made in there last week. I think you will approve of what God has done for her."

"What do you mean by that?"

"Nothing. I wanna surprise you."

"I'll do that; then I'll check out the rest of the town."

Bubba, with a troubled voice asks, "Why don't you stay here for a few more nights. That'll give me more time to talk you out of going into town."

Josh responds, "I wanna see the changes, and maybe a few more familiar faces. I'll be back later."

"I told you already that Sun Valley is gone and there's nothing but trouble in town. Why don't I go with you; we can take my old wrecker and I'll show you around."

"I promise I'll stay out of trouble."

"After what you did to Pete and his bunch, it's not you I'm worried about."

"I can take care of myself, and I'll be nice to everyone I promise."

Minutes later Josh walks out the front screen door wearing his tight-fitting jeans covered with leather chaps, black t-shirt and his leather jacket. He mounts the big bike and stretches his bandana over his head. He turns to Bubba, "I'll be back before you fix supper."

"Who the hell said anything about me fixing lunch? Bring me back a cheeseburger from Jill's place unless you wanna see how I fix horn toad stew."

Josh smiles as he fires up Elvira and yells over the rumbling sound, "Warm up the oven, I'll bring a dozen or so pizzas and cold beer back with me!"

Bubba screams back, "Now you're just teasing me. Come on, stay here and forget that town, it ain't for us!" He finally throws his hands in the air, "Crap, let me ride on the back! I can be your fat biker bitch and I want the meat lovers!" Josh lets out on the clutch and digs into the sand-covered asphalt. Bubba just stands there as the dust settles over everything in sight and Josh disappears down the lonely pothole ridden highway.

CHAPTER 7

Josh doesn't travel more than ten miles before he passes a nightclub with a large neon sign across the front, sporting large letters spelling out, 'The Cactus Rose' between two small neon cacti." He smiles as he thinks of the small cactus rose that he had placed on his mother's grave. It must have been hard having her only child sent off to prison in the prime of his life, leaving her all alone. Nobody can replace your mama.

A few more miles he comes across a railroad track and sees a small green sign with white letters written across the front; **'PLATTEVILLE, NEW MEXICO, POPULATION 6400'**.

He passes through three redlights before turning onto a side street leading into the downtown area and finally comes to a stop in front of Jill's Café. He kills the large and loud monstrous V-twin engine and then leans the big bike over on the kickstand. The cool morning air had long burnt off and he knew it was time to lose the leather chaps and jacket. He dismounts as a cowhand dismounts his horse after herding cattle all day, unsnaps his chaps, folds the leather neatly then his leather jacket and places them in the saddlebag. He makes an adjustment to his belt, but not just any belt, his father's old leather belt. It was an inch and a half wide, black and had thick, shiny Mexican conches fastened four inches apart, the entire length of the belt. He stands there stretching for a second or two when a dust covered light brown Crown Vic police cruiser eases up in the slanted slot next to him coming to a brake squealing halt. On the car door was a large star and under it was a logo that read, **'Platteville Police Department.'** A tall slim man in his late thirties wearing a slightly wrinkled uniform and sporting a beige Stetson hat with sweat stains around the inner brim steps from the car. He had a nickel-plated single action Colt 45 revolver hanging down his side resting in a shiny brown basket-weave holster.

Josh stands there with his two-week-old beard taking in the hustle and bustle of the main street. The officer walks over, not knowing who he was and says, "Nice bike."

Josh turns, "Thanks, nice Colt 45."

The officer places his hand on the dark walnut grips and lightly taps on the hammer with his index finger, "Yeah and I know how to use it too."

"Good thing; it's just a boat anchor if you don't." He starts to walk inside when the officer steps in front of him blocking his path.

"Is there a problem?" Josh asks.

"The name's Clint...Clint McNally."

Josh nods, acting as if he had never heard the name before, "Well that's a nice....and?"

"If that name doesn't mean anything to ya, you're not from around here. That name carries a lot of weight around these parts."

"It would be a lot lighter if you unloaded that ego, you got going on there."

Josh takes a step to the side and Clint counters his move staying in front of Josh blocking his path.

Josh smiles, "As much as I would like to carry on this agonizing conversation, I would like to get me some breakfast if you don't mind."

"I do mind. Why don't you keep going dude; there's a good place just south of here about thirty miles in a town called Lordsburg."

"I like it here and I'm hungry now."

Clint loses the fake grin, steps in close to Josh and says with a bad case of morning breath and in a low voice of authority, "Look buddy, those big arms don't scare me. I'm the law around here and the last damn thing the people of this town needs is Harley trash making trouble, so get on that damn Harley and get the hell outta here." With that, he makes an adjustment to his gun belt surrounding his thin waistline, turns and enters the café leaving Josh standing there on the sidewalk, wondering what he had done to piss Clint off. Clint didn't need a reason; he was a man who stayed pissed off at the world twenty-four-seven.

As Clint opens the door, a loud jingle came from a small bell attached to the upper metal stripping surrounding the door letting the waitress know that a customer had entered. He makes his way to the counter and pulls up a barstool. A beautiful brunette appears from behind the counter wearing a very short skirt exposing two of the fineness legs God had ever made and a blouse with coffee stains spread across the front of her apron. Her two top buttons were undone showing lots of cleavage.

She walks over to him and ask, "Let me guess numb nuts …free coffee?"

"That's all I can order sweet cheeks. You know how Papa feels about anyone buying breakfast here. He would skin me alive if I ate here."

"Yeah, wouldn't wanna upset the old bastard."

"You sure do look fine this morning. You'd look a lot better with me on top of you though."

"Yeah, and you would look a lot better if you would get your coffee somewhere else."

Clint turns and looks through the glass window as Josh stood there looking up and down the sidewalk. "Hey sweet cheeks, you know that guy standing out front?"

She turns and checks Josh out and liking very much what she's seeing, smiles and answers, "Young, good looking, big arms, wide shoulders, tight ass and one 'out of this world chest' huh! Nope, he's not from around here, that's for sure."

Clint turns back with an annoyed look in his eyes, "I wouldn't get too turned on if I were you. I just put that Harley trash on the road."

Jill, with a giggle replies, "Yeah, I can see him shivering in those fine black cowboy boots from here." Clint turns and takes a sip of coffee when he hears the bell above the door ring. He spins around on the swivel stool only to see Josh strolling over to a booth next to the large front windows.

Jill walks to the counter, grabs another cup and pours fresh coffee from the pot, "You sure put his fine ass on the road Clint. Just look at him run…I know, maybe he didn't hear you clearly over the sound of that big snoring noise you make when you use a word starting with any letter of the alphabet." She walks around the counter with coffee in hand and strolls over to where Josh is sitting. She stops and sets the hot mug down on the table.

"What can I do for you tall, dark, and handsome stranger?"

Josh turns and is stunned for a second over her beauty. He couldn't take his eyes off her and hesitated for a second, "You have a special?"

"Yeah, and my boobs aren't on it."

"Pardon me."

"You're staring at my boobs."

Josh with a grin, "Turn around."

"Excuse me."

"Turn around!" She turns and he slaps her on the ass and knocks a small brown scorpion from her dress.

She screams and a little turned on, yells, "Shit! You think you can just walk right in up in here and slap a girl on the ass?"

He points to the floor as the small scorpion scrambled under the table next to him.

She covers her mouth with a surprised look in her eyes, "Where did he come from?"

"Well, I would say that a mama scorpion and daddy scorpion did the old scorpion do, but if she had your attitude, it would have never got that far. So, I say check your flour sacks, they have a habit of crawling inside if you leave 'em open. Now what did I ask?" He thinks for a second or two and then, "Oh yeah, do you have a special?"

She tried to answer but was a little excited by his straightforward attitude and good looks. She comes back to reality and answers, "We have the hungry man special, a short stack with two eggs and bacon for $8.95 and the coffee is on the house." Clint could hear every word from where he was sitting.

Josh hands the menu back and says in a low sexy voice, "I'm hungry, so I guess I qualify for the hungry man special, and I'll have a big cheeseburger to go with everything on it and do you make meat lovers pizza here."

She giggles and, in a flirting, voice says, "Yes, I do. I don't know about the hungry part, but around here you definitely qualify as a man. Sorry about the smartass attitude. I get a lot of guys from the mines in here and they're always trying shit like that. Enjoy the coffee." She walks back to a small window cut into the wall where an elderly woman is cooking on the other side. Clint watches her as she places the order then turns to wipe the counter. She smiles with a glow on her face, glancing up every few seconds, staring as Josh poured the cream and sugar in his coffee.

Clint asks, "Why the free coffee?"

"I like him, he has manners and he's intelligent, unlike someone else I know and like I said before, he's tall, dark, and handsome and you're skinny, ugly and stupid looking. I've seen coyote crap with more intelligent than you. Does that answer your question Jackass?"

He turns on his stool, "I wouldn't be giving anything away if I was you. You'll be losing your business in a few weeks."

"I guess I can thank your father for that, him opening a big place two blocks over and all."

He shoves his thumbs in his belt, "You know pop; he likes running the whole show." He stares at Josh and shakes his head, "That dude sure looks familiar to me."

She shakes her head, "I don't think he's even close to being queer Clint."

"Wow, you're a regular standup comedian today."

"I try, but it's hard to be funny in this chicken shit town."

He gives her his usual frown. She nods, "Oh come on Clint; you say that about every stranger who comes into town. You're just upset because he doesn't scare easy."

Back at the table Josh is sipping his coffee staring out the window at Elvira. He turned back and couldn't help noticing that seven or eight customers were staring at him.

The elderly woman yells from the kitchen, "Order up!" Jill walks over, takes the order and strolls to his booth and gently places the plate and the bag containing the cheeseburger down on the table in front of him.

"The pizza will take a few."

"I've got the time." She just stands there staring, looking him over. He grabs the fork and knife and hesitates before asking, "You, okay?"

"I am now; do I know you from somewhere? Your voice sounds familiar, and I've seen those eyes before. I don't remember the scar though. Kind of sexy."

"I don't think so and I believe I would remember legs and a rear end like that. You really can't blame the scorpion for clinging to that."

She blushes and asks, "Where you from? I know you're not from around here."

He starts cutting his eggs, "Let's just say I'm from a little community west of Albuquerque and leave it at that."

She starts to take a seat across from him when suddenly Clint jumps down in the booth. She yells, "What the hell do you think you're doing!?"

"Just wanna ask him some questions, that's all. Wouldn't feel right if I didn't do my job."

She gets angry and blurts out, "Why start now?"

"Go wipe a table or something Jill."

She snaps back, "That's why I'm having so much trouble staying open; you keep running my customers off! I have an idea; why don't you go find a drunken Indian or go wipe your father's ass and stop harassing my customers!" She stomps off with the coffee pot in her hand.

He gives Josh a dirty look, and a sarcastic grin, "You don't hear so good do ya stranger."

"I hear just fine. It's lack of interest I have a problem with."

"I don't believe I caught your name dude."

Josh chews and swallows then replies, "That's because I didn't throw it in your direction."

Jill could overhear the conversation and giggles, embarrassing Clint. He reaches across the table and grabs Josh by the wrist as he was about to bite into a piece of sausage that is clinging to the end of his fork. "Look smartass, I could run you in right now if I wanted too."

Josh loses his smile and says in a nice low tone, "You've got three seconds to let go of my wrist or I'm gonna run a fork through it….you now have, two, one…" Clint could see that he was serious and turns him loose.

"I could make one call on this radio and have three officers over here before you can finish those eggs." Everyone in the place went silent. They had never seen anyone stand up to Clint before.

Josh takes another sip of coffee and with a snicker, "You'll be better off calling an ambulance instead, and three more buttholes like you is just gonna make a bigger mess to clean up."

"Are you threatening an officer of the law?"

"I don't make threats; I make promises and guarantees."

Jill walks over and interrupts, "Leave him alone Clint and go mind your own business. This is still my place."

Clint stands and in an angry voice, "Only for now, sweet cheeks."

He turns back to Josh who was smiling and taking a bite of egg, "And you Harley trash, take some good advice; when you're through eating, get on that maroon noise maker and get the hell out of my town."

Clint walks back to his stool as Jill takes a seat across from Josh. "Don't let him get to you; he gets bored and tries to show off in front of me. He spends the better part of a day trying to convince himself he's a man, which isn't going to happen anytime in this century."

He slides his plate over and with a grin, "I've known egotistical people like that all my life; I don't let it bother me. Is he your boyfriend?"

"When hell freezes over. Oh, he keeps asking me out, but I keep making up excuses like I have an eye lash missing or I need to water the pigs, or just watch reruns of anything on T.V."

"So, I take it you're not married."

Misunderstanding him, she gives him an angry look, "What does that mean?"

"I was just wondering why a good-looking girl like you hasn't been scooped up yet?"

"I guess the right man hasn't come around scooping! I'll clean the table and we'll finish this conversation." She smiles, stands and takes the plate from the table. She walks to the back and while she's gone Josh takes the bag in hand, places a twenty on the table and walks out the door. She returns only to find an empty booth but scans the room as if she was looking for her long-lost love.

Clint says with that nasty grin of his, "He left outta here a few seconds ago. I guess he got my message. Did he say anything else?"

"I never got his name." She gives Clint a frown and hesitates for a second before saying in a sarcastic way, "Damn! That makes me so mad. He left after promising me that he would bend me over and pound my… my…what is that you are always begging for? Oh yeah, now I remember, my ass."

Clint stands and watches as Josh kick starts Elvira and rides off. He turns to Jill. "You're working hard at getting on my last nerve today…let's see if you think it's funny after my dad closes this place down. Then you'll be begging me to bend that ass over."

She starts laughing, "I can hear myself now, 'Oh Clint, take me to that wonderland that only you can take me…give it to me skinny boy, oh yeah, you the man.' give it a rest, if I was stranded on an island with you and a monkey, I would be screaming, 'go monkey go, you arrogant asshole!'" She turns and watches as Josh rides off and then suddenly yells, "Well, I'll be that little bump on a fog's ass. I think I know who he is!"

Clint fires back, "Who!?"

"Never mind, go back and drink your coffee, I got to go see a man about a dog."

"I bet that dog rides a Harley."

"He sure the hell doesn't drive a dirty stinking police car. Now move it before I throw hot coffee in that little rat face of yours."

He grabs her by the waist and pulls her in close, "Look angel eyes, let's go out tonight and have a few drinks. I'll have you so turned on you'll forget all about that Harley scum."

"Oh my God!"

"Oh my God what?"

"I think I'm getting wet right now just thinking about it."

"Is that right?"

"Hell no! Just standing this close to you makes me dryer than the Flats. Now take your filthy hands off my waist before I break all your fingers with an iron skillet."

He removes his hands from her waist and takes a few steps back, "You'll come crawling to me when I take over for the old man."

"Yeah, that'll happen when ice cubes sprout from the desert in July." She removes her apron, throws it on the counter and yells to the cook, "Get that pizza for me, I'm stepping out for a while, cover for me!!"

The cook hands her a several pizzas and she quickly turns and runs out the door.

CHAPTER 8

Miles down the road out on Route 7, Josh hits the kill switch and Elvira silently coast to a stop under a large shade tree. He stares over the old log pole fence and scans the green pastures as far as the eye can see. It's just amazing how five minutes from the desert you can find beautiful, lush grass. It all depends on how much snow melts and finds its way through the foothills. He glances over at the steel gate attached to that wooden fence and could see a 'NO TRESPASSING' sign posted in the center just under another sign reading, 'McNally's Mines.'

Pondering on this for a few minutes, he starts Elvira, spins around making a three-quarter donut and travels a short distance before turning up a trail and then through a hidden brush covered driveway. He rides down the long dusty dirt trail and sees a pile of rubble where the large ranch house once stood. Over to his right stood the large old hay barn with a slight lean to it, where he had laid his head many a night.

The corridor through the center of the barn was wide and opened at both ends so hay wagons could travel through, unload the hay, and head back to the fields for more. That old barn could hold several thousand bales when packed full and had a small extra room up in the loft where he lived five years of his life. He parks Elvira in the wide corridor and stands there remembering all the good times. Well, not all good. At times the work could be so hard that he'd lose sleep because every muscle in his body would cry out in pain. Nothing would ever be the same now that Willie was gone.

Willie was from six generations of ranchers, but his father had trouble recovering from the depression of twenty-nine and lost almost everything. Like most folks during that time, Willie had to start over from scratch. Remnants of that era can still be seen around this old place. Perhaps it was the weathering of years gone by.

He scans the old barn and decides it was time to pay his old living quarters a visit. He walks over to the wooden ladder leading to the hay loft and climbs', hoping it's still able to support his weight. As he makes his way up the ten-foot ladder, he carefully peeks over the top and to his surprise his bunk and wooden rocking chair are just as he had left except for the cobwebs in every corner. Being there's no more hay to cut, the new owners must have overlooked the barn loft. A layer of thick dust covered everything he once called home.

He gently takes his hands and removes the webs from in front and makes his way to the bunk. At the foot of the bed was a small empty chest with a broken latch, where the police had found the murder weapon; a blue steel 45 colt Willie had given him. The old wool army blanket Willie had loaned to him was full of moth holes from many years ago. He just shook his head at the thought of Willie yelling for him every morning at five o'clock to get up and get started with the daily chores. He slowly strolls over to the doorway leading to the edge where a pulley system was rigged to pull bales of hay to the loft. He stands there remembering how many bales he must have pulled up and stacked. He wished he had a dollar for everyone he loaded and unloaded. He'd be a rich man for sure.

The memories were coming back clearer and clearer as he stood there looking out over the fields. He turns slightly to his right staring out the opposite end when suddenly he notices dust being kicked up from a fire red jeep traveling up the same hidden trail he had just taken. It was traveling fast and heading his way. He didn't remember anyone else knowing where that secret entrance was.

He knew the bike was hidden in the barn and just figured that he would wait them out. Maybe they would just pass him up heading for the mines, but instead the jeep pulls right up to the front as if the unknown driver is looking for him.

He squats down and leans against a large pole supporting the barn roof hoping whoever it is, wouldn't check in the loft, but knew as soon as they saw Elvira the cat would be out of the bag.

Maybe Bubba was right; coming back here was a bad idea. He hears the door slam and waits for the harsh trespass warning he was about to receive but listens closely hoping for the best. Suddenly he sees the top of the ladder begin to vibrate and can hear the wooden slats as they make a squeaking and popping noise for every step taken. He just sat there waiting to face an angry opponent.

To his surprise it was Jill, the young waitress from the cafe who topped the ladder. He was speechless as she came to a stop and stared at him with a disappointing and angry look on her face.

In a low voice he says, "I laid a twenty on the table, I swear."

"This isn't about the tab, mister tall, dark, and handsome."

"If it's about the pat on the ass, I figure it was far better than a scorpion sting."

"It's not about the slap on the ass either."

He starts to say something else, but before he could get the words from his mouth, she interrupted by saying in a slightly harsh tone, "Damn you Joshua Harley James, you made a fool out of me!"

He was at a loss for words and had no idea what she was talking about.

"Pardon me?"

She steps closer, "You gonna stand there and say you don't remember me?"

He steps closer, "I suffer from memory lost, so I've forgotten a lot of things over the years, but I would have remembered those legs for sure."

She steps even closer with a tear running down her cheek and in a sweet broken voice says, "Those legs use to be very skinny with knobby knees. I'm Jill, Jill Albright! I was the little girl who tried to follow you everywhere you went. I had the biggest crush on you."

"I'm trying to remember."

"You don't remember me because you never gave me the time of day."

In a low polite voice he says, "Okay, you have me over a barrel, jolt my memory."

She takes her hands and pulls her hair into two pigtails and then puts a wide grin on her face, "Now do you remember me?"

He steps closer and then it came to him, "The only girl I knew with pigtails and a wide smile back then was a small thirteen-year-old flat-chested brunette I called, 'Little Bit.'" He takes a closer look, staring into her big brown glassy eyes, "Well I'll be you are that little flat-chested thirteen-year-old who followed me around." He stands back, takes another look at her well-shaped breast and the legs of a super model and couldn't believe it's her. The waitress uniform she was wearing was very tight and showed every curve of her beautiful well-proportioned body.

She watches him as he checks out every inch of her.

"You broke my heart when you asked Susan to the prom instead of me."

"She was eighteen; you weren't even old enough to date. What happen to the pigtails?"

"I lost them about the time my breast sprouted out."

He was at a loss for words when suddenly she walks over, grabs him so tight he could hardly catch his breath and kisses him long and hard. She then steps back, "I knew I had seen that face before, even under that half-ass beard. I knew it was you and those black cowboy boots with silver plates on the toe and heels and that black belt with those Mexican conchos should have given me a hint." Josh could feel her heart pounding away as she stepped back then stepped back in and gave him another tight hug, but that was not what he was pressing against her. He tried to step back a little so she wouldn't notice the erection he was getting. Years of prison gave his penis a mind of its own. It's too late; she places her hand on each side of his face and asks, "Is that what I think it is?"

"If you think it's a hard-on, it is. It's been a long time since I've been this close to a woman."

"Oh, it's a woman now; whatever happened to Little Bit?"

He steps away, brushing the front of his jeans as he tried to shift the bulge in his pants in another direction. She steps closer and in a sexy voice asks, "What's wrong Josh…can't control those hidden, lustful desires?"

He smiles, "It's not hidden anymore thanks to that bump and grind you just performed on me."

She steps in close again and gives him yet another passionate kiss caus-ing his face to flush and a scalding fire to rush down his throat and burn his insides. He steps back, almost falling over the edge. She laughs, "You'll never believe this, but after all these years I've had two men in my life, but they could never fill those boots of yours. I'm twenty-nine now and my feelings for you are still just as strong."

"Your father would have shot me, and I wasn't about to go to jail over a thirteen-year-old with her hormones kicking in full blast."

She giggles as she walks over and takes a seat on the edge of the bunk, "You want me now Josh? I can promise you one thing, there's no jailbait under this dress."

He attempts to swallow the lump in his throat and then with excitement in his voice says, "Wow, you act like it was you who spent the last sixteen years in prison instead of me!"

"In my mind, I did spend sixteen years in that prison. Don't get me wrong, if it was anyone else but you; I would have slapped their face for rubbing their pecker on me."

"Me, rubbing against you; are you crazy? You were the one doing all the rubbing."

"I understand if you're too weak to control yourself around a young innocent woman. All those years in Prison with no woman to take care of that lustful desire just begging to get out." He just stood there with a funny expression on his face. She continues grabbing at her dress like a schoolgirl, "I could say you tried to rape me."

"Me, rape you?"

"Give me another one of those powerful kisses and I'll forget the rape charge." She pats the bed for him to take a seat. He reluctantly takes a seat. She turns his face toward hers and quickly grabs him again, firmly pressing her lips to his. He felt her tongue making its way into his mouth as her hands reached around his back pulling him closer to her. He pushes her away and being agitated says, "Slow down girl."

"What the hell is wrong with you? You have a young beautiful woman in bed, ready to show you the best time of your life and you act like an alley cat treed by dogs."

"It's been a lot of years."

"Have you forgotten how to have sex?"

"No, everything is happening too quickly that's all."

"You do know you can get into a lot of trouble being up here. Those goons working for McNally will kill you and bury you out back and no one would ever know the difference."

"I just wanted to check the old place out, that's all. I have a lot of fond memories here even if they are slow at coming."

"Yeah, I know all about your memories here. This is where that bitch Susan would come when she needed to be serviced like an old Jersey cow needing her udders milked. I would sneak over here sometimes and listen to you two up here panting, moaning, and groaning like two pigs fighting over corn mesh. I would get so pissed…and the pain I was feeling was breaking my heart Josh."

"I never had a clue you felt that way."

"You're lucky it's Saturday, otherwise McNally's workers would be crawling all over this place traveling back and forth to the mines. They could see that big chrome covered hog sticking out like a Jewish, queer, black man at a Ku Klux Klan rally."

"I'm not worried about that, but it is good to see another friendly face."

"You gonna stay long or are you just passing through?"

"I think I'll stay for a few days, but Bubba has only one bed, and he fills it with gas and yellow stained pillows to keep me from accidentally bumping into him when he's asleep. He has more gas shooting from his butt than he does from those pumps in front of his station."

"You can sleep with me." He gives her a look and she quickly snap back, "I mean you can stay at my place." She steps closer with a mischievous look in her eyes and continues, "I'll keep you warm at night. It can get cold in the desert at this altitude, but you already know that."

"Is Henry still alive?"

"Yep, Pop's still kicking, he just doesn't kick as hard or as high as he used to."

"Maybe he'll let me sleep in that old ranch house behind your place for a few days or has it fallen down?"

"No, it's still there, but it's a far cry from my bed."

"It will do for a few days."

"I can do you day or night, anywhere, anytime."

"You sure are the horniest girl that I've ever met."

She places her hands on her hips and asked in a loud voice, "Joshua Harley; have you gone homo from all that prison life? Because I've heard they do a lot of things in those places?"

He laughs, "Don't say that around Bubba, I already have him worried."

She gets angry, "Damn you Josh; I finally get old enough to have sex and you still treat me as if I was thirteen."

"It's gonna take some time to adjust to things Little Bit; I'm not sure I can handle all this at one time."

She unbuttons her blouse exposing her pink breast-filled bra and yells, "Does this look like a little bit, now stop calling me that, I hate that name!"

"Button up and tell me how long you've been working at the café."

She buttons up and leans back on the bed and crosses her legs. In doing so, she makes sure he gets an eye shot of her panties. She then says with a grin, "I don't work there, I own the place. Dad turned it over to me six years ago when he got injured. He's just lazy but tried to make me believe he wanted to spend more time fixing the ranch up or what's left of it. I only waited on tables because all my girls went to work for McNally's new restaurant. The only person that stayed was old lady Winfred and her arthritis is messing with her bad. I have to check every order to make sure she hasn't dropped anything on the floor. I'll be out of business in less than a few weeks unless I come up with a way to pay my mortgage payment. Yeah, McNally won't be happy until he owns the whole town. Oh yeah, I got your meat lovers pizzas out in the jeep."

"It's for Bubba, speaking of Henry, I never did get to thank him for testifying for me at the trial."

"He always liked you. That's how I know he wouldn't have shot you if he caught us playing doctor."

"So, he's still gets around uh?"

"He's having a lot of breathing problems, and his heart is giving him a little trouble, but it's his back that's killing him. Said he hurt it working with a horse, but I think he was trying to screw a nanny goat. That and he still thinks he's thirty. He's real slow now, so slow I bet he couldn't pull the trigger if he did catch us in bed together. Why he would be so happy at the prospects of grandchildren, he'll do back flips."

She sits back up straight and places her hands on his large bulging arms allowing her fingers to ease their way up to his hard broad shoulders. She leans her head over and kisses him on the neck and says, "You sure do fill out that t-shirt and jeans. You must have worked out every day in that place."

He slowly and gently pushes her back and asks, "Who's running your café now?"

She glances at her watch and yells, "Oh shit!!! I gotta get back for the lunch crowd, you go see dad and he'll show you where to unload. I'll be home later to fix supper and whatever else you may need fixing. Don't forget to bring that fat-ass Bubba with you. I know he hasn't had a good meal in months."

"As big as his gut is, you wouldn't think he was starving."

She stands and with slow casual steps, walks over to the top of the ladder, stops for a second and then slowly turns back to him for another glance, "I wouldn't go looking for Susan if I were you; that whore's spreading her snow white legs up there in that mansion as we speak, except she's not yelling out in the heat of passion, 'who's your daddy, who's your daddy…instead she's most likely yelling, 'where's your money, where's your money."

He grins, "So I've heard…so I've heard." She climbs down the ladder with the excitement of a little schoolgirl and runs toward her jeep waving back at him as she takes out the pizza and walks over to Elvira, lays it on the seat then walks back and jumps up in the driver's seat, starts the vehicle and spins off…

He shakes his head and then mumbles to himself aloud, "Who would have ever guessed that, that little homely, aggravating pain in the ass girl would have turned out so beautiful…Oh shit…Bubba's damn cheeseburger!!"

CHAPTER 9

Ten miles down the road, Josh turns and makes his way along the long narrow stretch of dirt, dodging the soft spots and mud holes created by the thunderstorm that night. As he pulled up in front of the old large, green painted house, surrounded by a wrap-around porch with log columns, he couldn't help but notice it needed a new coat of paint. Not as bad as Bubba's place, but still in need. From the corner of his eye, he sees a thin gray-haired man in his late fifties coming from behind the house sporting a hunched back and carrying two large metal buckets of water to an old wooden trough. The worn-out looking man sets the buckets down and wipes the sweat from his brow when he hears the loud rumble from Elvira's pipes as Josh came closer. When he stops and dismounts, the look of joy covers the man's weathered face. He slowly walks toward Josh with an awkward stagger and recognizing him right away. Josh pulls the old aviator sunglasses from his eyes and stood there for a moment taking in the joyous occasion.

Henry stops in his tracks, and tilts his head, "Well, I'll be a Billy goat's nut sack…if you ain't a sight for these old sore eyes."

Josh smiles wondering how Henry recognized him when no one else did.

"Why Henry, you old broken-down son-of-a-gun. You must have the memory of an elephant twice your age!"

They hug and then Henry steps back and glances over Josh before saying. "Boy, have you grown."

"Yeah, a little."

"A little my ass, you're a far cry from that skinny kid who put roadkill in my mailbox twenty years ago. Just wait until Jill gets a gander at you."

With a smile Josh responds, "You're too late, she already has."

"Did she try to rape you?"

"Yep, and I almost let her too. She sure has grown up. Prettiest girl I've ever seen." Josh is overwhelmed with happiness to see another friendly face. "I'm sorry about all the mischievous pranks Bubba and I pulled on you in the old days."

Henry responds, "That's alright son, and I'm sorry for pissing in that jug of white lightening you two stole from my back porch."

Josh just stood there in a daze for a moment or two and then says, "That's okay, I was already drunk from the twelve pack of beer I took from your icebox, so I let Bubba drink from the jug. He drank it so fast he never even noticed."

Henry just stares for a moment or two then says, "You are a pleasant sight for sure."

Josh pats him on his old, slumped shoulder, "What happened to your back? The last time I saw you, you stood straight and tall like a stalk of corn."

"Yeah, back then my pecker did too, but a lot of things have happened since those days. About a year ago, a young stud horse threw me on a fence rail. Doc said I'd never walk again."

Josh laughs, "You fooled him, didn't you?"

Henry laughs with him, "Sure did. My back makes me lean to the right a little, so I always walk to the left when I wanna walk a straight line. Overcompensating I guess."

"What happens when you wanna go right?"

"I don't, I just keep walking left until I wind up where I need to be." They both burst out in laughter.

Still grinning from ear to ear, Josh says, "I never got the chance to thank you for testifying for me at my trial."

Henry nods, "Well it didn't do much good with that bastard McNally knowing everyone on the jury and I mean in a personal way. A better lawyer would have gotten the trial moved north of here, maybe in Santa Rosa. Everybody liked you up there and McNally had no pull in that county."

Josh looks around at the rundown ranch and shakes his head, "The horse business must not be doing too well."

"Yeah, McNally shut the whole valley down for everyone who testified for you in court. I can't sell prairie dog shit if it looked like gold or lizard piss from mason jars if it looked like lemonade. Been paying the bills with what Jill makes at the café and it looks like that isn't going to last too much longer. Yeah, my bank account is all but dried up."

"Why don't you and Jill sell the place? There must be three hundred acres here."

"Can't, McNally holds the mortgage on it."

Josh, a little shocked at all he's hearing responds, "He owns the lease on Bubba's station, Jill's café, and he's gonna wind up with your ranch." Henry goes to pick the buckets up, but before he can grab them, Josh takes them in hand like he's carrying two coffee cups, carries them over to the watering trough and pours them out. He then turns to Henry, "How much do you need old man?"

Henry, misunderstanding him, rubs his chin, thinks hard and then says, "These two buckets should just about do it."

"I'm talking about money, Henry."

"Oh that. If I heard Jill right, I would say about five grand."

Josh laughs, "That's all?"

"Ain't that enough?"

"Not really."

"It's more than we got. Took everything we had in savings to bring the café up to codes."

Josh becomes silent as Henry smiles and says, "Don't let it worry you son; we'll make it one way or another. I've seen harder times. Let's go sit on the porch and I'll fix you a cold glass of water."

Josh scans the ranch and asks, "Where's all the livestock?"

"I have no idea."

"Then why are you pouring water in the trough?"

"I don't know; habit, I guess. I never know when they might decide to come back. It would piss 'em off if there wasn't any fresh water waiting for them. I think everything is hiding in the upper forty. Wouldn't want them to show up and find the trough empty."

They walk over to the porch when suddenly Josh goes into a seizure and falls on the steps rolling across the hard ground. He starts jerking all over and then passes out as Henry yells, "What's wrong boy!!?"

Two hours later, Josh slowly opens his eyes only to find Jill leaning over him. She's wiping his forehead with a cool wet rag. Bubba and Henry were standing behind her with looks of puzzlement and concern across their faces.

Bubba whispers, "Is he gonna be alright? This same thing happened early this morning. I thought he was a goner for sure. His eyes rolled back in his head like mine does after eating one of your cheeseburgers and then he fell to the ground like a wet noodle. Which reminds me; did anyone find a cheeseburger on him when he passed out? I bet it's in Elvira's saddlebag."

"Shut up about your damn cheeseburger. I think he's gonna be okay." Jill's rebuttal.

Josh smiles at everyone standing around him and in a garbled voice, "Uh! I went to a far-away land, and you were there Jill undressing me. Bubba was there and he needed a brain, but he was too busy eating and farting." He then turns to Henry and continues, "You were there too Henry. You kept yelling, "I need a stick in my butt to straighten my back up, and I kept saying to myself, 'there's no place like home, there's no place like home."

About this time Jill interrupts, "Yeah, he's all right." She turns to the two, "That smart-ass sense of humor just kicked in."

Bubba, "I think there are some pills that help in one of his saddlebags most likely right next to my cheeseburger."

She turns to him and gives him a provoking look, "Well, don't just stand there you dumb-ass, go get 'em."

Henry yells at him before he made it to the door, "If it's Viagra, save me some."

Jill quickly snaps her head around and gives him a look, "What are you gonna do Pop, go work on that old nanny goat we can't find?"

"I might smarty pants; just as soon as it gets dark, and she's drunk enough. That's if Bubba don't beat me to her."

Josh sits up, "How long have I been out?"

"About two hours," she replied.

He grabs his head and says in a low voice, "It's happening at shorter intervals."

Jill, with a worried look on her face, "What's happening in shorter intervals?"

"Oh nothing; just let me walk around a little bit."

Henry holds his hand up, "Hold it right there Josh. Your ass is naked as a Jaybird under that there blanket." Bubba walks through the door with a small bottle of pills in one hand and a crushed cheeseburger in the other just as Josh was taking a gander under the blanket. He clearly sees that he's been stripped of his clothes. He gives Bubba a drop-dead look and in a loud voice, "Where the hell are my clothes?"

Bubba raises his hands, "Why did you give me that stupid look, I don't care to see your naked ass. If I wanted to see a naked ass, I would squat over a watering trough and look at my own reflection."

Jill interrupts, "I took 'em off so you would be more comfortable."

"My boxers too?"

She smiles and places the cold rag back on his head, "Now don't be silly; who in their right mind would rather wear them boxers to bed than feel those crisp, sun-dried sheets against their naked body?"

"Me frankly; I feel just fine with my clothes on."

She leans toward his right ear and whispers, "I saw everything you got Joshua, even that tattoo of a cactus rose right on your…"

Bubba quickly interrupts the conversation, "Stop right there Jill! We can hear you and we don't wanna know. Just keep that information to yourself. I have enough horrible pictures running around in my head without you drumming up some more shit."

Henry gives Bubba a funny look, "Is one of those pictures Charlotte Evans?"

Bubba frowns, "It is now! Thanks for putting that back in there."

Henry turns back to Jill and Josh and blurts out, "I would like to know exactly where that little tattoo is."

Josh sits up hiding himself with the blanket, "Will everyone please leave the room so I can get dressed?"

Bubba turns to Henry and says sarcastically, "Well, if that's not a fine 'thank you' after giving him all that mouth to mouth!"

Josh just stares for a second when Henry starts laughing, "Don't worry, it wasn't Bubba that gave you mouth to mouth." He yells as he leaves the room, "It was me and I wasn't wearing my teeth!! I get better suction without 'em!!"

Jill laughs, "They're just kidding sugar; I'm the one who gave you mouth to mouth."

He grabs his throat, "So that's why my tonsils feel like they've been power washed and wet-vacuumed!"

"Somebody had to do it."

"Mouth to mouth doesn't work on the problem I have."

"Now how was I to know that?"

"Forget it. Now leave so I can get dressed."

Jill, "Why should I leave? I have already seen everything."

"You would understand better if you knew more about prison life."

She gets a serious look on her face, "How long have you been having these seizures and passing out?"

He just smiles and slowly places his hand on her knee and answers, "About a year now. Sometimes I can go three or four days without having one."

She shakes her head back and forth, "Bubba said you had a bad one early this morning."

He notices her staring at his hand on her knee, so he jerks it away, chuckles and says, "Get me my boxers please." She reaches under the cover and attempts to grab his man tool when he shoves her hand away and blurts out, "Do you mind!? You're still by far the horniest woman I've ever met."

She giggles and stands, "Only for you Joshua Harley James." She walks over to the dresser, takes his boxers in hand and throws them to him. "I washed your clothes and supper will be ready in five minutes, so wash up and don't be late. Bubba's been eyeballing the stovetop for hours, like a coyote watching a chicken pen."

Ten minutes later they're all sitting around at the table watching Bubba pile his plate full. Jill frowns, "You sure you have enough there, Bubba?"

Josh, "Will everyone bow your heads so I can bless this food."

"Wow, I did not know you got religion in the pen." Henry with a smile.

"I found Jesus two days after I got there, and he's been with me ever since. Now, bow your heads so I can bless this food."

They all bow their heads as Josh continues, "Lord Jesus, I wanna thank for this food and all the things you have bless me with. Thank you for letting me see my friends again and please forgive me for any foul language that Bubba causes me to say. Amen."

Bubba looks up at them still staring at him as he continues to load his plate down, "Sorry, it's been a while since I've had real fried chicken, biscuits and mash potatoes."

Josh, staring at Bubba's plate says, "He's right, last night we had what he called roadrunner, but it was shaped a little like a desert rat."

Bubba snaps back with his mouth full, "I assure you it was roadrunner. Damn!! Jill you sure can cook. Maybe we can get married and have a lot of fat children to carry on my legacy."

Josh, with a frown asked, "Let's get back to that roadrunner. How come it had four legs pointing up at the ceiling?"

"I guess he was a freak of nature. Don't look a gift horse in the mouth."

"It was a rat, not a horse."

"I said roadrunner and it wasn't four legs! Them other two was his little wings."

Jill turns her attention to Josh and gives him a wink, "How about you, has it been a while for you?"

He answers, "No, I had three squares a day for sixteen years cooked by my own hands. Then there was this big breakfast I had at your place this morning not counting that four footed roadrunner."

She smiles and without warning, places her foot under the table between his legs rubbing his crotch with her toes, "I wasn't talking about food."

He reaches under the table and pushes her foot away, "Pass the chicken please."

She licks her lips and replies, "Breast or thigh?"

"A thigh please."

"Good choice." She gently passes the plate of chicken, and Josh, having grabbed a piece, nods a 'thank you.'

Again, she licks her lips and gives him a sassy glance. "I personally like the leg; I like to chew the bone."

Bubba and Henry just stare at the two of them and then look at each other pretending not to understand all the sex chatter and innuendos. She starts to say something else when suddenly Henry blurts out, "Enough!! Me and Bubba are trying to have an appetite here!"

She snaps back, "What? I'm not stopping you two from eating. It hasn't slowed Bubba down."

"You don't think we understand what you're talking about with all that, 'I like chewing on the bone' crap?"

With a little sneer, she says; "I have no idea what you're talking about."

Henry fires back, "Even Bubba can read between those lines." Everyone looks over at Bubba and watches as he devours his chicken like it was the last edible bird on earth.

She stares at him ripping through his chicken like it was cotton candy, then gives Henry a glare, "Yeah, I'm sure all the talk has made Bubba lose his appetite. His fat ass could eat grits in a sandstorm."

Bubba notices everyone watching and says with a mouth full, "What were y'all saying?"

Henry shakes his head, "Nothing Bubba, just go back to your own little world. I bet you fall asleep at night counting chickens instead of sheep."

"I like pork chops too."

"Pork is from freaking pigs, not sheep. You're talking about lamb chops."

"I didn't know that. I thought ham came from a pig."

Moments later they sat back at the table as Jill goes back and forth placing dirty dishes in the sink. Henry reaches into his top pocket and pulls out a cigar. He leans toward Josh, "Have one of these. Taste real fine after a good hardy home cooked meal." Josh takes the cigar from his hand as Henry continues to pack his pipe full of imported tobacco and then lights it, "So where are you heading from here?"

"I was thinking about looking around town a little before traveling to Colorado. I didn't get a chance this morning after eating at Jill's place."

Jill, disappointed and upset at what she was hearing asks, "Why don't you stay here for a while and help Pop. The place needs fixing up and you can stay in the spare room."

"I might just do that; at least for a few more weeks."

She smiles, "Good, then it's settled, I'll go run your bathwater and then straighten the extra bedroom up." Henry turns to Bubba, shrugging his shoulders. She turns to them, "Bubba, you can sleep with Pop tonight and drive back to your place in the morning." Henry and Bubba just stood there staring at her, wondering what was going to come flowing from her lips next. She tilts her head and gives them a stare, "You two can go to bed now."

Henry fires back, "You're not talking to children here; we're not ready to go to bed. I was kind of thinking maybe we can stay up, have some of my homemade moonshine, smoke cigars and talk about the good-old days."

She gives him a dirty look, "You're tired and sleepy Pop, and take Bubba with you. You need to be up early to feed the livestock."

Henry shakes his head, "I don't have a particular time to feed nine chickens, one damn rooster, and a worn-down nanny goat."

Bubba pats his stomach and with a smile, "You have nine chickens?"

She gets angry, "Well hell, you need to get to bed early so you can milk the damn cow."

Henry with a puzzled look, "We don't have a cow, at least not one close enough to the barn to milk. What's going on here?"

She gets really ticked off and slams a plate in the sink and gives them another angry look.

Henry stares into her eyes, stands, and turns to Bubba and in an agitated way, "Sorry, I forgot to read between the lines again."

Bubba with a puzzled look on his face, "I'm completely lost."

Henry shakes his head back and forth at Jill, "Oh hell Bubba, let's go to bed before she decides to break all the dishes in the damn house. And another thing Bubba, don't start that farting game with me. I'll plug your ass with the bedpost. I'll take the moonshine to bed with us."

Bubba laughs, "Promises, promises."

An hour later, Josh is relaxing and soaking in a hot tub of water enjoying the pleasures of the moment. It's been sixteen years since he has had a good hot bath, that's if you don't count that bath at Bubba's place with all the rust in the water. Sure, feels nice. In prison they only had showers and he had to share them with ten other guys from his cellblock. Standing on the other side of the door was Jill who was reaching for the knob on the bathroom door but hesitated for a few moments while she pondered to herself. "What am I doing?" She asked herself. "What if he still thinks of me as the little girl he remembered before he went away?" She stood up straight, ran her hands down her pink lacy negligee, straightened it and said to herself, "Pull yourself together, he has been in prison for the past sixteen years, he will want you."

About this time Bubba peeks out of Henry's door and asks, "You get lost on your way to your room, Jill?"

She removes a candle from its stand that was resting on a small wooden table in the hallway and slings it at him with enough force to have taken his head off.

Bubba ducks and yells, "I guess not!"

Josh hesitates after hearing the thumping sound outside the door and then continues with his hot bath.

Jill turns her attention back to the door and slowly turns the doorknob and steps into the bathroom. Josh quickly looks up at her with a surprised expression, "What are you doing now? I'm taking a bath here." She just stood there with her back against the door and her hand on the knob, giving him a sexy stare. With her hands behind her she locks the door and that's when he really took notice of her. He knew very well what she came in for. She was no longer the little girl he remembered before he was sent off to prison. She had grown into a beautiful young sexy woman, one that he could very well lust after if he allowed himself, which at this point was going to happen whether he wanted it to or not.

He asks, "What are you doing in here?" As he looked her up and down and noticed her very well-proportioned body underneath her thin negligee. Her skin was so tanned next to the pink silky outfit that he could only imagine what she looked like underneath. What seemed like forever was only a few seconds as Jill stepped forward, pulling the thin straps over her shoulders, allowing her negligee to drop a few inches, exposing the flesh of her prefect shape breasts just enough to tease him. She hesitates and then allows the negligee to hit the floor. She hopes Josh wouldn't turn her down; she had dreamed of this moment for a long time. He just sat in the tub staring at her, as she slowly walks closer allowing him to gander over her tan, flat stomach. Then, she ever so gently, pushed her panties down, allowing them to slowly slide over her hips. Her body was just as he imagined, very toned and plump in all the right places. He was speechless as he just sat there and stared at her, already getting hard at the thought of what was about to happen.

She walks over to the tub, bends over and says in a soft voice, "It's yours, if you want it." He slowly reaches up and tenderly runs his fingers down her face; the touch and feel of a woman's skin sure was a big change from reading girlie magazines. He lets his hands move down her neck and shoulders and then very gently to her breasts. Her nipples responses with an unyielding sensation and stood out as if she was taking a walk in a cool rainstorm. She takes this as an invitation and leans closer giving him a gentle soft kiss on the lips. He takes her by the hand to guide her into the tub with him. She sits with her back to him and can feel his hardness as she snuggles between his ripped muscular thighs. He runs his hand across her bare breasts and begins kissing and nipping at the back of her neck. She leans back into him and enjoys the moment. She is surprised at how gentle he is with her.

"Why are you doing this?" He asks.

"I love you; I've always loved you and I'm horny as hell. Plus, I think you forgot to clean something, so let me help you with that. What kind of hostess would I be if I didn't clean you up in a proper manner….?'"

With that she turns to face him so she could look into his deep brown eyes. Without saying another word, she turns and slides her hot body down on top of him and starts moving up and down ever so slowly. He runs his tongue over her smooth breast until he can't take it anymore. He quickly stands, pulling her up with him allowing their wet bodies to mesh.

As they are standing in place, she slides her wet tongue across his tight sixpack and allows it to linger briefly, circling the entire surface of his abs. She then continues to lick him all the way down his muscular abs until she takes a firm grip. He gently places his hand behind her head and pulls it towards him, arching forward toward her. She continues until he is nearly about to explode. She rises back up kissing his stomach once again as she is fully aroused. He takes her face once again in his hands and kisses her. Then she grabs him by the hand and leads him from the bathroom and into the bedroom, still dripping wet. He gently lays her down and mounts her from the top. He eases into her and begins moving, slowly at first, then harder and faster. She says in a sweet, sexy voice, "This is what I have been waiting for all these years."

In the next room Bubba and Henry laid beside each other listening to Jill's bed springs squeak like someone was walking on an old tin roof. They can hear the headboard bumping out a steady rhythm against the thin wooden plank wall.

Henry slowly turns to Bubba, "Somebody needs to oil their springs and place a damn pillow between the headboard and wall."

Bubba smiles, "If they do that, than my imagination has nowhere to go."

Henry, "I can remember when I used to make noises like that."

Bubba ponders for a moment, "Whatta ya think they're doing in there?"

Henry smiles, "I hope they're making me a grandbaby."

Bubba responds, staring up at the ceiling with a blank look on his face, "I still can make noises like that, but with a silent pause in-between switching hands."

Henry turns and smiles. Bubba throws a crook in the corner of his mouth, "Don't get any ideas old man, I don't fly that way."

Henry, in a jokingly manner, "Let see how that goes after we finish off this jug of moonshine to loosen you up a little."

Jill could be heard yelling, "Oh my God!! Oh my God!! Faster...no slower...oh my God, that feels so good! Never in my life.....!!"

Bubba grabs a pillow and squeezes it around his ears, "I can't take this crap anymore. My pickle is harder than a fence post."

Henry laughs, "I do have that nanny goat out there tied to a fence rail. She's quite a woman if you're real gentle with her."

Bubba fires back, "You're one sick puppy; I'm not that bad off...Yet!"

Henry turns the other way, "Give it time fat boy, give it time."

The sounds that Jill is making gets louder as she keeps screaming out the words, "Oh, Josh, harder, faster, harder, faster."

Seconds later a small-framed picture of a running brook fell and almost hit Bubba in the head. Bubba asks in a real low voice, "Where did you say that nanny goat was tied?"

"I was just kidding; I haven't seen that bitch in months."

"So that was just a tease uh?"

"Yep, pretty much."

"How long do you think this will go on?"

Henry counts on his fingers, "Let me see; if my math is correct, Josh spent sixteen years in prison and she's been saving herself longer than that...I would say off and on about ten days and nights, that's if they stop to eat lunch."

In the other room Josh continues stroking her until he knows he can't take it much longer and rolls off. Jill looks over at him with a gazed look in her eyes, "Oh hell no you don't!" She climbs on top of him and places him back inside. She strokes faster and faster until she knows she will cut lose it any second. He pulls her down to him and starts nibbling on her nipples. This sends her over the top and she came so hard that the sound of her moaning makes him follow right behind her. Afterwards, they cling together in a sweaty entanglement. He held her tight for what seemed forever. Then she slowly and reluctantly rolls off the top of him.

He lies there breathing heavy and turns his head toward her, "You were amazing."

She reaches over and punches him in the arm, "It was just what the doctor ordered."

In the other room, Bubba smiles, "Finally somebody can get some sleep around here."

Henry laughs and starts a countdown, "Five, four, three, two, one… Suddenly Jill starts screaming and moaning. Bubba covers his ears again then quickly jumps from the bed.

Henry asks, "Where are you going?"

"To the bathroom!"

"You just went not more than twenty minutes ago!"

"I have the squirts if it's any of your business."

As he leaves the room, Henry in a loud voice, "Don't pull too hard. Ninety percent of all accidents happen in the bathroom!"

CHAPTER 10

Bright and early the next morning around six o'clock, Jill's running around the kitchen frying bacon and eggs like her adrenaline's maxed out. She checks the oven to make sure the biscuits were not burning, quickly wipes her hands on her flowered apron and runs to the cabinet to the right of the old ceramic sink. She takes out four plates and places them on the table next to the forks and knives. Out of the corner of her eye she catches Henry and Bubba staring from the doorway.

"What the hell are you two staring at?"

Henry, with a silly grin on his face asks, "Are you feeling alright?"

She places her hands on her hip, "Why do you ask that?"

Henry replies, "Because you're hopping around the kitchen like a lamb running from a starving wolf and it's not even light yet. And there's some kind of glow about you."

She snaps back, "I need to be at the café in an hour for the breakfast crowd. Somebody has to pay the bills around this rundown dump you call a ranch. Now wash up and eat, I wanna see some work done around here today."

Bubba starts mumbling as he turns to walk off while scratching his rear end, "I'll wake Josh."

She yells, "Don't you dare wake him! I'll do it. He had trouble sleeping last night. You two take your seat."

Bubba yawns and responds, "Yeah, we had trouble sleeping last night too. How would you know if he had trouble sleeping last night?"

She trots from the kitchen to wake Josh.

Josh is lying in her bedroom tossing and turning and sweating like crazy. He's dreaming he's streaking across the hot Flats at night, faster than a jet plane with police vehicles hot on his heels. There were helicopters throwing spotlights over the desert floor like opening night at the circus and bullet rounds are kicking up sand all around him. He's racing toward the mountains, but they seem to get farther and farther, when suddenly he takes a plunge into a deep washed-out gorge. Elvira buries herself deep in the sand and the rain starts to pour. The sudden stop threw him twenty feet. He slowly tries to crawl back when he feels a sharp pain in his leg. Headlights appear in the gully racing toward him. He couldn't move fast enough. The lights come to a stop and Jill jumps out and runs over gently placing her hand on his broken thigh. Bubba, steps out chewing on a chicken leg like there is no tomorrow.....

Jill's hand felt good on his broken leg. He smiles, still drifting in and out of his dreamland. Her grip gets tighter as he peels an eye open and sees her sitting on the side of the bed with her hand under the cover. He cuts his eyes and gives her a stare and in a slow tender voice asks, "Are you having fun down there?"

"I'm just waking it up for breakfast honey bunch."

"You have an unusual way to do that. You ever get enough sex?"

"Nope, you can never get enough especially when it's been that many years." She frowns and continues, "By the looks of that grin on your face, I bet you were remembering the pleasures of last night."

"Actually, I was having a nightmare."

"You sure you weren't dreaming about me?"

He drags himself from bed with the blanket still wrapped around him, "I was riding a beautiful buckskin mare with black mane and tail across the valley towards Ole Crooked Rock."

She smiles, "I bet you were. So, riding a horse around Crooked Rock makes your pecker that hard?"

"No, having a woman rub on it in the morning does though."

She slowly stands and walks around the bed and in a sexy voice whispers, "You want me again, right now? Because you can have me if you want."

He takes a step back, "I smell bacon. Are you cooking breakfast?"

"It can burn for all I care. Make love to me again Josh."

"You like to have killed me last night."

She gets frustrated, places her hand on her hips, "Damn your hide, most men would cross the Flats on foot to get a piece of me, now get washed and dressed for breakfast before those two pigs in there eat everything in sight." She starts to stomp out when he grabs her by the arm.

Bubba and henry could hear Josh banging her against the door.

They're are sitting at the table and turning ever so often towards the stove and then looking back at each other., "They're at it again, Henry. I sure hope he finishes quickly; I think the smell of that food is giving me a boner. Maybe we should turn the beacon and check on those biscuits."

Henry stands and walks over to the stove. He opens the oven door and with a rag pulls the biscuits out, placing the pan on the stove top and then turns the bacon in the pan for a few seconds before placing it on a plate with a paper towel underneath. Bubba poured the lemonade and then heard some crunching noises.

Bubba, "Are you doing what I think you're doing!"

Henry turns with a mouth full of bacon and barely able to speak, "No I am not!"

"Well, if you're not let me help you out."

Minutes later Josh walks into the kitchen wearing his usual tight-fitting jeans and black t-shirt and with an easy hand slides a chair out.

Bubba was grinning from ear to ear when he asks, "You have a hard night?"

Josh gives him a look and grabs a hot biscuit.

Henry laughs, "You must have a magic wand crammed in them there jeans boy. You had that girl running around this kitchen before daylight like a crazy woman on drugs. I can almost remember a day when I could do that to a woman. Do I have to replace the hinges on that door?"

Josh, "Give her a few boys and why do I see two biscuits and no beacon?"

Bubba blurts out, "You know very well why there's no beacon and what happen to the other eight biscuits, your guess is as good as ours…..Damn,

I just wish I had a woman like that."

Josh scoops some grits from a pot on the table, "You need to keep a ball and chain on that girl so I can wake up without her hands trying to pull on my 'you know what'."

Bubba shakes his head, "Now…let me get this right. You had a beautiful girl riding you so hard that it almost killed me and Henry in the next room and you're complaining? I've never seen someone so in love before."

Josh pauses from eating for a second, "I don't know if it's love yet."

"I wasn't talking about you.."

A few minutes later Jill comes walking in the room grabbing up dishes as all three just sit there sipping their coffee. She slams the dishes down in the sink and turns to the three, "Enough coffee; you guys can start earning your breakfast by cleaning up around this place starting with the old barn. I want this place to look like a real ranch when I get home." She rolls her hair up in a French twist and stalks out the door.

Bubba turns to Henry, "Well so much for that love shit. I've never seen a woman go from 'dancing around the kitchen with the look of joy on her face' to, 'get your asses to work,' that quick in my life. Maybe it would be better for me and Henry if you had stayed in there for a little longer."

Henry shakes his head, "Yep, why Josh here can turn 'em on and turn 'em off like a light switch."

Josh stands and follows her out on the front porch, but before he could speak, a police unit could be seen speeding up in the driveway. Jill turns to him with a nod, "That must be Clint getting started early. I figured it was just a matter of time before he came popping in here. Go back inside Josh and tell Pop to get me the shotgun."

Josh shakes his head back and forth, "You don't need a shotgun, just let him come. He can't do anything to me, I've done nothing wrong."

"It doesn't matter if you're right or wrong to Clint. He doesn't like you, never has liked you and never will."

The car pulls up to a stop and a large potbellied man with coffee stains running down the front of his wrinkled uniform steps out adjusting his gun belt. He brushes cake crumbs from his stomach and walks toward Josh.

Josh, with a grin, "Now I would recognize that fat belly anywhere. Even if it does look like Bubba's. You've got to be Big Jim Davis. You used to be the garbage man; sold hats and boots on the side."

The man stops a few feet from the steps leading up to the porch and with a sad look asks, "Am I too late for breakfast?"

Jill smiles, "Bubba stayed overnight; does that answer your question?"

"Yep, that boy doesn't leave a crumb."

Josh smiles, "By the looks of that belly, you don't leave a whole lot yourself. I bet there isn't a donut left this side of the Rockies."

Jim, with his frown turning to a grin, "I knew when Clint told me that a troublemaker dressed in black, sporting a belt with chrome Conchos and black cowboy boots, riding a big Harley that you were back."

Josh steps off the porch, "So, what now Jim, you gonna arrest me?"

"I just might! Why…Are you planning on giving me some trouble?"

Josh frowns, "What if I decide to run? How you gonna catch me with all that trunk space you're carrying around there?"

Jim slowly steps forward, "Too fat to run, I'll just shoot you in the back. Call it suicide. You see, we're not as refined as them there city boys up in Albuquerque."

Josh takes a step closer, "I don't think that's gonna happen, especially if you shoot like you used to throw garbage cans."

"I do have six tries, you know."

"You look a lot like a fat man who used to take me hunting all the time and if my memory serves me well; you couldn't hit that barn over there with a 12 gauge."

Jim stepped closer and by now they were standing within a few feet of one another. "I've been practicing over the last sixteen years; and now that you mention it, I do have that scatter gun in the car."

Josh replies, "That's the problem, it's in the car. What kind of fool would make you an officer of the law anyway?"

"I'm not just an officer, I'm the Sheriff now."

"Okay, I'll stand corrected; what kind of fool would make you the Sheriff?"

"Most likely the same damn fool that would let you out of prison."

Henry and Bubba walk out on the porch and stand there next to Jill watching the two.

Josh steps even closer, his large Harley belt buckle touching Jim's gun belt.

Jim asks, "Are you planning on kissing me stranger?"

"I would have to climb over that 'mountain you have for a gut' to do that, but what the hell, I'll give it a try." He reaches over and kisses him right on the lips. Jim jumps back spitting and wiping his mouth with his forearm and yells, "Damn you Josh, you turn queer in the big house!?"

Jill, being sarcastic, jumps off the porch and says as she makes her way toward her jeep, "I was asking him the same thing Jim, just yesterday, but after last night I can safely say he's still with us." She jumps in her jeep, starts it up and spins around kicking up dust everywhere as she makes her way down the driveway toward the main road.

Jim asks, "Wow! Who put a burr under her saddle this morning?"

Bubba, in a loud voice, "Josh put her in a bad mood. He cut the sex off too early!"

"Yep must have turned queer."

Josh smiles, "Even I can't go all night."

Jim shakes his head back and forth, "No matter, she sure is in a bad mood which means no free coffee this morning." He turns back to Josh and with a grin, "I didn't believe it when I heard it, so I had to drive out and see for myself."

Josh smiles, "How'd you know I was here?"

"Haven't you heard, I'm the lead investigator around here and we have them there new computer things that tracks people for us. That and I've had to listen to Jill talk about you for the last sixteen years, day in and day out, so I put two and two together."

Josh stands back and looks him over, "You haven't changed one bit."

Jim responds, "Well you sure the hell have. Where did you get all those muscles? You look like old man Eaton's prize-winning bull."

"I had free access to a gym and a lot of free time on my hands." Josh replied.

Jim grabs a hand full of his belly, "Maybe you can show me how to lose this."

Josh laughs, "It would take more than sixteen years to get rid of that. It would be like chiseling away at Chimney rock with just a screwdriver and hammer."

Jim laughs back, "You may be right, took thirty to get this way."

Josh leans over and places his ear just above Jim's gun belt, "I feel it kicking; is it a boy or girl?"

"Very funny, smart-ass!"

Josh, with a grin, "You're the only man I know that his waist size matches his height. You and Bubba must be running a race."

Bubba yells from the porch, "I...I..." He turns to Henry, "What's the word I'm looking for?"

"Resent' is the word you're looking for."

Bubba continues, "That's it, I resent that fat joke."

Jim looks Josh over again, "You're a sight for an old fat man's eyes and I'm glad to see you again and then in a way I wish I hadn't. You were wrong to come back here." Jim removes his beige Stetson and takes a seat on the steps.

Josh takes a seat next to him and asks, "What made you wanna be Sheriff? I thought you liked selling hats and boots and throwing trash cans."

"McNally bought me out and fronted the money to get me elected and then he married my daughter...And that's another thing; don't even think about seeing Susan. As much as I hate that bastard, she belongs to him now. She doesn't even speak to me anymore."

"So, you're one of McNally's boys now...huh?"

"Not really, he's my son in-law and as long as he makes my paycheck out, I'll pretend I'm one of the boys...Which brings up another point; get your ass outta town by sundown. They will be hot on your trail before you can snap your fingers. This town is about nothing but McNally and what he wants. And he is going to want you gone or dead. Not counting the run in with Pete and his bunch at Bubba's place. The whole town is talking about your encounter at Jill's place. They say you had Clint peeing on himself."

Josh loses his grin, "Get out of town by sundown'! You for real?"

Jim snaps back, "Nope, I've just always wanted to say that. I do have a few hats left over from the store and I'll leave you a nice black Stetson with Jill, so you can lose the bandana and blend in with your surroundings. I'm sorry to hear about your mama. She was a terrific woman. It took a lot of years for her to get over your daddy, but when you went to prison was more than she could bare." He struggles to lift himself from the porch, stands and starts to walk to the marked unit when he suddenly stops and slowly turns to Josh with great apprehension, "I do want you and that big scooter to stay away from town and out of McNally's way and I really mean that. Hell, he won't even know you're still here if you stay with Jill. I'll just say you left town for Arizona."

"Too late, you already know I ran into Clint yesterday morning."

Jim snaps back, "Yeah I just said that, and plum forgot that I said it."

"Yeah, we had some words over breakfast. I don't think he recognized me though."

"All the more reason for you to stay away from town."

Josh shakes his head, "I thought this was a free country."

"It's only free if McNally says it's free and he ain't gonna say that." He places his hat back on his head, opens the car door and struggles to get behind the steering wheel. He starts the car, places it in gear and looks over at Josh, "Take care of yourself and remember this, I have just so much control over what goes on around here. Maybe I can sneak out here sometime and we can go hunting." He drives off leaving Josh standing there scratching his head through his black bandana.

He turns to Henry and Bubba, "When it comes to the weather Bubba, you suck, but you're right about one thing; a lot has changed around here."

CHAPTER 11

Night takes over day at the Circle M Ranch as lights can be seen flicking on in various windows of the large white mansion on the hill with its tall white pillars setting off a faded gray glow in the dark. Acres of flowing green grass rolling for miles, hill over hill, in contrast to the hot sandy desert across the highway. The sky turns black as the sun makes its final glimmer behind the mountains. McNally walks out on the porch, places his Stetson over a thick head of gray hair and stabs a large hand rolled stogie between his lips. He was a man in his early sixties, of medium height, and stout, but had that control look about him. Before starting out, a beautiful woman with long flowing blond hair in her early thirties walks out wearing a long transparent gown and pauses before asking, "You going to be out late tonight?"

He turns with an evil glow in his eyes, "I think I'll go strike up a poker game if it's any of your damn business."

"I just wanna know if you need me to fix you a supper plate and leave it in the microwave?"

"Yeah, fix me a plate and if I don't get home in time, I'll throw it to the damn dogs...taste like shit anyway. Too bad you can't cook as well as you screw." He takes a few menacing steps closer, "You just have that ass of yours waiting for me in case I can't find another piece lying around tonight." She takes a seat on the swing and sits there in silence. He steps off the porch and into his black hummer. She watches as he drives off into the night on another one of his all-night drinking binges.

Minutes later she stands and turns to walk back inside when she hears a distance coyote howling at the moon then a very low voice is heard coming from the dark shadows, "I would have never in my wildest dream believed you would take that shit from anyone." The deep mysterious voice startles her at first and then she catches a dark figure out of the corner of her eye unfolding from around the end of the porch behind the last white column. Josh steps closer, but his face was hidden by the shadow from the second large porch column. She strains her eyes to make out who was speaking from the dark but couldn't make it out.

"Clint, is that you?"

"It's not Clint."

In a soft voice she asks, "Who are you? Your voice sounds familiar."

"An old friend from the past, who had to see for himself if it was true about what people are saying about her."

"Again, who are you?"

"You're still as beautiful as ever."

She steps even closer, only a few feet from the end of the porch. The voice strikes out into the night again, but this time she recognizes it. Taking a few steps back and in a broken, hesitant voice, "Oh my God, it's you!" He steps out of the shadows, and she covers her mouth to keep from screaming, realizing she had made no mistake. She tenses up and starts to shake and asks, "How did you…I don't understand how…you are supposed to be in…"

She takes a deep breath as he steps closer with a smile, "That's a lot of words for just a few incomplete sentences."

She swallows, "You should have never come up here. If he finds you here, he'll shoot you on the spot. We have top-notch security here and if they discover you here, they will string you up by your balls and you'll wish you were dead."

"I'll take that chance; just seeing you again is worth being shot for. There hasn't been a day gone by that thoughts of you weren't running around in my head. It's what kept me going."

She places her hand on her chest and takes another deep breath, "I belong to someone else now. My God how did you get so big?"

"He treats his horses better than that. I had a growing spurt."

"He takes care of me. I have everything a woman needs Josh, something that you could never have given me."

"Love; do you have love or is that even necessary anymore?"

Her lips start to quiver, "He gives me what I need; a future that does not spell poverty and that's enough. I didn't wanna wind up living in some rundown trailer park on the edge of the desert. I don't have to do anything but shop and keep him sexually satisfied. Now leave before somebody sees you."

"I can't until you tell me you have no feelings for me."

"I don't have anything for you, so just leave the same way you came."

"I don't believe you, not after all we've been through."

She turned her head to the left and then to the right, scanning the area making sure no one was watching. She steps back, "It's been sixteen years and a lot of changes have come to past. Now please leave before someone sees you."

"Say it, say you don't love me."

She hesitates before answering, "Alright then, I don't love you. Does that convince you?"

He replies, "That's the worst acting I have ever…" No sooner did he utter those words did a set of headlights light up the long-paved driveway and streak across the front of the house as a vehicle approached.

She yells, "It's him…run Josh, don't let him catch you here." He backs into the darkness as the vehicle pulls up in front.

Clint steps from the vehicle and sees her standing on the porch. He yells from the car, "Damn woman, it's cold out here; you're going to catch pneumonia!"

She glances over to make sure Josh was gone and then responds, "I'm okay, just walked out for a breath of fresh air." Clint steps up on the porch, grabs her and kisses her long and hard placing both hands on the cheeks of her rear end giving it a firm squeeze.

"You're shaking like a leaf."

"It's chilly out here." Being nervous over seeing Josh.

"I thought that old bastard would never leave. I see the cold air has your nipples standing up."

She grabs him by the hand and leads him toward the door, "Let's get inside before someone sees us." Josh, never leaving, peeks around the corner and watches as they step inside. He walks around to a window and could see Clint rubbing her breast before dragging her into the kitchen. He walks back a few more windows and sees her being thrown up on the table and Clint spreading her legs. He jerks his pants down in anticipation and makes his way between her thighs as she pulls on his uniform. He could hear her moaning as Clint had her gown pushed up around her waist and was already inside her making slow but strong stokes. He slowly turns, and for some reason, wasn't saddened nor upset at the events taking place before his very eyes, but more in a stupor shock than anything. What kind of man would throw his stepmother up on the eating table and bang the hell out of her five minutes after his dad left? He had no idea why he was surprised; it sounded just like something he would have done years ago. He took another peek and could see Clint hitting it so hard that the table was rocking back and forth. Not just any table, but a large oak table. He listens to their conversation as time passes. After watching for a little longer, Josh went to adjust his feet and knocked over a rake a worker had left leaning against the house. Clint stops stroking for a few second when Susan asks, "What's wrong?"

"I thought I heard something."

"Right, keep stroking before I lose the mood."

Minutes later they're sitting at the table smoking a cigarette. Susan leans back in the chair, "That was good stuff honey, but you need a bath. You smell like a damn pig from sweating all day."

"I didn't have time to take a shower."

"The old man won't be home for six or seven hours, so go take a bath."

He stands and walks closer to where she's sitting, "I'm ready for another piece of ass."

"After a bath!"

He grabs her by the head, pulls her up on her feet, bends her over the table and jerks her grown up around her waist again.

"You're hurting me, Clint."

"Shut up bitch and give it to me like I like it." He shoves it inside her and starts humping again like crazy; faster and faster.

"She yells again, "Did you hear me, I said for you to go take a bath before you have me smelling like a pig!"

He gets even faster and harder, almost pushing her small frame off the table. Suddenly he lets out a moan of relief; hesitates for a second or two and then slowly backs away and pulls his pants up. He takes two more cigarettes from his top shirt pocket, lights them and places one in her mouth and the other in his. He takes a long drag off of it, licks his lips and says, "Let's go take a shower together and then I'll break in the old bastard's bed like it should have been on your wedding night." He laughs, shakes his head back and forth and asks, "How do you crawl up in bed with that old nasty Billy goat anyway?"

With a chuckle she replies, "That old nasty Billy goat is worth about 10 million and for that much he can lay on top of me, sweat like a pig and have a freakin heart attack for all I care. Right now, you don't smell any better."

He places a hand on her breast and as he plays with her nipple he asks, "What makes you think he's gonna leave any of that money to you and not me and Pete?"

She moistens her lips with her tongue, as she gets turned on at the nipple rubbing, he was doing, and replies in a whisper, "He's gonna leave it to me unless you and Pete can take care of that wrinkled-up bean of his." No sooner did she get those words out, he gets an erection again, drops his pants and shoves it back inside her. She can't stand the odor he's giving off any longer, shoves him back and yells, "Enough for now; get that shower!"

He pulls his pants up shaking his head, "You never cared about the odor before; why are you so tense?"

"I'm tired of all the sneaking around; I think we need to speed things up a little."

"What are you talking about?"

"I'm talking about your father, stupid ass. I can't keep doing this sneaking around crap. I can tell by how hard the old bastard screws; his heart isn't gonna play out anytime soon. Trust me; I put some stuff on him that would make a Brahma bull fall over with a stroke."

"You have any ideas?"

"I say you two go for a horse ride up past Lonely Creek. Say you wanna go coyote hunting or something, then bash his head in with a rock and say the horse threw him. Nobody could prove otherwise, not that anyone would give a shit. The people of that stinking town will declare a holiday."

"Wow, you're one heartless bitch! I have a better plan; you can get him good and drunk and find that combination to the safe. I'll take the cash he hides in there and then you can sneak rat poison in the bastard's drink."

"Right and I'll be the first one they suspect."

"Not with me doing the investigation. I just say it was a heart attack."

"You ever heard of the phase, 'conflict of interest'? The Feds will flock into this town like ants on sugar.

Josh decides now is as good as any time to get the hell out of there. He takes off on foot across the yard and into the pasture. He fires up Elvira and takes off like a rocket across the meadow kicking up grass and dirt in every direction.

Clint stops talking for a few seconds, "I heard something."

She laughs, "How could you have heard anything over that moaning and grunting you were doing?"

"I'm talking about right now. I think I heard something."

"You're hearing things. Enough about that shit, there's another problem that's come up."

"What's that?"

"I just saw Josh."

"Josh who?"

"How many damn Joshes do you know?"

"Well, there's Josh Parker over in Red Valley and then there's…"

She quickly interrupts, "Joshua Harley James, you stupid ass! I swear Clint; sometimes I think you have less brains than a chunk of limestone."

"You couldn't have seen Josh; he's serving twenty years for murder."

"Maybe it was his damn ghost then…I'm telling you I just spoke to him minutes before you drove up."

Clint goes into deep thought, when suddenly he snaps his fingers, "That's why you are so tensed…..Shit!! That's who that bastard was!"

"What are you talking about?"

"Just before noon yesterday at Jill's place, I ran into a guy riding a maroon Harley, who looked familiar to me, but I couldn't put a name to that face until now."

She steps closer, "All those years of high school and you didn't recognize him."

"He had facial hair, a scar on his face and was wearing one of those motorcycle bandanas on his head and was built like an armored truck. It never crossed my mind."

"I swear Clint; you're as dumb as a damn mule. He could make trouble for us."

"You just leave him to me. I'll get a shower and we'll talk some more."

CHAPTER 12

Back at Henry's place, Josh pulls up on Elvira and sees Jill and Bubba sitting in rocking chairs on the porch with Henry standing at the end smoking on his pipe. He slowly dismounts and casually walks toward them, but before he could make it to the steps, Jill asks, "Where the hell have you been?"

He replies, "I was out riding the roads and checking out the sunset over at Look Out Point."

Knowing better, she gives him a look, "You've been out to McNally's place seeing that whore. It's written all over your face Joshua Harley James."

Bubba shakes his head and turns to Henry, "You can always tell when a woman's going off the deep end; she uses your whole name in a sentence when yelling at you."

Hearing Bubba, she quickly turns and gives him an angry stare. Josh breaks in and responds with a grin. "You're not my wife. I can still come and go as I please. I had to find out for myself if it was true."

Henry and Bubba look the other way, knowing how her temper could get out of control sometimes. She crosses her arms and gives the chair a little push with her foot, "What did she have to say? No wait, let me guess, 'I've missed you so much Josh and couldn't sleep at night just thinking about you in that terrible, cold, damp prison cell. Come on inside my mansion and let's make love like we used to up on Deer Lake.'"

He laughs at her mocking Susan and then responds, "You sound nothing like her. She said she hated me. That was just before McNally's son Clint walked up, grabbed her on the ass and gave her a mouth full of tongue."

Bubba jumps into the conversation; "Get out of here! You mean to tell me that son of a cigar-smoking whore-chaser is doing his mother?"

"Well, technically she's, his stepmother."

"Give us the dirty details and I mean the good ones." Henry leans in closer and tilts his head with his good ear toward Josh.

Josh gives Jill a look and she blurts out, "Go ahead; I would like to hear the details myself, not that I'm a bit surprised."

He continues with the story, "Clint gave her a big sloppy kiss as he was squeezing those nice round cheeks of hers." He gives Jill a wink and turns back to Bubba, "You remember how round those cheeks of her butt was up on Deer Lake, don't you Bubba?"

Bubba smiles, "You damn right I do. The memory of that ass is burned into my brain like the smell of fresh bacon cooking."

Jill gives Bubba a dirty look as Josh continues, "He pushes her well rounded butt into the kitchen and…"

Henry interrupts, "And what? Don't stop, I believe there's something happening between my legs!"

Josh responds, "Hold your horses Henry, this is the part where I was switching windows." He continues, "He grabs her by the waist and throws her up on the dining room table and spreads those legs back like a Thanksgiving turkey."

Bubba breaks out in a sweat, "Did he make a wish?"

Josh replies, "He did more than that. He stuffed that butterball turkey like two rabbits going at it."

Henry chuckles, "Wow, and I didn't think I would ever get a hard on again."

Jill stands, walks over to where Henry is standing and slaps him on the back before saying, "That's enough Pop."

"What? I'm not dead yet."

She snaps back, "You will be if you don't stop talking. You're just gonna give yourself a heart attack."

Josh takes a seat on the first step of the porch and leans against the support post, "Clint having sex with his father's wife, wow! That beats everything."

Jill yells, "What did you expect. She was a whore when she dated you, still is a whore, and always will be a whore. You're lucky you didn't get caught going up there to see her. Did you think she was just gonna lay out the welcome mat and open her legs for you?"

Josh frowns and slowly turns to her, "That would have been nice. Stop with the sarcasm. I had to know for sure."

"Well, now you know."

Josh, "There's something else. I heard them talking about getting rid of the old man. She wanted Clint to take him hunting and smash his head in and he suggested to her to give him rat poison."

Jill chuckles, "Again I'm not surprised at all." She walks toward the front door, stops, turns and says before going inside, "She will tell Clint and by morning everybody in the county will know you're back. Cold pizza is in the microwave." She walks inside, closing the door behind her.

Henry and Bubba lean closer as Henry asks, "Anymore details Josh?"

Josh adds, "She was screaming and yelling for more, which is pretty understandable considering Clint was never gifted in that area, and then he just jumped right back into it going for a second go around."

Bubba swallows, "What did she look like spread out on that table? Was she naked? Did it look good?"

Josh glances through the screen door, making sure Jill wasn't standing there and replies in a low whisper, "That girl looked so good I got an erection myself and had to stand a foot away from the window."

Bubba's mouth just drops open. Josh, seeing an opportunity to screw with his mind says, "She had the smoothest dark-tanned thighs, and they were shoved up around her…"

Bubba jumps up and yells, "Hold that thought Josh, I have to go to the bathroom!!"

Henry just shakes his head, "Now this is good gossip; would not surprise me if Little Pete ain't banging it too."

Josh stands and slowly makes his way to the door. Henry asks, "You gonna be alright?"

He turns and looks over his shoulder, "Yeah, it didn't upset me like I thought it would. I guess those years in prison has harden my heart."

Henry takes a puff off the pipe, "I guess you already know that Jill's in love with you and has been since she was eleven. As much as I hate to say it, I hope you decide to leave before it gets any harder on her. I don't want her to have to go through that again."

"Whatta, ya mean, Henry? Go through what?"

"After you were loaded on that prison bus, she didn't speak to anyone for several years. She would just lay in bed at night with her face crammed into the pillow and would cry herself to sleep. I've never seen a heart more broken."

"I never knew that."

"Yep, she wrote you every day, but when I took the letters to the post office, I just tossed them in the garbage. I wanted her to get over you and a letter back from you would have just made things worse."

"So, she thinks I never wrote her back. You shouldn't have done that, Henry. Does she know?"

"It's too late for that, and I'm not going to tell her now. Like I need an iron skillet upside my head."

Josh takes a few moments to think things over. He's thinking that Henry, being a wiser man than himself, probably did the right thing. He didn't know at the time how long the sentence would last or if parole was even an option. Josh also thought about how those letters could have given him some hope.

Henry finally broke the stupor Josh was in and says, "If she ever found out I was throwing her letters away, she'd cut my 'you know what off' in the middle of the night while I'm sleeping."

Josh walks back to where Henry had taken a seat in the rocking chair and takes a seat in the chair next to him. He could see that there was something else on Josh's mind, "What else is on that mind of yours?"

Josh places his hand on Henry's back, "I'm gonna let you in on a secret and I don't want Jill, Bubba, or anyone else to know about it."

Henry replies, "You got it."

Josh glances behind him again making sure no one was listening, "The blackouts I've been having are caused by a cancerous tumor that's placing pressure on the left side of my brain. A few years ago, they found it while I was getting tested for the terrible headaches I was having. I didn't even tell my mother. That would have been her undoing. Then these damn seizures started and have gotten more regular, and a little loss of memory is involved."

Henry was speechless and with a sad look asks, "Can it be fixed?'

"Nope; the prison doctor gave me a year to live. There's no telling how far it's spread by now. Look Henry, I'm still here, but I might not be here tomorrow. The pills I take temporary relieve the pain and also act as a blood thinner allowing the blood to flow past the tumor or some technical stuff like that."

"Damn, what can a man say to that?"

Josh replies, "Nothing…nothing at all. I just need a little time to tie up some loose ends."

Henry nods, "You can count on me for anything." Josh already knew he could count on Henry.

He stands and walks toward the door, hesitates and turns back to Henry again, "Glad to hear that, because I'm going to find out who killed Willie before my time comes and I will need all the help I can get." He turns back, opens the door and steps inside, closing it behind him leaving Henry sitting there puffing on his pipe, looking just like Snuffy Smith from the funny papers.

Josh walks by Jill's room and taps lightly on the door. She yells from inside the bedroom, "Come in." He opens the door very gently and sees her lying in bed with the blanket up to her neck. He walks over and takes a seat on the side of the bed and asks, "You alright Little Bit?"

"What did I say about calling me that?"

"I had to see her one last time just to put some ghosts to rest, that's all."

"You still love her?"

Josh thinks for a second or two and then answers, "I thought I did until I saw Clint riding her like a cowhand rides a wild horse; now I'm okay with it."

She places her hand on his hand and gently rubs the tops of his fingers and then says, "I have something that will take your mind off of her." She places his hand under the blanket and between her legs. To his surprise, she was naked as the day she was born.

"I guess you want sex now?"

"Yep, all you can give me. Now pull those blue jeans off and let me make those bad memories go away." He stands, undoes his pants, and tosses them across the room. In the next room Bubba was sitting up trying to remember all the details Josh had told them about Clint and Susan when suddenly he hears a loud bumping noise coming from Jill's room again. He crawls from the bed, walks over and places his ear to the wall. He could hear her bed squeaking like crazy and heard moaning and grunting. Henry walks in and sees Bubba's ear to the wall.

"I guess they're at it again?"

Henry walks over to the window and stares into the night and thinks about how Jill had had a taste for Josh since she was a little teenager. After all this time, she has finally had her dream come true, but little does she know the real story of Josh's medical condition. She will be devastated. Bubba turns to Henry and sees that he's in deep thought. He gives him a few minutes to himself before saying, "Come over here and listen to this. It's like a porn movie without a picture. That daughter of yours is by far the horniest girl I know."

"She gets that from my side of the family. Her mother hated sex, so I stayed out in the barn all the time."

"With that old nanny goat?"

"Hell no, it was the mama of the mama of that nanny goat. We're talking years here."

Bubba snickers, "That explains why that nanny goat has a funny lower lip."

They place their ears against the wall and listen to Jill screaming the words, "I'm coming, I'm coming."

Bubba shakes his head, turns to walk off mumbling, "I'm going, I'm going."

Henry asks, "Where are you going?"

"Back to the bathroom."

"You know something; you're gonna wear blisters on that thing if you don't give it a rest."

"I can't help it. A man has to have some relief."

Henry reaches over on the nightstand, grabs a bottle of hand lotion and throws it to him. "Here, this will help."

"Wait a minute; why would a man who could care less about how smooth his hands are, keep a bottle of lotion on the nightstand?"

"The bathroom is too far to walk for a man of my age and that toilet seat is as cold as an iceberg at night. When you get back, I need to tell you something about Josh's condition, but don't say a word to anyone. I'm gave him my word I wouldn't say anything, which is funny considering Josh has always known me for not keeping a secret."

CHAPTER 13

It's early morning just before light, Josh awakens to the strong aroma of freshly brewed coffee. He crawls reluctantly from Jill's bed and slowly drags his muscular frame to the footboard and puts his jeans on and walks into the kitchen and finds Jill standing there over the sink. She's staring out the open window with a mug in her left hand that's sporting a smiley face when suddenly she turns around and says, "It's a beautiful day. Take me for a ride."

"Didn't we spend two hours last night doing just that?"

"I mean on Elvira. I wanna see what all the Harley hype is about."

"I'm not sure she would like to share me with you. She can be a jealous girl at times."

"Come on, Josh, I wanna see that beautiful golden sunrise over Crooked Rock with you."

He shakes his head and gives her a smile as she pours a cup of steaming coffee and hands it to him.

He takes a sip, checks out the weather on the other side of the window and says, "Don't you have to be at the café this morning?"

"Are you kidding? My breakfast crowd has all but dried up, and what few that does come in can wait. I wanna feel the *wind* in my face and see the sun slowly rise over the desert floor; just you and me, and Elvira."

He blurts out, "What the hell, why not! Get a coat; it's chilly this early."

Ten minutes later they were streaking down Highway 146 at 70 miles an hour. Jill's hair is wavering in the wind as she held her arms tightly around Josh's waist, enjoying every precious minute. She's thinking, 'So this is what heaven's like.' The wind is beating at Josh's black leather jacket and the tail of his bandana flapping in the cool breeze. The roar coming through

Elvira's duel pipes is echoing through the canyons like a P-51 mustang in hot pursuit of a German Messerschmitt 109. She lays into the curves as if Elvira had a mind of her own. Chills are running up Jill's spine and it's not caused by the cold wind. She was now beginning to feel what he had been feeling for years about the 'machine.' He slows down to ten kicking it into a lower gear every few seconds and then looks over his shoulder, "You wanna see something my old man showed me?"

With a big grin and a young girl's giggle, "You bet I do!"

He tells her to slide back as far as she could get and lean against the short leather back support and hang on tight. To her liken,' he slides his rear end tightly against her inner thighs, throttles up the big twin and pops the clutch out at the same time causing the front wheel to lift smoothly off the ground until the bike was standing at a 45-degree angle. He walks her with the ease of a small mountain bike and says as he's controlling the throttle up and down, "Not many people can do this on a bike this size."

She yells over the wind and the roar of the engine, "How long can you keep it up like this!?"

He replies, "All night unless you're talking about the bike!"

"Yes, I'm talking about the bike, but the other is good to know."

"I guess as long as the road allows me." He throttles down and allows the big bike to level out, slowly letting the front wheel meet the asphalt with a gentle touch. He makes a quick turn down a small trail and over a small bluff then suddenly brings Elvira to a stop. The cool morning breeze raked across their faces as they took deep breaths. There in front of them lay the whole valley and its beauty as far as the eye could see. He steps off, pulling the zipper of his leather jacket down halfway. She follows as she reaches around his waist and tucks her hands into his side pockets to warm them up. The pink and orange morning sun are barely peeking over the far eastern slopes, giving them a glimpse of the desert floor at sunrise, rarely seen by city folk. Only at this time of morning could the desert speak to you with a gentle voice as the wind traveled over the sand dunes and scatter in all directions when it powders an occasional cactus tree. Tumbleweeds were bouncing across the cool rock formations as if they had a specific destination; a long journey that only they knew about and kept secret from the rest of the world. She realizes right then; this was a very special moment in her life.

She tightens her grip, "It's beautiful, isn't it?"

He smiles and takes in the beauty for a second or two before replying, "Nothing like it anywhere in the world. These southern mountain peaks overshadowing the hot desert is ingrained in my blood. It's amazing how it can be so cold and then turn so hot, so fast."

As the sun slowly makes its way up out of the east throwing its light on the face of the Rockies, its beaming light rays start to strike the scattered tin roofs of old wooden structures below giving the valley a Christmas tree effect.

He again sniffs the clean fresh air as a breeze meets his wind dried cheeks. The rising sun strikes their backs turning their jackets a bright glowing orange, leaving the pink fading behind the horizon. Jill has trouble speaking, but manages to say, "Let's make love; right here on the ground."

He slowly turns and gives her an awkward glance, "Its 45 degrees, that thing has all but disappeared back into its cave."

She licks her lips and with a sinister grin, "I bet I have something that will bring it back out." As always, when she's in this mood, she takes full advantage of every opportunity.

An hour later he shakes the sand off his clothes as he walks back to Elvira, mounts it and fires her up. She zips her jeans up, straddles the seat behind him and looks more refreshed and more in love than ever.

He turns to her, "I'll take you to work. I can use a heaping stack of hot pancakes this morning."

Moments later… they're running another 70 miles an hour when Jill yells in his ear, "You really get into this don't you!?"

He yells back, "Total turn-on, the sound, the smell, everything about it sends chills through my body!!"

She laughs, "So that's why your mind is so far away when we have sex; you're in love with a machine. Now I'm very, very jealous. It's not Susan I have to compete with, it's Elvira."

He yells back, "She's more than that; she's freedom on two wheels!" He makes a few turns, cuts through an alleyway and onto the main street. They come to a rest in front of the cafe. He dismounts, and then helps her slide off to the left and they enter the café.

Moments later he sits on a stool at the front counter taking in all the truckers who were just getting their day started. Jill places a large stack of pancakes on the counter in front of him and just stands there staring into his deep brown eyes. He gives her a glimpse, "Don't you think you should make your coffee rounds? You've got some customers staring you down."

Suddenly the front door flies open, and Clint appears wearing a freshly pressed uniform. He glances over the crowded room before his eyes came to rest on Josh sitting at the center of the counter. He strolls over and pulls up a stool next to him. Josh turns and smiles but says nothing. Clint turns his ugly mug towards him, "I thought I told you to get out of town."

Josh takes a sip from his coffee cup then slowly lowers it, "You did, but I didn't. You say a lot of things, but I don't think anyone pays any attention to you."

"I know who you are now, and I'm surprised you would even show your face around these parts after what you did to that old man. You should have gotten the gas chamber for that."

"Willie was my friend and I've never hurt anyone in my life, but that could change too if you keep screwing with me."

"You threaten me?"

"Wow, you're quick there, Johnny on the spot! You must have learned that in the book."

"What book?"

"That book for dummies. You know that book that tells you how to be an asshole cop and look stupid at the same time'."

"I'm the law around here and my job is to protect people from murderers like you."

Jill quickly fills some empty coffee cups before returning to the counter. She slams a cup in front of Clint, sloshing the hot java in all directions as it was filled to the brim.

"Don't start any trouble in my place, Clint, and I mean that."

"I was just talking about the good old days." Clint laughs. He couldn't help but notice that Josh is staring at her ass. He decides it's time to push him to the limits.

"So, Jill, you wanna go out again say Friday night?"

She stares at Josh from the corner of her eye and snaps back, "Shut up and drink your coffee Clint, so you can start a whole new day of doing absolutely nothing but riding around town and making an absolute fool out of yourself. And we haven't ever been on a date asshole."

Clint, with a grin, slowly turns back to Josh, "Is that ok with you, if I take Jill here for a ride in my police cruiser?"

Josh takes another sip of coffee and without looking at Clint, answers, "You might wanna wait for an hour or two. I rode her to work on the back of Elvira and it may take a while before she's in the mood again." He turns to Clint with a grin and gives him a wink, "Elvira, being my Harley in case you're wondering."

Clint with a look, "What the hell does that mean?"

Josh, as his smile gets wider, "It means, dumb ass, that Jill here has been sitting on my face since I've been back, and it could use a rest."

She gives Josh an angry stare before filling his cup again, "Thanks Josh; do you mind keeping our business to ourselves?"

Clint slams his cup down and in an agitated state, "You've always been nothing but trouble as long as I can remember you, but those days have come to an end. Things have been peaceful around here until you showed up."

"You mean boring as hell." Josh responds as he takes a sugar container and pours a small amount in his cup. "And don't sell yourself too short here; you've always been a spoiled little shit who never had to work a day in his life. Your father had to pay the teachers off just to get you outta high school."

Clint getting angry, "I could put you in jail right now if I wanted to, but I'm going to give you a chance to walk out that door and never come back."

Josh pushes his clean plate back, "You can try."

"Those big arms don't scare me. I can get on this radio and have ten guys over here in three minutes."

"The other day it was three. Platteville must have hired some more assholes since the other day, and I don't care if you can shit a National Guard unit; you have no idea what I can do to you in three minutes."

"I'm gonna make your little visit here a living hell."

"You have me nauseated right now with that smell coming from you. That shower you took last night isn't working. Susan failed to tell you where that bar of soap was?"

Clint's eyes open wide, and he spits his coffee all over the counter and his clean uniform.

Josh laughs, "So that's what it sounds like when an asshole has a blowout."

Clint grits his teeth, "So you did pay her a visit last night?"

"Yep, sure did and you'd be amazed at what all I saw and heard through the kitchen window."

"My father will kill you for that. I think I'll give him a call right now."

Josh lets out a small laugh again, "Stupid ass, I'm sure he will wanna know why you were there."

"I check on the place from time to time. My father has a lot of expensive things in that house like silverware, jewelry and shit like that."

"It wasn't the spoons and forks you had spread out on the dining room table."

Clint reaches for his pistol and before he can clear the holster, Josh kicks his stool out from under him, causing him to hit the hard tile floor. Josh quickly places his boot on the wrist of the hand Clint had around the pistol grip, "One move and I'll break it." Everyone in the place was watching as the tension grew. Josh and Clint's eyes meet in a fearsome staring contest. Josh with anger and Clint with fear.

A voice could be heard near the doorway, "He's had enough." Everyone turns to find Sheriff Jim standing there. He walks over to where Josh still had Clint pinned to the floor with his black boots, "Let him up."

Josh eases his boot back, "He started this mess, Jim."

"I know he did, he manages to start shit everywhere he goes."

Clint gets to his feet, "This bastards under arrest Jim for assaulting an officer."

Jim steps closer, "You're a poor excuse for an officer, now go write some tickets out on 87. I'm getting complaints about speeding trucks."

Clint gives him a mean look, "You ain't gonna arrest him?"

"Nope, looks like a misunderstanding to me, now get going."

Clint walks toward the door picking up his hat that flew from his head as he hit the floor, "This ain't over. When my father hears about this, he'll have your sorry ass behind bars, or worse and you're in trouble too Jim." He walks out the door.

Jim turns to Josh and with a grin, "I enjoyed seeing that, but you should have just got up and left town like he said. His father will have his big goons looking for you."

Josh places a ten on the counter and walks toward the door, "A few more days and I'll be out of your hair for good." Jill, listening in disappointment, runs around the counter and follows him out the door. As he mounts Elvira she asks, "What did you mean by 'a few days? You just got here."

"You saw what just happened in there. I'll just bring trouble down on everyone."

"I don't give a damn I'm not letting you go. You can't do this to me now."

"You knew this visit was temporary when you first figured out who I was. I'll have Bubba pick you up after you close."

"I wanna go with you. We can go to Albuquerque, and I can get a job waiting on tables until you get back on your feet and we can have kids. You can sale Elvira and we can buy a truck and be a real family."

He reaches up and gently runs his fingers through her long silky hair and rests his hand on the back of her neck. He pulls her closer and gives her a slow gentle kiss and then says, "Get rid of Elvira and buy a truck' you're kidding me, right?"

"Well, you could keep her and have a truck too."

"Little Bit, there are a lot of single men in this town that would give their right arm to have you."

"I don't want them, I want you!! I've been waiting half my life for you to come back and I'm not letting you go. And stop calling me Little Bit."

"I'll see you back at the ranch and we'll talk about it." He starts the bike and takes off heading out of town. That rumbling sound could be heard at least a quarter mile away as he shifted through the gears.

Jim walks up next to her, "You have got to get him out of this county, Jill. He's a good man and all he needs is a good woman. You two make a good couple. Your temper and his gentle attitude should even things out." He pats her on the shoulder and walks off. Jim, being a good soul, knew very well the dangers that lay ahead for them two. He had been around this town for many years, way before Josh was born. He also knew Josh was innocent of killing Willie, but if he kept hanging around, there would be another murder and Josh, most likely, would not come out on top.

Sitting between a building and the railroad tracks on the outskirts of town was a patrol car watching as Josh slowed for the railroad tracks. Giving him a little distance, the car eases out of his cubby hole and then over the tracks. Josh is staring out across the desert when he glances in the side rearview mirror and sees the marked unit quickly catching up. He checks his speed and plainly knew he was under the limit. The car approaches and Josh just continues to ride on as if nothing was wrong. Two miles past the city limits, the blue lights come on. Josh reduces speed, pulls over to the right side and before he could put the kickstand down a shot rang out. He felt a sharp pain in his shoulder as the round tore through his dad's old leather jacket. He kicks it down in low gear, spits gravel and like a sling shot, hits the pavement. He was traveling so fast he failed to see that the marked cruiser had turned off somewhere. He never got a glimpse of who was driving it, but he had a very good guess.

Later he pulls up to the ranch. Bubba smiles and waves as Josh ran up to an old well and bumped it with the front tire. He lays Elvira over and falls to the ground. Henry was working on a fence and sees what's going on and limps over to where he had fallen. By this time, Bubba had made it over and is trying to lift Elvira off his leg. Henry places his arm under his head, "Another seizure?"

Josh turns his head up to the side, "Not unless my seizures are developing bullet wounds. Somebody in a police unit shot me. I think it was Clint, but I never got a glimpse of his ugly mug."

Henry sees blood oozing from the sleeve of the leather jacket, "Looks like you've lost a lot of blood."

"I'll be okay." He glances over at Bubba struggling to get the bike up, "Help him Henry lift Elvira and push her in the barn. Then you two can drag my ass into the house, I'm feeling a little dizzy." They hesitate for a few seconds, push Elvira in the barn and then return to help him from the ground. They walk toward the house with Henry under one arm and Bubba under the other; then they enter the house, place him on the sofa and remove his leather jacket.

Josh reaches in his pocket and takes out a small knife and hands it to Henry, "Cut the t-shirt off, it hurts too bad to pull it over my shoulder." As Henry cuts the shirt off, Josh looks out the window to make sure he wasn't followed.

Henry glances at the wound and tells Bubba, "Go get me some hot water, peroxide and those bandages from over the washing machine." He turns to Josh, "Looks like it went clean through the fleshy part. Just tore some outer flesh."

Josh responds, "Good, I didn't feel like having you dig that bastard out. It sure is bleeding a lot."

Henry, "It took a chunk out so it's bleeding a lot."

Hours later, bubba comes driving up with Jill jumping out and running to the house. She quickly opens the door in a panic. Josh is lying on the sofa but turns his head when he hears her yelling, "I came as fast as I could!!"

Josh gives Henry a look, but the look on Bubba's worried face gave it away.

"You just had to tell her, didn't you?"

Bubba, "Like I needed her being pissed at me for playing the silent game."

She makes her way to the sofa and fluffs a pillow, "You should be in the hospital."

"It's not that bad. Henry said it went clean through and missed the bone."

She turns to Henry and then back at him, "Right, that's coming from a man that has trouble treating jock itch. I bet he didn't even wash his hands…Infection! That's just what you need."

Henry gives her an awkward glance, "I never claim to be a damn doctor, but I'm good enough to see it barely nicked him, and you're right about not washing my hands."

Jill asks, "Who did it, Josh?"

"Henry."

"Henry shot you?"

"I thought you were asking who put the bandages on."

"Smart ass; I'm talking about who shot you."

"I never saw a face. It was a marked unit, most likely Clint."

She fires back, "It had to be Clint, only he's stupid enough to ambush a person in broad daylight. That sorry no-good son of a …"

Bubba turns to Josh, "Boy, why is Clint so pissed, or do I have to ask?"

Josh replies, "I pulled a stool out from under him and embarrassed him in front of a café full of people. I should have known he would try something like this. I let my guard down and that's not my way." He lays his head back on the pillow?"

With a frown she answers, "McNally heard about what happened and sent the Health Department over and they closed me down just before me closing up." She continues by turning to Henry and Bubba, "You guys leave the room; I need to undress him and fix him some soup."

Bubba shakes his head, "How come he needs to be undressed to eat soup? You get pissed if I eat cereal in my underwear in the morning."

Jill snaps back, "Have you seen your fat ass wearing holy underwear in the mirror?"

"Like I wanna see my own ass in the mirror, and I'm not fat. I was an oversized baby when I was born."

Henry laughs, "You were so skinny when you were born, they had to tape splints to your legs with duct tape."

Josh interrupts, "Bubba's right, leave my clothes on if you don't mind."

She snaps back, "You should be comfortable."

She turns to Bubba and gives him an angry stare. Bubba shrugs his shoulders, "Me and Henry will go finish up on that fence, and I think we'll do it naked, so we'll be more comfortable! I've never seen a woman so anxious to undress a man before."

Jill catches Henry before he walks out, "Call Doc Seymour and have him stop by."

Josh overhears her, "No! I don't need a doctor, it's just a flesh wound, and I'll recover just fine on my own!"

She slaps Henry on the back, "Never mind; the stubborn ass doesn't need one. It was just a 45." She turns to Josh, "That bandage looks like shit. I'll get a new one and do it right."

Josh, "Bubba and Henry got me all fixed up, babe; just let it be…I can't take anymore probing right now. I could use a shot of whiskey though."

CHAPTER 14

The next morning Josh is filling the water barrels without a shirt. Every muscle in his upper torso is flexing with sweat, pouring down his pecks, when Jill, still wearing nothing but a see-through nightgown, spots him from the window and yells, "Damn you!!" She runs out the door, down the steps and across the clearing toward him as he's pouring the water from the buckets, "What the hell do you think you're doing!?"

"I'm trying to help out around here. Life goes on, Jill."

"You're hurt and should be in bed resting."

"I'm okay. I feel a little throbbing, but other than that, I feel great."

About this time Bubba rounds the corner of the barn stretching his arms and wearing nothing but long johns with holes everywhere. She places her hands on her hips and yells again, "Damn you, Bubba; get some clothes on!"

Bubba yells back, "Look who's talking. It's hot as hell out here and I'm trying to be comfortable."

Josh steps back and with a grin, "He's right, I can see right through that gown. By the way, white lace panties are my favorite."

She turns to him and asks in a low voice, "You like what you see?"

"Yes, I do, and I'm sure Bubba likes what he sees, but I believe we're about to have company." She turns to the driveway and sees a new black Hummer and a patrol car kicking up dust.

She yells, "Shit!! Here comes more trouble!"

Bubba shakes his head, "I was wondering how long it was gonna take before they came out stirring up more crap."

They come screeching to a stop near the front porch. Jill takes off into the house passing Henry at the door.

"Where's the fire sugar?" Henry asked, not seeing the vehicles pulling up at first.

She yells back, "Not now pop, where's the shells to the shotgun?"

"In the gun, where else would they be?"

Bubba steps next to Josh. Glancing down, Josh nods, "You look stupid, Bubba; get some pants on."

"I'm not going to the prom. Screw them. Way too damn hot to worry about wearing pants now."

Henry walks out and leans against the porch column and fires up his pipe. He yells to Josh, "Go inside Josh, this is bad!!"

Josh smiles, "I'll stay, I can take care of myself and I wanna hear what they have to say."

Several men step out with clubs in their hands with one opening the rear door of the Hummer. Walter steps out with his men gathering around Josh.

Walter shakes his head, "Well I'll be damned; I thought Clint was full of shit when he told me you were back. So, it was you that whipped my boy Pete and his friends the other day at Bubba's place."

Bubba yells, "Bubba's place is right, it's still my place for another three weeks!!"

Josh with a grin, "Yeah, I whipped Little Pete. Looks like you spent more time chasing whores and ripping people off than trying to raise your kids and teach them some manners."

"Speaking of whores, I heard you paid mine a little visit last night."

"I wasn't the only one." He turns to Clint, smiles and gives a wink. Clint frowns and turns the other way hoping his father didn't catch on.

McNally blurts out, "You should have never come back here. Willie had a lot of friends in this town."

"Yeah, and you weren't one of 'em, Walter. I see you bought the old place. Wow, what a coincidence, being ole Willie having the only access to that part of the mountain range and you owning all those old mines with no access."

"Are you insinuating something?"

"I'm not just insinuating something Walter; I'm stating facts."

"You were trespassing last night and me and the boys here are going to rough you up and run you out of town or I could have Clint here arrest you and violate your probation."

Josh smiles, "Are you sure your boys are up to it?"

"These ain't Pete and his friends this time."

About this time a large man steps forward and swings a club, but Josh ducks and pops the guy right in the knee, snapping it like a twig. The man grabs his knee and falls to the ground screaming in pain. Clint starts to pull his gun when a loud blast from a shotgun went off and sprayed the front windshield of the Hummer. Everyone stopped and turned to see Jill holding an old ten-gauge double barrel shotgun. There's anger in her face like no one has ever seen before, blushing like a red-hot tart.

She yells, "I have one more load of buckshot, who wants to be the lucky one to get it!!"

McNally glances at his windshield and yells at her, "Damn you, Jill, that vehicle is only two weeks old!"

Jill smiles, "Like I give a shit. You wanna see what the other barrel can do to your fat overlapping belly? Now get off my property and take that bunch of trash with you."

"You're bringing a lot of trouble down on you and Henry."

She snaps back, "You have already pissed me off lard-ass by calling the health department and having them close me up, so don't make it any worse." Josh walks over to Clint and snatches his pistol from his holster. He kicks the cylinder out and ejects the cartridges on the ground with one being an empty shell casing.

He takes it in hand and makes a short examination of the shell casing, "Been doing some hunting, Clint?"

"I don't know what you're talking about." Josh knees him in the groin causing Clint to double over and grab his crotch.

"You need to learn how to shoot before you ambush a man in broad daylight." Josh kicks the other rounds out on the ground and shoves the unloaded pistol back in the holster.

Jill yells again, "I'm gonna start counting and when I get to three, I'm gonna splatter assholes all over the driveway. One…two…"

They all bump into each other trying to get back into the vehicles as McNally yells out, "This ain't over by far! When I get through with you Josh, you'll wish you never left that prison you came from! And if I catch you at my place again, I'll kill you for sure. Susan is my wife now and ain't nothing you can do about it!"

Jill, still holding the shotgun walks out to where Josh was standing, "You got that shoulder to bleeding again." She turns to McNally, fires a shot in the air and as she quickly breaks open and reloads, she asks in a loud voice, "You idiots still here?" They quickly take off down the dirt driveway like crazy, throwing dust and rocks into the air as they went.

She turns to Bubba with a frown, "Go get your pants on so we can get started with some work around here. It looks like we might have to put this place up for sale after all."

Henry steps closer, "Let Bubba get back to his station and me and Josh will finish the fence."

She turns to Henry, "Josh ain't in shape to do any work. He needs some rest, and Bubba needs to work off that ten pounds of food he ate this morning."

Henry, "Your ass hasn't given him any rest either. I'm surprised his penis isn't blistered."

Josh interrupts, "I feel just fine. Will you stop over-reacting?"

"Get back inside; I'm in the mood to use this damn thing." Jill says in anger.

Ten minutes later Bubba is met at the front by Josh. Josh grabs his hand and places a small, black, thick, leather pouch in it.

Bubba asks, "What's this?"

"There's twenty thousand dollars in that pouch, I want you to go by the bank and pay Henry's mortgage off, pay some on Jill's place and there should be enough left over to pay your place off."

Bubba with a puzzled look asks, "Why don't you give it to Jill? Are you going somewhere?"

"Yeah, I brought a lot of trouble on everybody."

"You're gonna need this money, they ain't a lot of people out there willing to give an ex-con a job."

"I'll do just fine, Bubba. Will you do that right now before you go home? I'll see you at the station later."

Jill walks out the door hearing some of the conversation, "What do you mean you'll be there later; you're staying here. I told you to get into bed."

"I can't; McNally will send his damn goons back here and tear this place apart."

"He does and I'll open them up like a can of bad beans."

"It's better for me to hide out at Bubba's and I'll leave first thing in the morning."

Her eyes start tearing up and she yells, "No!! You just got here!"

"I know that, but the padre was right, there's nothing here for me."

"I'm here Josh."

"I don't want them to hurt you three."

"I got a whole box of buckshot, let 'em come back, and I'll pepper their asses up good."

"This isn't gonna work."

"What about me? You expect me to just marry one of these local desert hicks?"

"I can't stay here. It really was a mistake to come back!"

"I'm going with you."

He turns to Bubba, "Will you please go take care of that business, Bubba?" Bubba shakes his head and heads for his tow truck.

Josh steps closer to her, grabs her by the hands and in a gentle way says, "That's no way to live, riding the roads with your ass strapped to the seat of that vibrating bike."

"I don't care, I can think of worse things to have strapped to my ass. I wanna go with you, if I have to run behind Elvira all the way."

"Whatta, we live off of, sex?"

She smiles, "Works for me."

He laughs and just shakes his head, "You beat all. I'll tell you what, I would like me, you and Bubba to have a few drinks tonight at the Cactus Rose and I'll think it over and let you know then."

"Why can't we just stay here and have a few drinks; there's nothing but trouble there. You act like you wanna run into Walter's goons. After Henry and Bubba pass out, I can do things for you that will keep you from leaving."

"I wanna see if I recognize anyone before I leave and I promised Bubba that we would go over some old stomping grounds."

"Bubba will understand, and you should be more interested in spending time with me."

Josh, in a joking manner, "Yeah, but Bubba doesn't wanna hump me every five minutes."

"That's real funny; he wants to hump everything else every five minutes." She places her arms around his neck, squeezes tight and whispers in his ear, "I'll be packed and ready to go in the morning." She turns and walks back inside saying as she went, "I'll go fix us something to eat."

He nods with a grin and then turns to the mountains scanning as far as his eyes could see. He strolls over to the barn and bends down on his knee, running his hand over the fuel tank of Elvira allowing his fingers to rake the silver-plated Harley medallion. He says to himself out loud, as if she understood every word he's saying, "Well, girl, I feel some bad times are coming and I'll need all the help you can give me." He pats her marron six-gallon tank and then strolls toward the house…

In town and thirty minutes later, Bubba steps from his wrecker, and wobbles his heavy frame across the parking lot of the 'First Bank of Prattville,' with the money pouch in hand. Suddenly, a loud squealing noise is heard as Little Pete speeds into the parking lot on his scooter followed by his bunch of worthless thugs. He locks up the back tire causing the bike to slide a short distance coming to a stop right in front of Bubba. He quickly jumps off the bike, pulls his pants up to his waist and yells, "Well lookie here, it's none other than our fat ass friend Bubba! Where's your bodyguard lard-ass?"

Bubba smiles and steps back, "He's resting from whooping y'all's asses the other day. You boys know how exhausting it can be throwing dog shit against the wall."

Pete steps up closer with a grin, "I wouldn't get too smart if I was you. Me and the boys here are in the mood to slap some fat ass around."

"Look Pete, I'm kind of busy right now, so can I take a rain check on that ass whooping? Maybe you and your bunch can come around the station next week when I have more time to piss away."

Pete reaches out and snatches the thickly packed pouch from Bubba's hand. Bubba quickly tries to retrieve it, but Pete jerks back, "Not so damn fast fatso." He opens it and pulls out the money.

"Shit, just look at this." Pete says as he counts the money out. Another young man watches closely as Pete counted and then turns to Bubba and asks, "Where in the hell did you steal all this money? We know damn well you're not bringing in that much at that run-down shack you call a service station."

Bubba gets angry, "That's none of your business you little shit where I got it, now give it back." He struggles to reach for it, but Pete passes it to another and then to another as Bubba tries relentlessly to get his hands back on it. Soon it made its way back to Pete. Bubba in a loud voice, "It's not my money now give it back!"

Pete, "Well, if it's not yours, it must be ours." Bubba just stands there getting angrier when suddenly a patrol car shows up with Clint sitting behind the wheel.

He slowly steps out and walks over to where everyone was standing, "What's going on little brother?"

Pete laughs and gives Bubba a glancing stare, "Nothing much, that's if you don't think it's funny that Bubba here is carrying a whole lot of cash around with him."

Clint snatches the overstuffed pouch from Pete's hand and turns to Bubba with a menacing glare, "Where'd you get this, chunky butt?"

Bubba snaps back, "It belongs to someone else."

"Yeah, I just bet it does."

"I'm taking it to the bank for somebody else now give it back. You have no right to take that."

Clint shakes his head back and forth, "I think I'll turn this money in at headquarters until we locate the rightful owner and when you see Josh again, tell him he won't always have a woman around with a shotgun to protect him." He crawls back into his car. Bubba walks over to the car window and leans close.

Bubba, "If you take that money, Josh will shove his fist so far up your skinny ass, you won't be able to shit right for the next ten years of your life. His forearm is so large that your rectum will be permanently damaged."

Clint smiles, "We'll see about that fat ass." He speeds off as bubba turns to Pete.

Pete nods his head back and forth, "Well, Bubba, as they say, easy come, easy go." He punches Bubba in the gut causing him to crunch over. They all jump on their motorbikes and speed out of the parking lot doing wheelies as they went. Bubba painfully walks back to his tow truck and drives off wondering how he was going to explain to Josh about what had just happened...

CHAPTER 15

Later that evening, the hot sweltering day was beginning to cool down a little with a nice breeze coming off the Flats. Jill is in her room running around getting dressed, finding the tightest jeans and the lowest cut blouse she could muster up. Bubba was sitting at the kitchen table with a blank expression on his face and had large sweat balls rolling down his temples. Josh strolls into the kitchen still pulling his tight black T-shirt over his well-built frame. As he took a seat across from Bubba, he could see that something was bearing down on his mine.

"You're sweating like crazy. You act like you're playing a game of chest with a diamondback and bet your left nut on it. You gonna be alright?"

Bubba chokes on his own salvia for a second or two and then replies with a slight stutter in his voice, "I wish I had been bitten by a diamondback. It would take my mind off some bad news."

Josh reaches over and places his hand on Bubba's shoulder, "Well tell me what's troubling you my old fart-master."

"You remember when you sent me to the bank to pay the mortgage note this morning?

"Let me see." Josh acts like he's trying to remember. "Yeah, I think I do remember something about sending you to the bank with twenty grand."

"Good, because I ran into Little Pete and his bunch, and they really hassled bad…"

"And, let me guess they took it from you."

"And then that asshole Clint came into the picture."

"And?"

"Well, you know with Clint and Pete in the picture, things can't be good.

They kind of took the…"

Josh interrupts, "Tell me you didn't let them keep the money!"

"What could I do Josh? Pete snatched it from my hands, and they played keep-away, then Clint showed up and took it from him."

"Why the hell were you carrying it in your hands? They wouldn't have even known you had it if you had been carrying it in your pocket."

"Like that much money will fit in my back pocket. That leather pouch was as thick as a phonebook. Look, I'm sorry, I don't know what to do."

"'Sorry,' that's all you have to say about it? Sorry don't cut it. That money would have allowed you, Jill and Henry to keep your homes and businesses."

"Maybe Clint will give it back when he finds out that it's not really stolen."

"Listen to what you're saying. That'll happen the day you grow some bull balls and stand up for yourself!!"

"It could happen. I've never known Clint to be a thief."

Josh shakes his head as in not believing what he was hearing and responds, "The man is screwing his stepmother and he ambushed me in broad daylight and tried to kill me. Yeah, I'm pretty sure he has some morals buried somewhere deep in that conscience of his."

"What was I supposed to do, there was six of 'em and then Clint came up and he has been looking for a reason to beat my ass."

Josh slides his chair back, "I'll get it back in the morning. Whatever you do, don't let it ruin our evening out and remind me to show you how to kick seven asses at one time."

"You know I've never been much on confrontations."

"Just don't let her know anything about it." He stands and walks over to the icebox, takes out two cold beers and hands one to Bubba, "If I was as big as you, I would rule the roost."

Bubba snickers, pops the top on his beer and with a funny expression, "You confuse fat and lazy for brains and muscle."

"A hippo is fat and lazy, but nothing in Africa will go near it."

"Because he's fat and lazy?"

"No, because he has teeth eight inches long and the guts to use them... that's why."

A few minutes later Jill comes walking into the room all decked out with her long dark hair pinned in a ponytail. Her pants were cut so low that Bubba spit his beer across the table, "Damn, any lower and your prairie dog's gonna show."

Josh corrects him, "Its beaver, not prairie dog."

Bubba nods, "Same damn thing to me."

Jill runs her hands over her hips and gives Josh a sexy glare, "What about you Josh?"

Josh, pretending to not notice, "What about me?"

"You like it?"

Bubba yells again, "Yes, yes and hell yeah!!"

Jill says without taking her eyes off Josh, "Shut up Bubba! I wasn't asking you."

Bubba responds, "I was answering for him, because he looks like he's at a loss for words."

Josh just sat there speechless, staring at her well-rounded curves.

She licks her lips and in a slow smoothing voice, "The reason you don't see any pantie lines is because I'm not wearing any...You wanna check it out?"

Bubba yells again, "Yes, yes and hell yeah!!"

She gives him another pissed look, "Shut your freakin face! Don't you have something to do outside?"

Bubba snaps back, "I'm his agent and I say let's see if you have panties just to be sure. I don't want my client getting into anything without me checking it out first."

She quickly turns and grits her teeth, "I'm gonna close my eyes and count to three. You better not be sitting there when I open 'em."

"So, do I need to be gone when you count to three or when you open your eyes?"

"Move it fat ass!!"

Bubba jumps up and quickly runs out on the porch as fast as his chubby body would allow. About this time Josh gives her a once over and says, "I like it."

She steps closer, "I'm having trouble getting my belt through the rear loop; you wanna help me before we go?"

Bubba yells from the porch, "Yes, yes and hell yeah!!"

She walks over and yells before slamming the door shut, "Go feed the livestock."

He yells back through the door, "I can't do that with two ears of corn and a hard on!"

Josh, with a chuckle, "He can't take the hint." He yells out the door, "We wanna be left alone for a few Bubba!"

Bubba blurts out, "All you had to do is say so! I'm not a child! I can understand plain English!"

Back inside the kitchen, she straddles his lap and says in a cunning voice, "You wanna go another round sugar before we go out?" She gently starts kissing him on the face making her way to his lips when suddenly Henry walks in, "You guys need to get going if you're going."

She slaps her knee and jumps up, "This place is busier than an ant farm." She leaves the room in frustration.

Henry smiles, "What put sand in the crack of her ass?"

Josh stretches his arms back over his head, "Women don't need a reason; they just need a place to do what they do. I need to go check my oil and gas anyway."

Back in her bedroom, Jill's standing next to her bed facing the wall and folding a pair of shorts when Bubba decides he should apologize for not taking the hint sooner. He lightly taps on the door and cracks it open, with a loud squeak, knowing she had already gotten dress, but before he could say a word, she lifts her head and stares at the wall, "So, you've changed your mind and decided you need some relief before we go out huh?" Bubba looks around to see if anyone else was in the room. After thinking she was talking to him, he innocently shrugs his shoulders. She bends over and in a soft voice says, "Why don't you come on over here sweetie and rub that thing on this tight ass."

Bubba smiles and walks with an erection pushing hard against his jeans and presses it against her jeans. Jill, with a grin says, "Work that thing baby…work it."

Bubba says in a loud voice, "I'm trying, but I can't feel anything through those tight jeans!!"

Josh was in the barn gently wiping the dust from the chrome primary cover when he hears Jill yelling from inside the house, "Damn your hide Bubba, I'm going to kill you!" Bubba comes running from the house toward Josh when she steps out with the same double barrel shotgun she pulled on McNally. He takes refuge in the barn behind Josh.

Josh laughs, "What the hell did you do this time?"

Bubba replies, "I thought I was doing what she asks me too; crazy ass woman… they never know what the hell they want."

Jill, being extremely pissed, yells from the porch, "Keep that horny over-weight tub of shit outta my room!!"

Josh walks over with Bubba still trying to hide behind him, "What the hell did he do to make her wanna shoot him?"

"He tried to poke me in the rear with that dried up little bean of his!"

Bubba yells, "You know very well with this gut, that's impossible."

"He tried what?" Josh responded.

She yells again, "He tried to stick me in the ass!"

Josh turns and gives him a frustrated look, then steps out of the way, leaving him standing there with a guilty look on his face, "Okay, go ahead and shoot him!"

Bubba steps sideways and gets behind Josh again and yells as he went, "She ask me to, Josh. I was just going to apologize when she asked me to check her ass out and rub my big man tool against it!"

Josh turns back to her, trying not to laugh, "Damn, your standards are getting lower."

She snaps back, "I thought it was you until I felt his wilted stalk rubbing against the crack of my ass."

Bubba yells, "Now that is totally uncalled for!!"

Josh starts laughing when she lays the shotgun down and places her hands on her hips, "There's nothing funny about it!" She steps off the porch and asks, "Are we riding Elvira to the club?"

Josh replies, "Why do you ask?"

"Because, if we are, I'll need a jacket."

Bubba peeks around Josh, "We can take my tow truck and you won't need a jacket or a shotgun."

She quickly responds, "I like riding on Elvira with Josh if you don't mind...pervert!"

Josh, still trying not to laugh, "Yeah, we can take the bike; go get your jacket."

Jill, with a grin yells, "Alright! Now you're talking!" She quickly runs back into the house to retrieve her jacket.

Josh glances over as Bubba as they both walk from the barn, "Whatta we do about Henry, Bubba? The last time I left an old man alone, he ended up dead."

Bubba, "He likes staying home and watching T.V... He'll be okay. Unlike Willie, Henry doesn't trust a soul. You do know that it's a bad idea to go to the club with everything that has happened?"

He places a hand on Bubba's shoulder, "I'm leaving in the morning after I get the money back. I would like to show Jill a good time before I go."

Bubba shakes his head, "She thinks she's going with you.....you do know that, right?"

"Yep, my plan is to get her drunk and then let her sleep right through the leaving process."

"I'd hate to be around when she wakes up. She's gonna be as pissed as a hornet. She'll be so mad she'll shoot me and Henry just because she's angry with men."

"I'll hide the shotgun."

"And the skillet!"

Josh takes his leather jacket from the saddle bag and then hesitates for a second, "You take good care of her after I'm gone."

Bubba with a sad look on his face, "Why don't you come live with me, maybe we can fix the place up and turn it into a real profitable station?"

"That won't work. We like sitting around on the porch drinking beer too much."

Jill comes running from the house with her denim jacket on as Josh mounts the bike. He turns to Bubba and asks, "Are you coming or not."

"Yeah, I'm coming. I'll see you two there."...

CHAPTER 16

Josh and Jill turn into the empty parking lot of the Cactus Rose. It was early, so the regular crowd had not gathered yet. He comes to a stop in front of the large window facing the road. Jill's jeans were so tight she had trouble getting off Elvira's wide girth. Josh hit the kill switch shutting her down and gently leans her over on the kickstand. He slowly dismounts and stands there staring at the neon sign stretching across the front just below the roof line. She sees the puzzled look on his face, "Changed a little, hasn't it?"

With a smile, he thinks of all the good memories he had dancing around the dance floor into the wee hours of the night, "Yes it has. I can remember when this parking lot was hard dirt covered with a thin layer of oyster shells and the sign was painted across the front."

She pulls her jacket off, "We're catching up to the twenty-first century. It can hold over two hundred drunk desert rats now."

He grabs her by the hand and with a snappy tone in his voice, "Well, let's go in and grab a table before the crowd shows up."

Jill, with a smile and lots of anticipation, squeezes his hand tightly in her grip, "Let's do."

They step into the place and take a table next to the front window. Jill stares out through the large plate glass window at the big black and chrome machine, "Let me guess, you want a good view of Elvira?"

He places his jacket on the back of the chair, "You got that shit right."

No sooner did the words leave his mouth, Bubba came driving up in his old beat-up tow truck. He parks next to the big bike, steps out and strolls through the front door like he's part owner of the world. Josh laughs as he watches him make his way toward them, "That Bubba acts like he doesn't have a care in the world."

Jill, with a giggle, "We need to get him laid and fast. I think I heard him in the bathroom making groaning noises."

Josh responds as Bubba made his way around some tables, "You sure he didn't have a pillow in there."

"He better have not had one of my clean pillows in there."

"I've seen him on a double date, trust me a pillow is a step up for him."

She loses her smile and in a sarcastic tone, "When you say double date, you mean when you had that whore hanging all over you."

Getting tired of the smartass stabs, he turns to her and with a grin, "Yep, those were the days."

She gives him a pissed look and then turns her attention to Bubba as he pulls his chair out.

She laughs, "What's wrong, Bubba, forget your date?"

He snaps back, "Nope, I'm with Rosie Palmer tonight."

She doesn't catch on and asks, "You leave her in the truck?"

Josh laughs. She quickly flips around in her chair and asks, "What's so funny?"

"Bubba's talking about his hand."

"I don't get it."

Bubba starts laughing also and holds his right hand out.

"I beat it until my palm is as red as a rose. Now do you get it?"

"Nope!"

She turns to Josh. "Explain."

"Oh, come on, he whacks his own worm."

"That's stupid."

Bubba interrupts, "Hey, a man has to have some relief and the good part is, I can switch hands and have a different date without having a shotgun pulled on me over a stupid misunderstanding."

She quickly fires back, "You're getting worse Bubba at being a sick pervert."

"Is that right? One man's junk is another man's pot of gold I always say."

"That's right; well, you don't see Josh pulling on his own thing."

"That's because you've been pulling on it for him every ten minutes since he hit town. And another thing, you should have sat up late at night years ago and watch Elvira, mistress of the dark with him."

Josh as a big grin takes over his face, "Bubba's right, every young man does it."

He decides to have a little fun. "I can remember when Bubba and I would chase nanny goats for hours. Good thing we didn't catch any."

A sick expression takes over her face, "You mean you two would have had sex with a nanny goat?"

Bubba smiles, "Sure, that's if she's the prettiest nanny goat in the bunch."

Before she could reply, a young waitress wearing short shorts and a sports bra strolls over to the table and asks, "What can I get for my first customers of the night?"

Bubba shouts, "I'll take some of you Canya."

"The name is Tanya; get it right, Bubba."

"I like Canya, as in 'can ya sit on my face?'"

She snaps back, "In your wildest dreams."

"How'd you know?"

Tanya, with a smirk on her face, "Because I know you so keep your damn hands off my ass tonight."

He shakes his head back and forth, "I'll try sweet cheeks, but you know I have those stubby wandering fingers."

She pops the back of his head with the palm of her hand, "Yeah, I do know that and if you don't want those stubby wandering fingers broke chubby, keep 'em away from my ass."

Jill interrupts, "If you two are through flirting, Tanya; my date and I will have two ice cold beers in the bottle."

Tanya turns her attention to Josh, "Coming right up.....Wow! Who's the new stuff in town?"

Jill gets angry and jealous, "That new stuff, as you say, belongs to me, so, as you just told Bubba, keep your damn fingers to yourself if you don't want 'em broke."

Tanya gives Josh a smile, "So you must be the owner of that burgundy iron horse parked outside the window."

Bubba, seeing Jill getting more pissed, yells. "It's maroon and make that three cold beers and crank up that jukebox." Tanya returns to the bar leaving Bubba staring at her rear end.

Josh pats him on the shoulder, "We need to work on your approach; you couldn't get old lady Conner's sow with those moves."

Bubba turns to him, "Too late, smarty pants, I have already got...... Hey, wait a minute, what does that mean?"

Jill kicks Josh on the shin under the table, "Nothing Bubba, you just keep being you."

The music starts up and Josh asks, "You wanna dance?"

Bubba replies while still watching Tanya standing at the end of the bar waiting for the bartender to bring the drinks, "Not right now, but maybe later, after a few beers."

"I was talking to Jill, not you. You just keep an eye on Elvira."

Bubba glances out the window and says as Josh takes Jill by the hand and leads her to the floor, "Okie dokie...whatever you say. I'll watch it like she's my own bitch."

A few seconds later, they're out on the dance floor with Jill holding Josh so tight, he could hardly breathe. He whispers in her ear, "Loosen up Little Bit, any tighter and I'm going to up-chuck."

"What did I tell you about calling me that?"

"Sorry, I keep forgetting. Old habits are hard to change."

A few hours pass and the bar is crowded with elbow room only. All three are drinking and laughing when five motorcycles pull into the parking lot.

Jill looks out the window, "It's time to go; trouble just showed up."

Josh places his hand on hers, "We'll just mind our own business, and they'll leave us alone."

Bubba jumps in, "Yeah, that's what I always say right before they hold me down and beat my gut black and blue."

Josh places his hand on his arm, "Not this time. If they come this way, just let me do the talking; hell, they might not even notice us sitting here."

As the young men dismount their bikes, they take notice of Elvira and stand there for a second or two staring at her, knowing very well who the owner is.

Pete shakes his head and with a grin, "This is going to be one hell of a night boys."

Mike nods, "Why don't we just leave him be for now Pete. I would like to just sit back and enjoy a few drinks and dance a little before getting the shit kicked out of us again."

"Shut up Mike. He's not that tough."

"Where in the hell were you when he was kicking our asses at Bubba's place?"

Jill, staring through the window says, "Too late, I think they know we're here."

Bubba with a snicker responds, "How could they not know? There's eight hundred pounds of American steel sitting out front like a big ass billboard sign."

Little Pete and his bunch come strolling in the front door and make their way across the room to the bar. They scan the place until their eyes come to rest on the three of them sitting at the table.

Bubba just shakes his head and says in a low voice, "I knew coming here was a bad idea. When all this is over, y'all just remember what I said."

Pete and his bunch walk over to the table with Pete placing his knuckles flat on the tabletop.

Jill, with her usual angry stare, says, "Not tonight, Pete. You guys go play with yourselves somewhere else."

Pete, not paying attention to her, looks Josh in the face. "That was the most stupid thing you could have done coming back here dude, especially after what you did to old Willie. They say you blew his brains all over the back porch, not that the old bastard had much to begin with."

Bubba stands, "Why don't you and your asshole buddies take that bad breath of yours and go back to the bar before you get some shit started."

Pete pushes him back down in his chair and with a grin, "He's already started some shit by coming back to town riding that hunk of oil dripping scrap metal sitting out there."

Jill quickly stands, "Look, I've had just about enough of your crap. Now you can go back to whatever rock you climbed out from under, or I'll call the bouncer and he'll throw you out."

Pete, with a smirk on his face, "You forget who owns this town, bitch."

Josh reaches up and grabs him by the hair of the head and slams it down on the table, breaking his nose. He stands and flexes every muscle in his body as if he is about to rip his shirt. He lets Pete fall to the floor then turns to the others, "Anybody else got any magic words they wanna say?"

Mike shakes his head back and forth and steps back. Another grabs a chair and swings toward Josh, but he ducks and kicks him in the chest knocking the breath out of him. Another grabs a beer bottle and breaks the end off, leaving a jagged bottom. He walks a small circle as Josh just smiles. The man lunges at him. Josh sidesteps him and elbows him in the mouth, taking out a few teeth then takes the man's feet out from under him. Pete stands with blood gushing from his nostrils and yells, "Somebody call my brother!!" With that he throws a punch. Josh catches his fist in his hand and crushes Pete's fingers together. Another runs up behind and gets Josh in a bear hug but gets head-butted and kneed in the groin. They struggled to get to their feet and then surround Josh with one trying to work in behind him, but Josh had managed to place his back to the wall.

He says with a snicker, "You boys sure you wanna fish in the hole? We can call it a night and just let the whole situation drop right here." They all relax, stepping back, losing their desire to fight, when suddenly Josh feels a sharp throbbing pain in his head causing every muscle in his body to go on the blink. He struggles to place his hand on both temples and then falls to the grit covered floor.

Pete yells, "Get his ass boys!!" They all pile on top with Bubba and Jill trying to pull them off one at a time. They were kicking him in the ribs and face as he just laid there in an unconscious state. Jill was grabbing at Pete's arm and yelling, "Enough Pete, he's sick and can't move!!" One of the others pushes her to the floor as they continue their relentless pounding. About this time a loud shot rang out causing everyone in the place to become motionless. There standing in the doorway was Clint holding his Colt revolver in hand and pointed at the ceiling.

Bubba yells, "I was going to say, 'It's about damn time!'"

Jill runs over to Clint, "Your brother and his bunch started a fight and then Josh passed out. They kept kicking and punching him. We need an ambulance."

Clint walks over and just stares down at Josh lying there on the floor, bleeding from cuts and abrasions. "Yep, he looks bad, doesn't look good at all. Then on the other hand does he really need an ambulance or is he just too drunk to stand?" He makes a haft circle around Josh, staring down with a nasty grin on his face.

Jill yells, "Did you hear me!? I said he needs medical help!"

He smiles and glances over at his brother Pete, "You say he attacked you, Pete?"

Pete slowly scans the room, hesitates, then replies, "Yep, me and the boys were just minding our own business when he came over and started a fight. The bastard broke my nose and I think he got some of my fingers too."

Jill can no longer hold her anger back, "You liar! That's not true; we were sitting at that table by the window when your brother and his bunch of asshole friends came over and started a fight."

Bubba breaks in the conversation, "She's telling the truth, Josh wasn't messing with anyone, but I can see what's gonna happen here already."

Clint glances around the room at all the blank faces and yells out, "Anybody else see it the way Jill and Bubba saw it?"

Nobody says a word knowing Clint and Pete ran the town. He turns to Jill, "Sorry Jill; nobody else saw it that way." He pulls his handcuffs out, rolls Josh over on his belly and places them around his wrist.

She yells, "What the hell are you doing!? Bubba and I are telling the truth." She hesitates for a few seconds, "But I guess that wouldn't matter to you….would it?"

He turns to her and with a smartass grin, "Looks like Josh just started trouble with the wrong people."

Bubba steps up, "You and your crooked family have managed to take this whole valley over and you have everyone in it scared to do or say anything about it, but you don't scare me."

Clint walks over to Bubba, "You better shut up before I put your fat ass in jail next to him."

Jill pulls Bubba back, steps closer and slaps Clint in the face, "If something happens to him, I'll shoot your balls off and I mean it."

He replies, "Are you threatening a police officer?"

She snaps back, "I don't see a police officer, just another one of Walter's spineless puppets."

Clint motions for help and they take Josh out to the patrol unit, laying him in the backseat with Jill and Bubba following them closely out the door. Bubba turns to find Pete using his good hand to paint Josh's Harley with a can of yellow spray paint.

He yells, "Damn you little bastard!"

Pete laughs, pulls out a switch blade and cuts both tires. He then takes the gas cap off, unzips his pants and pisses in the tank in front of everyone.

Jill turns to Clint, "You gonna just stand there and let him do that?"

"Do what?" He jumps behind the steering wheel. "Look Jill, why don't you and Bubba go home and let me handle this."

She leans her head in the window and says in a low voice, "If he dies, I'll make sure you never walk again, and you know I mean what I say. I will personally blow both your legs off at the knees with a shotgun." Clint takes off burning rubber as he left the parking lot heading toward town.

Jill turns to Bubba, "Take me to my Jeep."

"Why, where are you going?"

"I'm going down to the station to make sure nothing happens to him."

Bubba nods, then hesitates for a second before saying, "He's bad off right now. Let me go with you. If you have a plan, I want in on it."

"After letting me off at my jeep you can come back with the tow truck and get Elvira."

Bubba looks down at the ground and kicks his other foot, "I wanna tell you something, but Josh asked me not to say anything."

"Tell me what?"

"Josh gave me twenty thousand dollars to put in the bank and Clint took it from me."

"Why would Josh give you twenty thousand dollars to put in the bank if he was planning on leaving?"

"He wanted me to pay the mortgage on your dad's place, your café and my station." She steps closer and places her hand on Bubba's shoulder and in a low, sweet voice, "It will be alright after tonight, get his bike fixed so we can leave first thing in the morning." She smiles and then suddenly without warning slaps him in the face. "Josh must be the only real man within a thousand miles."

He yells as everyone standing around starts laughing, "What the hell was that for!?"

"That's for keeping secrets from me, now let's get going before Clint has a chance to do anything to Josh."

CHAPTER 17

Roughly twenty minutes later, back at the Platteville Police station, Clint is dragging Josh's limp, battered and bruised body into a cold empty damp cell and leaves him lying on the filthy, concrete floor, then slides the iron bars closed. He stares down at him with a sinister smile and says with an arrogant attitude, "This will teach you to come back and screw with us, Harley trash. That face doesn't look so good now." He turns, places the large keys behind his belt and walks from the cellblock corridor and back to the office.

Thirty minutes pass when Jill comes strolling into the station, finding Clint the only one there besides Josh back in the cell. He was sitting at his desk with his feet propped up reading an old dirty magazine that had been hidden in a desk drawer. He catches a glance of her standing there in the doorway wearing a short, short brown skirt and the top three buttons of her white blouse unbuttoned showing an abundant amount of cleavage. He stands and licks his dry parched lips with anticipation.

She asks, "You like what you see?"

He walks around the desk and leans back on the corner, "What is there not to like."

"You've been trying to get this stuff for a long time...well here's your chance."

"Yeah right; you're wasting your time if you think I'm going to let him go."

She steps closer, "I didn't come down here for him; I came down here for you. I only like him because of the bike rides. The authority you showed at the club got me to thinking and I was impressed with what I saw."

"Huh, that's funny; an hour ago you wanted to blow my balls off over him."

"I still do, I just don't need a gun this time."

"Is that right?"

She slowly swaggers across the room swinging her luscious hips from side to side until she's only a few inches from his wet salvia dripping lips. She places one arm around his shoulder and her right hand on his crotch. She slowly works her fingers massaging him ever so gently.

Clint, getting turned on says, "Okay, you want some of this, let's go back in the sheriff's office." To her surprise he grabs her by the hand and quickly pulls her into the back office. He places his hands around her narrow waist and lifts her up on the desk.

She tries to stall for some time by saying, "Slow down, let's take it nice and easy."

He lets out a chuckle, "You have your way and I have mine. I wanna hurry up before that fat ass Jim comes back. I won't take more than a few minutes to do what I got to do." He reaches down and pulls his man tool out through the zipper and places her hand on it. She gently strokes it as he starts kissing her on the cleavage moving lower until he was shoving the blouse down with his chin placing his lips on her nipple. She tries to push him back, but he forces her back on the desk even harder.

She whispers, "Slow down. Let's make this last at least five minutes." Knowing that things were not going according to plan, she tries to push him off again.

He reaches down and pulls her skirt up around her hips, "Now I'm going to show you what a real man feels like, then you'll know what you've been missing." He grabs her white lacy panties and pulls them down to her knees.

She starts to panic and yells, "Okay, that's enough."

He places his member on the surface of her thigh. She keeps trying to push him away, but he holds her down with a firm grip and the weight of his body.

"That's it baby, struggle more, I like a lot of action. I'm gonna make you forget all about that bastard back in that cell." She was getting tired from all the struggling, so she reached over and grabbed a cast iron paperweight within arm's reach and slammed it hard in the back of his head, knocking him unconscious. It sounded a lot like an overripe cantaloupe being broken open. He laid there like a limp noodle on top of her for a few seconds before she managed to push him over and to the floor.

She quickly stands, pulling her panties back up and her dress back down. She kicks him in the face and yells, "You say you like a lot of action uh! You have your way and I have mind uh! I hope you die you rotten son-of-a-bitch!" She reaches down, places his hand on his penis then grabs the keys to the cell from his waistband and as she heads for the door, she remembers what Bubba had said about the money Clint had taken from him that morning. She walks back over and goes through his pockets. She walks back out to Clint's desk, opens a few drawers and there she finds the thick leather pouch stuffed with money. After removing the money, she runs from the room toward the jail cells. While making her way down the hallway through the rancid odor of puke and human waste left by old drunks the night before, she stops and finds Josh holding his rib cage and trying to pull himself up by the bars. She unlocks the cell door, slides it open and quickly reaches down and helps him to his feet.

In a broken stutter, "I'm not sure, but I think I have some cracked ribs. What happened?"

"You passed out…Pete and his bunch roughed you up, and then Clint brought you here, now let's get you back to my place and doctor you up before anyone shows."

Disorientated he asks, "Although it looks familiar, where's here?"

"You're in jail; now pull yourself together a little so I can haul you to the Jeep."

He responds, "Not your place, that's the first place they'll look. Take me back to Bubba's and I'll figure something out." She struggles as he makes it to his feet and then before they left the cell, Josh asks, "How did you get the keys?"

"Don't ask, let's just say I made the ultimate sacrifice and leave it at that."

They stagger from the rear and Josh hesitates when he sees Clint through the open door to the sheriff's office lying on the floor holding his tool in his hand.

Josh, "Wow, was clint playing with himself?" Josh trying hard not to laugh says, "That's funny as hell......I wish I had a camera."

They walk from the building and into the deserted parking lot at the rear with Josh painfully struggling for every breath. She helps him up in the passenger's side of the Jeep, and then she makes her way around to the driver's side. She hastily turns the key and starts the engine. Abruptly slamming it into drive and they speed off into the night…

CHAPTER 18

Jill slowly pulls up to Bubba's service station checking in every direction for any unfamiliar vehicles before coming to a stop. Josh is leaning over with his head resting in her lap as she eases around to the rear of the station. Bubba runs out the backdoor to assist her in carrying him inside shaking his head from side to side, then sees Josh's heading lying in her lap, "What a man, still trying to eat that thang. Man, those bastards did a number on him. How did you get the keys from Clint?"

"What is it with you men and ya damn twenty questions? Put it this way, he will have a big ass headache when he wakes up, if he wakes up."

Josh looks up at Bubba, "We left, leaving Clint lying on the floor playing with himself."

Bubba laughs, "Yeah I can see how prone he would be to doing that with that face of his."

Josh turns to her, "Now you're in trouble for helping me escape and they'll be looking for you."

She snaps back, "Clint will be so embarrassed that he won't even mention me. He'll be too busy looking for you."

They carry him into the garage, and he hesitates when he sees Elvira sitting there covered with streaks of yellow paint and both tires flat.

Bubba says with sadness, "They pissed in the gas tank too, but it's not that bad. I will have it cleaned up by tomorrow."

Josh grits his teeth, "Now I'm pissed. Payback will be hell when I get back on my feet. Those son-of-a-bitches better find a big rock to hide under."

Bubba tells Jill, "Let's lay him down in my bedroom."

She fires back, "They will be looking for him and they will check every room."

"Look, we can move him to a storage place under the kitchen floor when they show up looking for him. You can see a vehicle coming for miles before it gets here."

She gives him an awkward look, "He's in too bad a shape to be put under the floor."

"It's okay; I have a small mattress for him to lie on, fresh water, and a year supply of potato chips and beer. I use the room when a bill collector shows up."

"That's stupid; just don't answer the damn door. They can't come inside unless you invite 'em inside."

"Obviously you don't know how far behind I am on some of my bills. I take no chances. The other week, a man came to the door wearing a suit. He knocked and knocked and then knocked some more. I thought he would never leave. And when he did, I think he took a truck tire and that old red rooster that I could never catch for dinner."

She nods in discuss, "Forget I said anything. Let's lay him down." They carry him into the bedroom and gently place him on the bed. She glances around the room and with a frown, "Looks worse than a pig pen."

"It just happens to be the way I like it."

She signals for Bubba to leave the room as she fluffs the pillow. "Go keep an eye out in case we were followed."

He asks as he leaves, "How come you have to undress the man every time we turn around?"

"For your info, I need to wrap some bandages around his ribcage. He may have some cracked ribs smartass!"

"He doesn't have to have his pants down for that, does he? His ribs ain't around his nut sack."

Josh, trying to get his shirt off, interrupts. "When you two are through you can help me with my shirt here." She gently pulls the black t-shirt over his arms as Bubba walks out the door. His midsection is covered with blue and purple bruises.

Josh lays back and says to her, "He's right, just leave my pants on. If I need to make a run for it, I want my pants. How bad does my face look?"

"Just a few cuts and abrasions; I'll have you fixed up in no time. Then I'll fix you something to eat, that's if he has any food in this nasty damn rundown dump."

She steps out and catches Bubba popping a beer open, "How come you're always interrupting me when I'm trying to get laid?"

With a smirk he replies, "He can't screw with cracked ribs. What are you, part rabbit? Show some mercy on the poor bastard. And did you see Josh's facial expression when he saw Elvia? He pissed!"

"He can't screw with you hanging around all the time either."

"Well, if I can't have sex, nobody else can."

"Why didn't you just say that in the first place?"

"You mean you're going to give me sex?"

"Read my lips, 'I'll have sex with you when hell freezes over'. Now move it or lose it."

"You're a very funny girl. For your information, I live here. This is my damn place. I'm the boss around here."

She grits her teeth and steps closer, "I'm sorry Bubba, for disrespecting you in your own house. I'll tell you what, why don't you fix Josh some of that famous lemonade you make, just before I kick you so freaking hard in the nuts, your teeth rattle!!

He pauses and then in a loud voice, "Yes ole horny queen bee, whatever you say!"

"Right now!!"

"Okie dokie; I'm moving already." He quickly strolls toward the kitchen mumbling, "It's still my house....for a few more months anyway."

She goes looking through the kitchen cabinets and finds nothing, then turns to him and asks, "How can anyone be so fat and have no food in the cabinets?"

"I have beer."

She turns to him, "Drive to town and pick up some things, I'll watch after Josh."

He slowly walks over to where she's standing, "I know what you're up to young lady. Don't let this stupid look fool you."

"Now what are you talking about?"

"You want me to go all the way to town to get some food, so you can rape him and take full advantage of his condition."

"That's crazy talk. I would never take advantage of an incapacitated man."

"I believe you'd jump right up in the casket at his wake! Why don't you go to town, and I'll stay here and take care of my little buddy?"

"Right, you'll give him a sponge bath?"

"No, he's clean enough. He's not going to a banquet you know."

She steps closer, reaches up and runs her fingers through his hair. She kisses him on the cheek and says in a soft sexy voice, "Please go for little ole me. You know for a fact sweet Bubba, that if you don't do what I say I will shove a cactus so far up your ass."

"I don't think so. I know what you're doing here."

"I'll tell ya what I'll do for you, if you do this one little favor for me."

"What's that?"

"I'll try to remember I'm a lady and refrain from breaking your spine and biting that fat nose off!!!"

Five minutes later Jill had Bubba's arm pinned behind his back.

Bubba, "You are going to break my arm!"

She pushes even harder, "You going to the store?"

"Yes!"

"You gonna back talk me again?"

"No!"

"I'm gonna get you some money to buy some things and you're not gonna let anyone take it from you, right?"

"Right!" She releases him with him holding his arm. "That hurt Jill!! But for some unknown reason I have a hard on….uh." He smiles and walks out the door. She returns to the bedroom and takes a seat on the edge of the bed.

Josh, in severe pain slowly turns to her, "Everything will be alright, I'm just bruised up a little. I think I have a chipped tooth though. I'll be back on my feet in a few days and be on my way."

She snaps back, "You mean, 'we'll be on our way'."

"Yeah, that's what I meant."

She leans over and gives him a gentle kiss on the forehead.

He smiles, "You really care that much about me?"

"I love you and nothing is going to change that."

"Hand me my medicine, it's in my jacket pocket." She walks over to the dresser, reaches in his leather jacket and takes out the small container of pills. She empties one out in her palm and walks back to the bed, "You only have five left."

He quickly replies, "I've been popping them like candy."

"What are they for and what's going on in that hard head of yours?"

"The pills are for severe headaches when I have an attack."

"What kind of attack? You've never told me what's wrong with you."

He places his hand in her hand, "I'll be okay, just get me a glass of water and let me rest."

She places her hand on his crotch, "You want me to take your mind off those cracked ribs? I can put some red lip stick on and paint your….."

He interrupts, "Water please."

She gets angry when she sees him avoiding the question. "I also got the money they took from Bubba. When was you going to tell me about that?"

"Before I left, I mean before we left."

She steps out of the room to get his water.

CHAPTER 19

As Bubba drove into town, he could see police units driving around in every direction with their blue lights flashing and their spotlights checking down alleyways like someone had declared a state of emergency. He steps out at Dan's small drug and convenience store and casually strolls to the door as if he had not a trouble in the world. As he pauses for a second looking to his left and then his right, he steps through to glass doors, grabs a small basket and walks down one aisle after another gathering bandages, a few cans of soup and other assorted items. He walks back to the counter where Martha, a young, petit female clerk is wiping down the countertop with a wet paper towel.

"Helloooo Martha, I'm so hungry I could eat a horse and I'm talking Clydesdale here."

With a grin she replies, "Knowing you Bubba, you could eat a whole herd."

"You flirting with me my little butter covered muffin? What say you get off early and lets both grab a bite to eat?"

"Is food and sex all you ever think about?"

"Pretty much and I'm not getting much of either here lately." He glances out the large plate window and asks, "What's all the commotion about?"

"Haven't you heard?" She wiggles her index finger indicating to Bubba to step closer.

"Joshua James jumped Clint in the cell tonight and hurt him bad, then escaped. Busted his head pretty good I heard. McNally has the state police and everybody else he can find, out looking for him as we speak. They say they found him lying on the floor with his you know what in his hand."

"You don't say. You know I've had my hand on mine in every room in the house and sometimes on the front porch of my station."

"I'm not surprise at all…. They're looking all over town; he's on foot, so I'm sure he won't get far. I don't understand Bubba; Josh was always a nice young man. And if I remember correctly, he was very polite and a handsome devil at that. I even heard he has muscles from head to toe and can fill a pair of jean tighter that a full sack of potatoes."

He shakes his head back and forth, "Drugs, Martha, this damn world has just turned to shit; it's not even safe in the police station anymore. They say that good looking devil raped ten women the first day he was out of prison. They say he raped one twice and she begged for a third go around. They say he's hung like a stallion. Must have it strapped to his leg to keep it from getting out. Lean closer." She leans closer and he whispers, "They also say he raped a young clerk about your age, height and build at a little convenient store just like this one in Albuquerque and now no man can satisfy her. She's been ruined. They say she awakens in the middle of the night screaming for more. Her boyfriend needs to wear clown shoes to keep from falling inside her now."

Martha gets shivers up her spine, "You don't say."

"I swear on my next meat lovers pizza. Now be careful if he comes in here and make sure you always have a stick of butter with you." He leans even closer, "They say Josh gets in there so deep and hits it so hard and fast; so, fast the butter melts and runs down your thighs. Wow for some reason I'm craving butter."

She quickly grabs a hairbrush, "You think he'll come in here?"

"He could, you never know. That's if he's still in town. If he does, put plenty of butter between your legs, because, if my information is right, he'll wreck that thing of yours."

"Crap! Is my make-up, okay?"

"Lip gloss."

"What?"

"Lip gloss… he likes a lot of lip gloss on the women he rapes."

"She quickly takes some lip gloss from her purse, applies it and wets her lips with her tongue.

"How about now? You think he'll rape me now? I mean I sure hope he doesn't come in here."

Bubba stares closely as her tongue works itself back and forth like a little lizard, smoothing out her lip gloss.

"That's goooood Martha, now unbutton your blouse and show a little cleavage. They say he likes a lot of cleavage."

She undoes several buttons and shoves her breast up, "How about now?"

"I'm not sure, let me think about what else he likes…" He pretends to think hard and then says, "Oh yes, I almost forgot, he likes a certain kind of panties."

She gets more excited and asks, "What kind Bubba, what kind!?"

He places his thumb and index finger on his chin like he's thinking again and then answers, "I'm not sure, let me see the ones you have on."

She stares in every direction, "Don't tell anyone about this."

"Hey, mums the word girlfriend."

She slowly unzips her pants and pulls them down a tiny bit exposing the top of her red panties."

Bubba gets excited, "Red, that's nice, very nice. Are they thongs?"

"No, but they are small and have lace around the edges. Maybe he'll like that."

"I'm not sure about that. Pull your pants down a little lower."

She pulls them down even lower.

"A little lower?"

She takes them down even more when he nods his head, "Wow!! I'm not sure about Josh, but I sure would like to take a shot at it right now."

She gives him a dirty look and pulls her pants back up, "Damn you horny bastard! That's not funny. Seriously, you think he really did all those things?"

"He's a dangerous man Martha. Prison life will do that to ya. Sure, hope they catch the son-of-a-bitch before he rapes another. If you get scared, you can come over to my place and I'll protect you……for a small price."

"What kind of price?"

"The kind of price that will allow me to eat those red panties off your ass!"

"If anyone's gonna eat my panties off it will be Joshua Harley James, now go get me a stick of butter out of the cooler and get the hell out of here right now Bubba Hannon before I hit you with a roll of freakin nickels."

Bubba smiles, walks to the cooler and grabs a stick of butter and hands it to her, "Would you like me to apply that butter between your legs, because Josh might not give you the time."

She grabs the butter from his hand, "Now leave Bubba! He's not gonna come in here with you standing there."

Bubba smiles, turns and walks out the door carrying a bag load when he almost runs over Sheriff Jim.

"Where's the fire, Bubba?"

"How the hell would I know; do I look like a fireman? Might be between Martha's legs after I got her all turned on."

"It's a rhetorical quest …oh crap…just forget I even asked. How's it been going lately?"

Bubba stands there holding the bag of groceries and with a stupid look on his face, "Just fine up until now. Sure, is a lot of activity going on tonight. Haven't seen this much commotion since old lady Sinclair's bull got loose and tore the town square up."

Jim steps closer, "This maybe a stupid question, but I guess you've heard about Clint?"

Bubba acting sad responds, "Man I hate it happened, Clint's a good man. They say he was found on the floor holding his tally whacker. You think he'll live?"

Jim trying not to laugh, "Cut the shit; nobody cares if he lives or dies. Clint's a spoiled rotten little shit who was always up to no good and you know it. Now tell me where Josh is."

"I haven't seen him since his arrest at the Cactus Rose early tonight."

"Then where's Jill?"

"Haven't seen her since the arrest either; have you checked at her place?

Henry might know."

Jim glances in both directions and then steps closer, "Listen, I know it was Jill that helped him escape tonight because Clint was found unconscious in my office as you say with his hand on himself."

"Must be an epidemic because as I was just telling Martha that I've been in every…."

Jim interrupts still trying not to laugh, "This is not about you Bubba."

"You know as well as I do that he has about as much luck with women as I do, unless he's banging your daughter."

"Whatta mean by that Bubba?"

"I'm sorry Jim my mind is still on Martha's red panties."

"Just tell me where he's at before McNally's boys catch up to him. I can get him out of the county where he'll get a fair trial."

Bubba hesitates for a second, "Haven't seen either one, sure wish I could help you though."

Jim looks around and then in a low voice, "If they find him first, they'll kill him and ask questions later. I don't want Jill caught up in the middle and getting hurt."

"If I see 'em, you'll be the first I call." Bubba starts to walk off but stops, turns and says, "I wouldn't be too worried about Jill. That girl comes closer to hurting someone else before getting hurt. Between her and Josh, I believe they could clean this town up."

Jim glances down at the grocery bags in Bubba's arms, "You have a lot of food there. You have company staying at your place?"

"Oh my God, Jim, I didn't get this fat eating desert thorn bushes."

Jim yells as Bubba starts to get in his truck, "Tell him to get outta the county and ASAP, before they block all the roads. I will be out to your place in the morning say around 8:00 a.m. if you get my drift."

Bubba smiles, "What drift you talking about, and what the hell does ASAP mean?"

"You know very well what drift I'm talking about."

"Oh, that drift…I will have fresh coffee made, looking forward to your visit. Bring some porn; I have plum worn out my tapes."

On the way out of town Bubba runs up on a roadblock. A Platteville police officer walks over to the window and scans the inside of the truck cab.

Bubba with a grin, "Hey booger eater!"

"How's it going tonight, Bubba?"

"Same ole, same ole. What's the roadblock for?"

"Have you heard? Every law enforcement officer within a hundred miles is looking for Joshua James; they say he almost killed Clint early tonight. Put him in the intensive care unit over at Riverside. He may die. They say he was found with his hand on his man tool where he was playing with himself…."

Bubba interrupts, "I did hear that… Yeah, now that you mention it, Martha did say something about all that. She didn't say his was in that bad of shape though."

"You haven't seen him, have you?"

"Nope, thought you said he was in the hospital."

"I'm talking about Josh, stupid."

"Why I sure have, he's right here in my glove box taking a shower."

"Very funny." Dave leans over in the window and whispers, "I hope Clint's sorry ass dies. You know that bastard had me working a school traffic intersection the other day in a hundred and ten degrees."

"Well hell, what's so bad about that? It is your job you know. Who else is gonna help the little children across the street?"

"That's just it, there are no children. School let out a month ago."

"Then why the hell did he have you standing out there?"

"You're as stupid as a wood rat, Bubba. That's my whole point. Clint was just being mean. They say he was found lying on the floor with his pecker in his hand."

Bubba, "You said that already. Bubba laughs, "Could have been worse, could have been somebody else's pecker he was holding in his hand."

"Sounds a little funny to me."

Bubba snickers, "It sounds a lot funny to me. I can just see Clint laying there holding onto his little pencil eraser with a big old smile on his face and a knot on his head."

"I'm not talking funny as in funny, Bubba."

"Look Dave, there's nothing unusual there. I've had mine in my hands ten times this week already. Hell, I bet even you've had yours in your hands a bunch this week. Hey, Martha, up at the drug store, just showed me her red panties. I think I saw bush."

"Why would she do that?"

"I'm not sure but it's got me wanting to go home and play with my pecker right now. Hope nobody hits me in the head while I'm stroking it."

"You think she'll show me that thang?"

"Hell Dave, whatta ya got to lose?"

"I'll check it out right now."

"What about this roadblock duty you're on?"

"I don't give a shit. Josh just did what we were all thinking about doing."

"When you speak to Martha tell her Josh just raped another girl at Jenny's convenient store. Say shit like, she can't even stand behind the counter straight, then talk about red panties and then ask her to show you... Now...if you don't mind, I'm in a hurry...you know, while the mood last."

Dave laughs, shakes his head, steps back and waves for him to drive on.

CHAPTER 20

Later Jill finishes up with the wrapping of Josh's ribcage when she hears a bumping noise out on the front porch. Josh cocks his head when he hears it too and in a low voice, "Turn out the lights."

She stands with caution and slowly makes her way across the floor to the light switch and flips it off leaving nothing but the light beaming from the moon, streaking through the front window. Across from the bedroom, the light was casting a shadow from the curtains on the wall. She eases out in the hallway and makes her way to the kitchen where she sees a shadowy figure easing its way across the porch, passing in front of the window over the sink. Carefully grasping the wooden handle of an iron frying skillet from the countertop, she slides in behind the door as the knob jiggles. She nervously wets her lips with the tip of her tongue and brings the pan up slightly over her head as the door slowly opens with the hinges making a loud squeaking noise. A large bulky figure eases inside and she nails him over the head causing him to fall to the floor like a large sack of potatoes. A bag of groceries scattered across the wooden plank floor as she turned the light on to get a glimpse of who she had just laid out.

There in the light she discovers Bubba lying there with a large reddish colored bruise overlapping a golf size knot on the right side of his head. She covers her mouth for a few seconds, realizing what she had done and says to herself in a loud piercing voice, "Oh my God, I think I just killed Bubba!!"

An hour later Bubba awakens and finds himself in bed lying next to Josh. Jill was placing cubes of ice wrapped up tight in a rag on his right temple. He reaches for his head with his right-hand yells, "Ouch! That hurts damn-it!"

She gives him a frustrated look, "Serves you right for sneaking up on us like a damn old alley cat looking for a free handout. I thought it was one of McNally's boys searching around the place for Josh."

He frowns, "Why the hell would one of McNally's boys be carrying groceries in his arms?"

"I didn't see any damn groceries, you overweight piece if shit until it was too late. I never heard that loud ass tow truck of yours pulling up."

"That's because I ran out of gas a half mile down the road, which by the way seems like ten miles when you're carrying a bag full of freakin can goods!"

She snaps back, "Let me get this right balloon belly boy; you own a gas station, and you ran out of gas?"

"For your information wicked witch of the east, the gauge doesn't work, and I've been so caught up with all that has happened lately, I forgot to check it with my stick." He flares his nostrils as he sniffs the air and asks, "Did you give me a sponge bath? I smell as fresh as a pine forest."

"Hell no, you fell on the floor that I mopped down with Pine-sol two hours ago. This place smells of chicken shit and beer and I wouldn't give you a sponge bath if you were the last man on earth. How crazy do you think I am?"

"Crazy enough to mop worn out wooden floors with one-inch cracks between the planks. How did you get me in here?"

"I dragged you by the feet."

"That would explain why I have a splinter in my ass. I sure hope a house falls on your ass soon."

Josh starts to laugh but the pain running through his ribcage quickly put a stop to that.

She nods, "Stop making Josh laugh, and what the hell took you so long anyway?"

"Did you hear what I just said? I ran out of gas, plus Jim caught me at the store."

"What did he have to say?"

"Clint's head was busted wide open like an over ripe melon, and he told everyone that Josh did it. Jim knows it was you that helped him. For some reason, he wouldn't say anything about you. I guess it's too embarrassing, so he thinks it's best that they believe Josh did it. They're calling in state troopers and a helicopter from the state guard first thing tomorrow. Get this; nobody gives a shit about his head. But everybody knows about him lying on the floor with his pecker in his hand. Now that's a Kodak moment if I ever heard of one."

Jill, at a loss for words, just stared for a second and then with frightened stutter in her voice asked, "He's hurt bad you say? I didn't think I hit him that hard."

"Yep, you smashed his peanut brains out, if that's possible."

"Oh my God, what have I done?"

"Stop worrying, I don't think it's as bad as all that, maybe a few stitches. It got worse every time somebody told the story. If I hadn't gotten out of town when I did, I would have had to attend the funeral."

"I didn't wanna kill him just knock him out for a little while so I could get Josh out."

Josh attempts to sit up and says to Bubba, "Nobody needs to know the truth. It's best that everyone thinks I did it."

She starts crying, "I can't let you take the blame for that."

Bubba interrupts, "I say he had it coming. Nobody seems to care one way or the other what happened to him. McNally is more interested in finding Josh. They still think you're in town hiding out. Now what do we do from here?"

Josh goes into deep thought for a second or two and then gives Bubba a wink, "How soon can you get my bike ready?"

"I can have it looking brand new in a few days, that's if Jill here doesn't kill me first. I will have to get the tires from town. Now if Jill doesn't want to see me whack off, she better give me a few. That Martha has my you know what about to jump out of my jeans."

Josh lies back down, "Okay, I'll stay hidden for two days and then Jill and I will leave."

She wipes the tears from her eyes, "By then they'll have every road and goat trail blocked for miles; how will we get out of the county?"

He again winks at Bubba, "I'll figure something out sweet cakes, now go heat me up something to eat, I'll be a needing all my strength in a few days."

She stands and heads for the kitchen, still very upset.

Bubba leans toward Josh, "What's all the winking about? You know very well you won't be well enough in two days."

Josh places his hand on Bubba's shoulder and in a whisper, "I know that, I need my bike fixed by tomorrow night. That will give you and me a day to figure some things out."

Bubba snaps back in his version of a whisper, "But you told her you weren't going to leave for two days."

"That's what all the winking was about. I'm leaving without her, I'm gonna need to travel fast and she'll just slow me down. I'm not going to turn her into a fugitive from the law too."

Bubba thinks for a second, "I do not wanna be around when she finds out you're gone. I don't think my head can stand another run-in with that iron skillet. What is it about that girl, if she's not having sex, she's gotta be busting everybody upside the head or throwing buckshot in every direction."

"Everything will be all right; you just take good care of her after I'm gone. I will be lucky to live another week or two anyway."

Bubba asks, "What do you mean 'live another week or two' that's not very...very..."

Josh interrupts, "Optimistic...the word you're looking for is optimistic."

"Yeah, that's the word I was looking for."

Josh says, "Everything will work out old friend."

Bubba with a sad look on his face, "I have been lost ever since you were sent off, and then when you returned, I thought things would be like they used to be and now you're going again. What will I do for fun?"

"Jill lifted my money from Clint. You can fix things up around here and make a real service station out of it. Jill will forget me one day and find her a good man to take care of her."

Bubba just sits there wondering how things were going to be with Josh gone again....and then with a snicker, "You don't really think for one second, she'll ever forget you, do ya?"

"Let me rest; I have a lot to think about."

CHAPTER 21

The next morning Bubba comes running into the room yelling at the top of his lungs. "Josh, wake up, Jim's pulling around back!" Still haft asleep, Josh struggles to get out of bed as Bubba places his arms under his armpit. They struggle to walk into the kitchen and as Josh leans against the counter, Bubba pulls the table away, folds the tattered rug back and opens a trapdoor in the floor. Josh, very painfully makes his way down under and Bubba closes it, flips the rug back and slides the table over it. Seconds later Jim walks through the rear garage staring at Elvira sitting in the corner. He then knocks on the back door.

Bubba yells, "Checks in the mail!"

Jim yells from the other side of the door, "It's me Bubba, Big Jim; not a bill collector!"

Bubba yells back, "Come in, the doors open!"

Jim walks into the kitchen scanning each room as he went as if looking for something or someone and then walks right past Bubba and takes a chair.

With a fake Grin, Bubba says, "Coffee's brewing. It will be ready in about five."

"Smells good; where's Jill?"

"I would say she's fixing Henry's breakfast right about now."

"Nope; went by there before coming here. Henry says he has not seen her since last night."

Bubba gets a little nervous and responds, "No telling with that girl."

"I see Josh's bike is still here and you've managed to clean the yellow paint off."

Bubba stands and walks over to the coffee pot, "Cream and sugar?"

He replies, "Please." Bubba places the sugar and cream in front of him. Jim takes a teaspoon and stirs the coffee, mixing the ingredients in with the strong brew and takes a sip. "Damn, that's the worst coffee I have ever tasted."

"So…are you surprised. I'm not a damn chef. I ground my own beans and I'm sure there's a little chicken shit in every sip. You can't make a move in here without stepping in it; although Jill has done a wonderful job of making it livable."

Jim shakes his head, stands and walks with coffee in hand. He makes his way out into the rear garage toward Josh's Harley with Bubba right behind him.

"Thought you said you haven't seen Jill."

"I didn't say nothing; you said Henry hadn't seen her since last night."

Jim runs his hand across the shiny maroon fuel tank and slowly turns to Bubba, "I can remember fishing with Josh when he was about fourteen years of age and all he talked about was buying a big Harley like his dad's." With a smile he continues, "She sure is a fine-looking machine."

Bubba smiles, "We call her Elvira after the Mistress of the Dark. She's almost like having another mouth to feed around here."

Jim gently runs his hand across the leather seat then suddenly stops, turns, and walks back to the kitchen.

Bubba slaps his hands together and in a loud voice, "Well, I guess you need to get going and do whatever a sheriff does! I bet you have your hands full looking for that evil bastard Josh. Poor old Clint."

"Why are you in a hurry to get rid of me?"

"Me? Hell no…you can move in with me if you want, as a friend though. I…I…got nutin to hide."

"I never said you had anything to hide. You're as nervous as a chicken with you staring at it after not eating for two days."

Bubba does a fake laugh, "Me and chickens…that's funny Jim. You really got it going on this morning."

"How did you get that big knot on your head?"

"I think I slipped taking a shower."

"You don't have a shower."

"I do if I hold the hose up high enough."

They sit there in silence for a few minutes when suddenly they hear Jill walking in the front door yelling, "Damn you Bubba, I wouldn't have to buy all this crap if you had gotten the right stuff last night!! I swear, sometimes I think you have your head up your ass." She walks into the kitchen with a grocery bag filled with canned goods, "I knew better than sending you to the store last night. You forgot the bandages." She steps around the corner and is so surprised to see Jim sitting there with Bubba, she drops her groceries.

Jim lets out a chuckle, stands, walks over, and bends down and picks the items off the floor when suddenly a wide grin appears across his face. "Let me help you with that." He places the stuff back in the bag and sets it on the table. Bubba is winking and nodding his head toward the floor. Jim continues, "Lord, that's a lot of stuff you have here." He starts picking the goods up and placing them on the table one item at a time, "Sure is a lot of soup and here we have some large bandage wraps."

Jill with a lump in her throat snaps back, "Yeah, Bubba was about out of groceries, so I figured I'd stop and bring him some." She glances over at Bubba and can see him motioning toward the floor with his eyes and then his index finger. Suddenly he puts his finger in his nose when Jim turns around to give him a look.

She asks, "I didn't see your car out front; you sneak across the Flats?"

"Nope, even the smell of dying lizards won't travel in the wind on the Flats. No, I parked around back." He continues as he takes a chair. "Who are the bandages for? Bubba's out of those too?"

She was at a loss for words and then Bubba jumps into the conversation, "You never know when I'm going to need bandages around here Jim; you know me, always falling over shit. Why I was sleepwalking the other night, I walked right off the porch. Damn nearly broke my neck. Now I remember; that's where I got this knot on my head."

Jim lets out a chuckle again, "Last time you were injured bad enough to need bandages, was when you were thirteen. You unzipped your pants, took a pissed and then caught your nut sack with the zipper and damn near cut them off. I think you were playing with yourself. Yeah you were one horny little kid; scratched your nut sack all to hell and back. Has Jill set up housekeeping with you Bubba?"

Bubba walks over and places his arm around Jill's shoulders, "You didn't have to tell that story in front my new girl. Yeah, Jim, me and my girl have decided to move in together. Why I had that girl in bed screaming this morning an hour before you showed up….right Jill sweetie pie."

She gives Bubba a fake smile, "Yeah Jim, I have been pulling on his little nub all night and that story doesn't surprise me at all, I already know you're a pervert. Your secret is safe with me."

Jim looks under the table and then gives her a smile, "I sure hope he's long gone from here. I'm wondering how he made it out with all the roads blocked."

She grins, "I'm sure he'll do just fine, Jim. He knows this country like I know my way around a kitchen. He's most likely halfway to Mexico right about now."

He fires back, "I can't see him leaving his bike here. I sure hope he doesn't try to use Twin Peaks Road; the state has that blocked also."

Bubba, catching every word he was saying jumps in and asks, "So, if a man was trying to get out of the county and make it to Mexico, how would he go about doing that?"

Jim turns to Jill and winks an eye, "I would say the only way out of here would be across the Flats and then the mountains. That's the shortest route to Mexico. A good man on horseback who really knows this territory could make it into Mexico in two days if he has enough water and the weather holds out."

Bubba, with that puzzled look on his face as he always gives when he can't follow the conversation, "There's no way anyone could make it across the Flats in that length of time, he would have to carry enough water for his horse and that would slow him down. The heat would kill him and his horse before he made it to the mountains."

Jim laughs and looks under the table again, "I didn't say it would be easy, but it is possible if he was to travel by night and rest during the day. I once knew a young lad who did it in eighteen hours riding on an old buckskin horse of mine, but that was a long time ago." He stands and stretches, "Well, I guess I need to get going and check on some roadblocks." He starts to walk off and then suddenly stops in his tracks,

"I don't think they'll check the Flats, but if they decide to, they'll use one of those choppers from the state guard unit in Albuquerque with that new thermal imaging camera and night vision equipment. I'm sure a smart man with good friends can figure something out." He walks to the door and turns to them again, "I sure wish I could have told him before he left how much his friendship meant to me."

Jill, with a smile replies, "I'm sure he knows Jim, thanks for stopping by." No sooner did he walk out the door, than Bubba slid the table over a few feet. They jerk the rug back and lift the trap door.

About this time Jim comes walking back in. They just stood there holding the trap door open. Bubba asks, "You forget something Jim? We were just about to start house cleaning."

He glances down at the trap door then replies, "I just remembered I parked in the back. You two continue with your cleaning, I'll just show my way out the rear." He walks around the table and out the backdoor.

Bubba takes a deep breath, "That was damn close."

She slaps him on the shoulder, "He's not stupid: he knew what was going on. Didn't you see him checking under the table? Hell, he just caught us holding the trap door wide open."

He reaches down and helps Josh from the cramped space.

Josh, in pain, "Get me back in bed; I'm hurting all over and it's hot as hell in that hole."

Bubba laughs, "Once, they came looking for me because I was three months behind on the tow truck note and they hung around for two hours. It was in January, so I liked to have frozen to death. It was like a damn icebox down there."

Bubba helps him to the bedroom as Jill runs to get his medicine. As Bubba lays him in bed, Josh looks up and asks, "You think it can be done?"

"Yes, I guess it can be done, just pull your clothes off."

"Very funny Bubba."

"What can be done?"

"Taking on the Flats; you know that damn God forsaken, almighty piece of hot scorching sand bed you call a backyard."

Bubba laughs, "With a good horse, perfect weather, and a lot of luck, nope, not a chance."

Josh gives him an awkward look, "I did it a long time ago. I'm the lad he was talking about."

"I know that, but you're a lot older and that horse is dead now."

"I will not try it this time with flesh and bones. This time I'm gonna use an Ironhorse, she needs no water and she doesn't get tired."

Bubba laughs, "Yeah right, like that's gonna happen."

"I mean it; I'm gonna cross the flats with Elvira."

Bubba with a shocked expression on his face comes back, "No way, the sands too deep and there are washouts to deal with."

"Everybody else thinks the same. If I travel by night, I can make it to the foothills of the mountains by daybreak."

"Elvira will overheat as soon as the sun comes up."

"As long as I can keep a speed of ten to twenty miles an hour it will be okay. I need you to find me a small tank of compressed air."

"What for?"

"Ten miles into the flats I will have to let some air out of the tires to give me more contact with the ground. Once I make it to the foothills, I will inflate them back up."

Bubba shakes his head, "Well, tomorrow night is out of the question; you need more rest, maybe a few weeks."

"I don't have a few weeks. You know as well as I do, McNally and his boys will tear this place apart looking for me."

"Can't do anything but make improvements here…and I'm damn serious about that; there are a lot of problems when a man takes on the Flats and what about Jill?"

Jill walks into the room and catches part of the conversation. She walks over with a mysterious look on her face, "You know, again, I'm always walking in and hearing half a conversation. What about Jill?"

Josh gives Bubba a glance and then nods for him to leave the room.

He taps the bed for her to have a seat. She hesitates, "I already know what you're going to say and you're not leaving without me."

"Look, I have a small chance without you and none with you. It's going to be hard enough traveling across the Flats and then I have the mountains to deal with."

She takes a seat on the bed, "I was listening to Jim, and I have it all worked out. Pop is going to pick up two good horses and a mule from Doc Cooper's place and together, we can make it. You'll need me to look out after you."

"I'm not using horses, I'm taking Elvira. I can travel a steady twenty miles an hour or maybe more on a hard surface."

Bubba sticks his head in the room and interrupts, "Bullshit! You'll be lucky if you can travel a mile in an hour and Elvira will light up like a spotlight if Jim is right about that thermal imaging stuff or whatever you call it."

Jill takes one of Josh's boots from the floor and throws it at Bubba and then turns back to Josh, "Bubba's right for a change and you're not leaving without me and that's final."

"Then I'll just turn myself into the authorities. My chances will be the same."

"I love you and I can't live without you!"

This is the defining moment for her. She realizes her love for him, but she also realizes the risks that are about to be taken. Not being a stupid female, she can sometimes come across as angry and controlling, that's just her nature. So, her persistence here is so obvious, but she's not going to be left out under any circumstances.

He thinks for a second and then says, "I have an idea. You can meet me in a few days in a little town of Samora just over the border and then we can move south from there."

Her eyes start tearing up and she responds with her bottom lip quivering, "What if you don't show? What if something happens to you out there in that stinking desert or what if you have another one of those attacks? Who'll get your medicine for you?"

"I'll be okay. The attacks will pass all by themselves. If you wanna help, you can start by running my bath water and fixing me something to eat."

Bubba walks to the door, "I need to go back into town. I forgot to get those red panties…I mean the two new tires. You want me to get anything else?"

"You can pick up a few cans of heavy duty compressed air with that fix-a-flat for me."

"I can pick that up too."

Josh turns to Jill, "Get Bubba some more money from my jacket pocket."

She walks out into the kitchen and removes some cash from his jacket pocket and walks with Bubba out on the porch and quietly asks, "What are his chances of making it to the border?"

"Slim to none, but he keeps his cool under the most stressful of situations and if he can't do it, nobody can. He made it one time with nothing but a canteen and a 22 rifle for killing rattle snakes." He turns and walks to his tow truck he had retrieved earlier, starts the engines and with a smile takes off………

CHAPTER 22

Back at the Sheriff's Office, Jim is pulling up front and notices several vehicles in the parking lot and five or six small motorcycles parked to the side of the building. McNally's Hummer dominated the parking area. He shakes his head and enters through the door and not to anyone's surprise, McNally is sitting there with a large ten-dollar stogie resting between his teeth and surrounded by some officers and other men volunteering their help. Standing in the corner is Little Pete and his five friends. He slowly removes his Stetson and places it on a hat rack by the door. McNally yells across the room, "Where have you been!?"

He slowly strolls over, "Out making sure all the roads are covered. I also checked Henry's and Bubba's place out."

McNally props his feet up on the desk, striking the heels of his cowboy boots hard against the hardwood surface, "I was going to have Pete and his bunch check Bubba's place out."

He fires back, "The only thing they're good at is punching on that man. I said I have already checked Bubba's station out and Josh isn't there."

"You sure about that, I mean you've always kind of favored that bunch. If I remember correctly you used to take that boy on hunting and fishing trips."

Jim pulls up a chair, "That was a long time ago. Now I'm the Sheriff and one of my officers has been assaulted. I want the man who did it as much as you do."

McNally stands and walks over to him, leans over and looks him in the face, "I want that son-of-a-bitch dead, you hear me, Jim. Nobody hurts one of my boys and gets away with it. When Clint gets out of the E.R. he will be pissed. Hell, this is your entire fault for letting him stay in the county."

Jim snaps back, "He broke no laws."

McNally slaps him in the top of the head as Jim quickly stands to his feet in defiance, but scans the room making eye contact with everyone, then realizes he's in no position to stand up to him. McNally, with a grin, "I own this county and your ass too, so what I say goes. You do what I say when I say. I want that bastard found. If he makes it out of this county, I'll kill you in his place, understand? I have a National Guard chopper coming in first thing tomorrow before the light of morning and I want it to cover all the pig trails. I don't want that bastard going around any roadblocks. That bastard may try the Flats again, so I want every ranch between here and Mexico told that if they loan that boy a horse, I will burn their ranch down."

Jim asks, "Why the Flats? Nobody can travel the Flats and if he does try it, the Flats will kill him for you. He'll be dead in hours."

McNally replies, "I know that, but I also know that son-of-a-bitch is one tough bastard and I'm not taking any chance. You have all the back roads covered?"

"I do."

"I want that big ass Harley found and I want every square inch between here and that state line covered. I want every rock looked under; every gulley checked out. I want this county locked down tighter than a prairie dog's ass." He turns to the others, "Why the hell are your asses still here!? Get out there and remember if you spot him, call me first on my private radio. I don't want those state boys catching him first."

Jim turns and watches as each one leaves through the door. He turns to McNally, "I wasn't able to find the assault report Clint made out when he arrested Josh."

McNally walks over, takes his hat from the rack and places it on his head as he slowly turns, "Josh must have taken it with him or maybe Clint hadn't got started on it before that coward attacked him. You fill out another and make sure it reads right. I don't want all those federal boys snooping around here."

Jim sits back down in his chair as McNally leaves, shakes his head and says aloud to himself, "Damn you, Josh, what have you gotten yourself into now?"

An hour later Josh was soaking in the tub when the door slowly opens, and Jill comes walking in dressed in a bright red flowered sundress. He sees something different in her eyes and asks, "Okay, what are you up to now? It seems you're always catching me in the tub." She says nothing, just steps closer and allows her dress to fall from her shoulders showing every smooth curve of her dark bronze color skin, perfectly tanned from being in the hot New Mexico sun too long. He shakes his head, "Not again. Who's keeping an eye on the road?'

"Bubba's back and I have him watching from the porch."

"He's supposed to be putting two new tires on Elvira."

She giggles, "First things first. This may be our last time together so I'm going to rock your world."

He gets a little worried and says as she steps into the tub, "Look, I'm sore to the bones, so you'll have to be gentle here....Okay? Crap!! The sun must be recharging your batteries." She doesn't say a word, just shoves his legs against each side of the tub and crawls in-between them.

Bubba is sitting on the porch and could hear water splashing, moaning, groans and grunts from the bathroom. She's screaming and yelling so loud Bubba is turning red in the face and getting a little embarrassed. Just when he didn't think the noise could get any louder, five F-16's came across the desert floor at Mach 1. When they passed over, he couldn't hear a sound from the bathroom. He strolls into the kitchen to get a beer when Jill with wet hair walks in placing her shoulder straps back over her shoulders.

With a smile, Bubba asks, "Is he still alive in there? Didn't know you liked watersports so much."

"He's worn slap out, but he's still alive…What a man. Now mind your own damn business jackass."

He slowly makes his way over to the door and peeks inside. Josh glances over with an exhausted look on his face, "Lock the damn door and stand guard! If I didn't have cracked ribs, I do now." Bubba glances down on the floor and can see where water had been splashed everywhere.

He shakes his head in amazement, "You lucky bastard. If you take a bath again, let me know and I'll bring you an inflated innertube." He turns and closes the door.

A few hours later, Josh comes slowly limping out on the back porch and takes a seat in the swing next to Bubba. He asks, "Where's Jill?"

"In the kitchen cooking and watching from the window to make sure no one comes up from the north and I'm sure she's plotting her next sexual encounter with you."

He shakes his head, "Anymore sex like that and I won't have the energy to go anywhere."

Bubba laughs, "That's exactly what she's up to. She must be making up for lost time. Funny, I can remember when we looked all night for sex, now you can't even take a bath without it being poured on you."

Josh pats him on the shoulder, "I see the tires are on Elvira and you have her looking as good as ever. Great job dude."

"Yeah, you'll never guess who I saw in town when I was getting those tires."

"Who?"

"Clint…he was standing around yelling orders and mad as a rattlesnake that's been pissed on and he had that bolt action 30/06 in his hand…Oh yeah, he also had this bandage wrapped around his head. He looked like a mummy from hell. That was so funny."

Josh chuckles, "That Jill must have really whopped him good. I guess it doesn't pay to piss her off."

Bubba rubs his head, "You got that shit right!" He turns to Josh, "Changing the subject, just how are you going to cross those Flats? It gonna take a lot more than screwing to get across that. Even a desert lizard has to hide from the heat."

I should be at Twin Peaks by daybreak. I'm going to travel as fast as I can by the cool of night…"

Bubba briefly interrupts, "You mean by the cold of the night."

"Yeah, as I was saying earlier before I was interrupted; I'll let the air out of the tires when I get to the sand pits and then air them back up when I hit hard ground again. I need enough water to make it to the mountains, and some chicken sandwiches. I also will need about a hundred feet of good rope."

Bubba, a little surprised asks, "Are you sure you don't need the kitchen sink?'

"Nope, that should just about cover it."

"What time are you leaving?"

"About two hours after dark."

"Why so late, you'll need those two hours if you're going to make it to the mountains before light."

He smiles, "Me and Elvira have a little job to do just after dark, which reminds me, I'm also gonna need about ten feet of chain just big enough to drag four hundred pounds."

"What are you planning in that head of yours?"

"I'm going into the towing business for about thirty minutes; let's just say I'm gonna make you proud of me and Elvira before I leave."

Jill comes walking out on the porch with a plate of fried chicken. Bubba, in a loud voice, "Wow!! That looks good. Listening to watersports can make a man hungry."

He reaches over for a piece, but Jill slaps his hand, "Yours is in the kitchen Bubba, this is Josh's plate."

He shakes his head, stands and heads into the kitchen mumbling, "Yeah, this is Josh's, its Josh's chicken, its Josh's coffee, it's Josh's sex. It's always about Josh." She takes a seat on the swing next to Josh and holds one hand as he eats with the other.

A few minutes later Bubba comes back out on the porch with a plate loaded down with chicken. He sits on the steps and scans the horizon. "I don't understand how you manage to catch those chickens when I can't even get close."

She snickers, "They never saw me coming. In other words, you need to be smarter than the damn chicken."

Bubba turns to Josh, "Well I may be more stupid than a wood rat, but any idiot can smell a breeze coming out of the west and I notice the clouds are coming in between Twin Peaks which means that there's a storm brewing and I don't mean a brief evening shower. It should move in about eight in the morning maybe earlier."

Josh smiles, "Do you just make that shit up as you go?"

"Pretty much, but I think I'm close this time. Bound to hit it right once in a while."

"That may be the edge I need. A chopper can't fly in that shit."

Bubba interrupts again, "It also means they'll be checking the Flats sooner than you think."

Josh goes into thought for a second or two before saying, "A good rain will keep search parties out of the mountains."

Bubba, shaking his head, "You're forgetting something; riding in sand is one thing, riding up and down mountain trails in the mud is another. McNally wants you bad, and he'll have search parties up there even if there's a blizzard."

"You have a better idea?"

"I say me, and Jill smuggle you past the checkpoints in a hay wagon."

"Hey, that should work. It always works in the movies, up until they start poking the hay with a pitchfork."

"You really think so?"

"Hell no; even a dumb ass like Pete wouldn't fall for that." Josh turns to Jill and asks, "What's wrong? You haven't said a word in ten minutes."

She responds, "Just thinking. If we had left when we should have instead of going to the Cactus Rose, we would be long gone from here. If you're leaving tomorrow night, why would the storm make a difference?"

Josh avoids the question and sidetracks with a nod, "You're right, but it's not the first bad decision I've made. Coming back here was my first and I was warned by an old padre not to come." He lays his plate on the porch and stands, "I have a lot of planning to do, and you need to start getting those things I need together."

She stands also, "You need to lie down and rest." He just stands there for a minute or two knowing she is worried to death about him, but there was nothing else he could do. He's running out of options.......

CHAPTER 23

The sun is ending its journey across the sky as it gives off its last glimmer of light before setting behind the dark gray mountains of the New Mexico's dry southwest corner. Josh straps his leather chaps over his tight-fitting jeans and then pulls his black leather flight jacket over his black t-shirt as he prepares to go out. Jill and Bubba just sat there on the sofa as he forced the jacket closed, zipping it up midway to his chest. The jacket was one size too small, but it belonged to his father once and Josh, working out in prison, didn't make it fit any better. That wasn't about to stop him from wearing it.

Jill, with a frown, "Where are you going?"

Bubba breaks in, "He's going to the Cactus Rose."

Again, she's lost in the conversation and asks, "I don't understand. What could possibly be there that would make you go back?"

Bubba interrupts, "Pete and his asshole buddies."

Josh walks over to where she's sitting and places his hand gently on her cheek, "I have a little unfinished business to take care of before I leave. Something I need to let Elvira do this time." He then walks over to Bubba, "You get the chain and yellow paint I asks for?"

"I did indeed. Not bright yellow, but baby shit yellow." He replied, then walks over to a cardboard box on the floor and pulls out a small ten-foot piece of chain all rolled up with a hook on each end and a can of off yellow paint.

Jill widens her big brown eyes at the sight of the chain, "What's that for?"

Josh grins, "I'm going to use it to improve foreign relations a little." He reaches for his keys on the table and walks to the doorway leading out to the rear garage. He turns and hesitates for a second and then says, "I'll be back in about an hour." He then walks out the door leaving them sitting there wondering how far Josh was going to push his luck. They hear Elvira fire up and the rumbling sound vibrated the walls throughout the rundown house.

Bubba glances over at Jill and reassures her by saying, "If he's going to do what I think he's going to do, he'll be alright. It's something that needs to be done. It's a man thing, you wouldn't understand. I just wish I could be there to see it. You know something?"

"What's that?"

"It's times like this that makes me proud to be called his brother."

"Do you just talk to be talking?"

"Yep, sometimes my words are a lot like my farts, no control whatsoever."

Twenty minutes later, **J**osh eases to a gentle stop just a few hundred yards from the parking lot of the Cactus Rose wondering what the best approach would be. The club was really booming. He takes off, getting up some speed before shutting Elvira's engine down. He allows her to coast into the lot in silence and to the right side of the building where Pete and his bunch had parked their rice rockets. He leans over on the kickstand, dismounts, and walks over strapping the chain to the front forks of little Pete's new bright muti-colored bike and hooking the other end to Elvira's rear crash bar. Then he paints the others, not forgetting to urinate in each fuel tank only to run out on the last one. He cuts their fuel lines and mutters to himself aloud, "I told Bubba I didn't drink enough lemonade!"

Minutes pass and with a loud scraping noise, he comes slowly dragging Pete's bike around to the front of the building. A young woman wearing a short, tight skirt is crossing the parking lot headed for the door when she sees him sitting there with a great big smile on his face.

"Joshua Harley, well I'll be damned! Look what the cats dragged in!"

"Hello Janet, longtime no see."

"I heard you were back in town. You made a big impression on your return. They're looking all over for you. How come you haven't looked me up?"

"I've been busy for the last few days taking care of a lot of unfinished business."

"Yeah, I heard that too. You busted Clint's head pretty good."

"Yeah, I really feel bad about that."

"I just bet you do. Well, if it makes you feel any better, he had it coming. That asshole has been pushing people around ever since he started wearing that badge. He wanted oral sex to rip up three tickets he wrote me. What a dickhead!"

"What'd you do?"

"Paid the tickets. I'll rather suck a jackass off."

"How's the family?"

"They're doing great. Are you planning on staying long?"

"Nope, I'm leaving tonight."

"You wanna have a few drinks? Then maybe we can go to my place and talk about the old days, or we can do whatever makes you feel good."

"I'm doing something right now that makes me feel pretty good."

"Maybe I can help you with whatever you're planning to do with that bike you're dragging around. I bet you have a lot of sexual energy built up after being in prison that long." She places her hands on his bicep and rubs it gently with her fingers. Martha said you raped a whole bunch of women after you got out of prison. You don't have to rape me."

He says with a grin, "Maybe some other time. My ribs are killing me. I think you can help me though."

"Just name it!" She blurts out with anticipation.

He gives her a wink of the eye and says, "Go inside and have Pete and his bunch come to the door. I do not want them to miss this."

She looks at Pete's bike lying on its side and starts laughing. As she walks toward the door she stops and turns, "Only you would have the balls to do what I think you're going to do." She opens the door and disappears into the club.

She walks over to the bar where Pete and his bunch are laughing and drinking beer. She lightly taps him on the shoulder, and he turns with a grin, "Oh hey Baby, you wanna go for a little ride on my new bike. Maybe you can show me and the boys a good time in Lonesome Canyon."

"I don't think so; that's why it's called Lonesome Canyon. I don't think I can fit on the back of your bike anyway."

"Sure, you can doll face. It sits two."

"It did sit two."

"What the hell are you talking about?"

"Your new bike is going for a bumpy ride without you."

He can tell from the grin on her face that something is wrong. She starts to walk off when she turns back toward him, "Oh yes, I almost forgot. Josh is out front waiting for ya."

He loses his smile and runs for the front door with everyone else pouring out behind him. He stares at Josh and then sees his bike laying there on the pavement with the short piece of chain strapped to the front forks.

"Oh shit!! Easy there Josh, that bike's brand new and set me back thirteen grand."

Josh shakes his head back and forth, "You're right. It's just too nice of a bike."

"That's right, nice and easy, just unhook it and I'll buy you a nice cold beer. We can forget all the misunderstandings we've had in the past."

"Yeah, and I'll just forget all about what you boys did to Elvira here."

"Me and the boys were just having a little fun with ya, that's all. We meant no real harm. Seems you've cleaned her up damn good. It was Clint that put you in jail."

Josh starts to step off the bike when he suddenly stops and places his ear to the gas tank, "What did you say girl? Uh… uh…is that right…a little fun you say? Well, you have a point girl." He turns to Pete, "I was going to forgive and forget, but Elvira says your bike could use some new pin stripes, so screw you, Pete." With that he pops the clutch and takes off like a rocket dragging Pete's bike as he goes. Sparks fly in every direction. The horrible scrapping noise was so loud it made everyone laugh.

Pete yells, "Get that son-of-a-bitch and somebody call my dad!!" His buddies ran around the corner of the bar only to find their bikes spattered with yellow paint and the fuel lines cut.

Two police units are parked quietly side by side at a crossroad. The two officers are carrying on a boring conversation about their wife's cooking when one stretches his arms out behind his head and says, "I bet that Josh is a thousand miles from here by now."

The other laughs, "Have you lost your mind? McNally has this county so locked down a scorpion can't take a piss without someone seeing it."

"He sure did a number on Clint. That knot on his head is bigger than my mother's old Dodge."

"Yeah, I'm still laughing on the inside about that. I've wanted to do that for years. Bastard had it coming. They say Mark has a photo of Clint holding his dick as he laid there on that floor."

"Oh, shit I would give my left nut to have a copy of that. You know Seth; I always had my suspicion about Willie's murder. I mean Willie and Josh were close, almost like father and son."

"Oh hell, we all know McNally had Willie murdered. He needed access to the mines and Willie wouldn't budge an inch. I personally hope Josh gets away."

The other officer leans forward adjusting his rear end to the seat, "Yeah, me too…You hear something?"

"Yeah, it's my belly growling. Let's go to Charlie's Meat House and get a burger."

"Not that…Listen closely, I think I hear a motorcycle coming."

"It's most likely Pete and his bunch coming from the Cactus Rose. I bet they're heading for Lonesome Canyon to smoke dope and whack each other off."

"I don't think that's Jap bikes I hear. Way too loud. Sounds like thunder. Too late in the evening to be those jets."

"What's that terrible scraping sound with it?" They waited a few minutes as the awful sound kept getting louder and louder until they could see sparks flying in the dark endless night air, but no headlights were visible. Then suddenly Josh goes by at about sixty miles an hour with Pete's bike grinding and jolting against the asphalt. He waves his hand as he passes by.

One officer waves back at him and then slowly turns to the other, "You were close; it is Pete's bike alright or what's left of it."

The other officer smiles, "I do believe that's Josh riding the Harley out in front dragging it."

They start laughing and then one asks, "You think we should give chase?"

"I'm sorry, I didn't catch the question. I vote Charlie's Meat House."

"We should at least pretend to give chase or say we gave chase?"

"Let's give chase, I'm bored as hell and wanna see the expression on Pete's face when he finds what's left of his bike. We can always say we lost Josh in the dark."

They take off kicking up dust, one behind the other. They attempt to catch up, but miles down the road, Josh slows to a stop and unhooks what is left of Pete's bike and leaves it in the middle of the road. He then takes off burning rubber as the two patrol cars come flying down the highway with blue lights flashing and sirens blaring. The officer in the first unit suddenly sees large pieces of Japanese steel and plastic in the road and swerves to miss it, running off the road and flipping upside down. When it came to rest the officer struggles to crawl from the unit as the other car turns around to check on him. He yells, "You alright?"

"Yeah, let me in." He staggers over and jumps into the passenger's side of the other cruiser, and they take off with smoke boiling from the tires. As the unit closes in, Josh shuts down on the throttle and increases his speed. They can see they're losing ground.

Seth, "Damn that bikes fast." The driver takes the mic in hand and starts to call on the radio for additional units to block the road up ahead but changes his mind hoping he gets away. Suddenly Josh makes a quick turn off the pavement and on to a dirt road. The patrol unit follows until the road runs out. Josh jumps a small, hardened pile of dirt pushed up from previous road construction and clears a deep gulley. The two officers follow but go air-borne and end up in the washout nose first. Elvira's pipes could be heard batting out a rhythm echoing in the night and bouncing off that rocky desert floor. The two crawl from the open doors on their hands and knees as one says to the other, "That boy sure can ride a bike!!"

"Hold that thought, I hear Josh coming back this way." He shakes his head and continues as he stands, grabbing his back in pain, "The old man is gonna be extremely pissed about this." The other says, "Maybe we can make up another story that sounds better."

"I'm working on it as we speak."

Josh comes across the desert sand and slows as he approaches the two officers standing there covered with dirt. He slows down and yells over Eliva's rumbling pipes, "You boys, okay!?"

One of them yells back, "We are, thanks for checking on us!"

Josh, "Just making sure! It's good to see you boys again and thanks for all the good times we used to have in the old days!"

"No, thank you Josh! They say you knocked the shit out of Clint while he was whacking off!"

"You boys take care of yourselves I gotta go, I have a date with destiny!" He takes off like a rocket…

CHAPTER 24

Back at Bubba's service station, Jill was pacing back and forth with panic written all over her face as Bubba just sat there sweating like he was sitting in a sauna. She suddenly stops pacing and yells at him, "What's keeping him!? Something has gone wrong I tell you!!"

He shakes his head, "Give him some more time, after all, he needs to avoid every law officer within a hundred-mile radius. Damn it's forty degrees outside and I'm sweating like a pig."

"I'm just worried sick. You think he went to see that bitch?"

"Not unless he's gonna tie her up with ten foot of chain and drag her ass down the road."

"That would be okay with me. He should have been here by now."

"He's not going to see that whore. In another ten minutes, you're gonna hear those pipes come roaring up."

Bubba sees that the coffee has finished brewing, "Coffee is ready." He starts to stand, "I'll fix it."

She walks over to the counter, "I'll get it; you just sit there on your fat ass."

He gives her a look, "You don't have to take it out on me just because he's a little late."

"Sorry, I didn't mean that." She starts fixing two cups of coffee when Bubba sees that she's placing scoop after scoop of sugar in his cup.

With a chuckle, "Okay, I could use a little coffee with that sugar."

She bumps herself in the head with the palm of her hand, "Sorry again, this waiting game is driving me insane." Again, she asks, "What do you think he's up to?"

"You can bet its some neat shit. I'm thinking he's dragging Pete's bike down the highway at this very moment."

She walks over to the table placing his cup down in front of him and then takes a seat herself, "You guys and your pride. Do you seriously believe he has a chance at crossing the Flats on that stupid bike?"

"Don't let him hear you call Elvira stupid and stop asking me that. It will be a breeze for a man with his skill."

She thinks for a second and then shakes her head, "You really believe that?"

"Not a word of it. To pass the time let's go over the good and the bad while we wait for him to show. The bike will be too easy to spot from the air. The heat from that big twin against the cold desert can be spotted for miles with them looking through those new thermal cameras they got."

"Heat? What the hell are you talking about? Men with that Harley jargon drive me nuts."

"Don't ask; I saw something about it on the military channel. Now once spotted, McNally will set two or three guys with rifles ahead and just wait until he passes and blow his brains all over the Flats or they can just pin him down until the heat kills him."

That just makes her even more upset." So she asks, "And the good?"

"That was the good."

"Thanks a lot for putting my mind to rest."

He places his hand on her hand, "He can do this, in a few days he'll be sitting in a Mexican cantina somewhere over the border, drinking a cold draft waiting for you to just pop in. He has one thing in his favor. No one in their right mind would believe he will even try to cross the Flats on a big Harley, and like we all know, he has done it before on a horse."

A soft voice is heard in the background, "And he can do it again…"

They are startled and turn to find Susan standing by the door dressed in tight-fitting jeans and a shear white blouse with a white fur coat over her shoulders.

Bubba with a frown, "Like I said, no one in their right mind would."

Jill jumps up and with an angry tone in her voice, "See what happens Bubba when you leave the damn doors open; all kinds of scorpions, lizards, and snakes crawl in!!" She turns to Susan, "How long have you been standing there?"

Susan, with a grin, "Long enough to know you think I'm a bitch and Bubba thinks I'm a whore…and about Josh making it across the Flats. I know he can do it."

Jill gets really pissed, "Why are you here, you slut from hell?"

"I knew when I found you and Bubba, he wouldn't be far behind."

"Well, I'm sorry to disappoint you, but he's gone already." Jill snaps back.

Susan steps closer, "Now I've been standing here long enough to know he's coming back."

Jill turns to Bubba with a grin, as she reaches over and takes a frying pan from the stove.

Bubba slowly stands, "What are you gonna do with that skillet?"

"I'm going to whack this bitch in the head; she knows too much. She'll just go right back and tell Walter, her so called sugar daddy, of Josh's plans."

Susan glances down at the pan and then back into Jill's eyes, "Look, all I wanna do is explain things to him."

Jill steps even closer, "Yeah right, explain how your legs accidentally got spread open and Clint just accidentally fell in between them on your big fancy kitchen table."

"How did you know about that?"

"You should have closed all the blinds. Josh saw you and Clint playing stuff the whore turkey on the dining room table. I'm the only one not surprised."

Susan steps even closer, "For your information, I'm still in love with Josh."

Bubba interrupts, "Wrong thing to say if you're trying to avoid the iron frying pan! If you tell anyone of his plans to use the Flats, he won't have a chance."

Susan responds, "If you let me stay, I won't tell a soul."

With a laugh Jill responds, "I bet if I bust your ass with this frying pan, you won't tell a soul either."

Susan, with a lump in her throat, "Now you wouldn't really hit me with that frying pan...would you?"

Bubba jumps in, "You might wanna ask me and Clint about that before you ask that question. I have a knot just above my right ear to prove it."

Jill jumps in asking, "How's the old knot on Clint's head doing now that the subject has been brought up?"

"How would I know; I just came from the house when I heard about Josh."

"I just figured since you've been screwing Clint and possibly little Pete behind their father's back, that you wouldn't be worried too much about Josh."

"Josh and I had a lot of good times. And I wouldn't do Pete if he was as rich as his old man."

Jill snaps back, "Like I was saying just this morning, once a whore always a whore."

"I know it doesn't look like it, but I really do love him."

"You don't have a clue to what real love is, and this conversation is going in the wrong direction if you don't wanna wind up like Clint."

Susan nods, "Maybe not, but I know enough to know you're in love with him too."

Jill with a sarcastic smile across her face, "Wow, you must be psychic. I have an idea; tell me what these stars mean."

She raises the pan over her head when a voice comes from the living room doorway, "Put the pan down Jill." Everyone stops and turns to find Josh standing there covered with dust.

Bubba, "I didn't hear you come up."

"That's because I shut the bike down when I saw the strange vehicle parked out front." He steps across the room and slowly takes the pan from Jill's hand and places it back on the stove. He turns back to Susan, "What brings you here?"

"You do, we need to talk…I'm still in love with you."

Jill lets out a fake giggle, "Yeah right, it took you about three hours to get over Josh the day of the trial." She turns to Josh, "This bitch is going right back to Walter and tell him which way you're going."

Josh slowly takes a seat, "Take Bubba out on the porch and give me a few minutes with Susan."

Jill, shocked at what she's hearing snaps back, "Go ahead, who's stopping you?"

"I mean a few minutes alone."

"You're kidding me, right? This bitch is going to get you killed."

Josh thinks for a second and gives her an awkward look, "Take Bubba and go outside like I said."

She grabs Bubba by the arm, pulls him out onto the porch and slams the door shut. Bubba with a smirk, "Now you know how I feel all the time with that 'Bubba, take a walk, Bubba take a hike, and Bubba we need a few minutes alone…'"

"Okay, I get it; now shut the hell up so I can hear what they're saying."

Back inside Josh walks over and closes the kitchen window. He turns to Susan and asks, "What really brings you out here?"

"I love you and I just wanted to explain things to you."

Outside Jill and Bubba had their ears pinned to the wall when Jill gets pissed and whispers to Bubba, "That slut, I shouldn't have hesitated so long with the skillet."

Back inside Josh with no expression on his face asks, "Why him, of all the men you could have had, why him?"

"Walter offered me security and things that you could have never given me."

"I gave you my heart and that's something you can't buy with McNally's money."

"I didn't need love; I needed a future. What was I supposed to do? Wait for you to get out of prison?"

He shakes his head, "I would have felt better if you had broken down a little in court or waited a few years before getting married."

"We had nothing, and Willie stood in our way. We could have been rich."

Back outside Jill whispered again, "That lying white trash."

Bubba responds in a whisper, "Will you shut up, I can't hear what they're saying. Maybe the conversation will get juicy."

Back inside Josh continues, "We had each other, wasn't that enough?"

"We had each other when you weren't running around with your buddy's drinking beer. Maybe if we had gotten married things might have turned out different."

"Marrying you would not have spared Willie. I was with you when Willie was killed, and you could have saved me sixteen years if you had told the jury that. You drove my Mama into an early grave."

"Willie had it coming. He wouldn't sell and all he had to do was sign the damn papers; he was stubborn. Two hundred thousand dollars was more than enough for a rundown ranch with a few head of cattle and some horses."

All expressions leave his face as he hesitates a few seconds then asks, "How did you know how much McNally offered? Willie and I never said anything about that to anyone."

Susan gets nervous, "Walter told me; that's how I knew."

"Before Willie was killed or after?"

"What are you implying?"

He thinks even harder and then it hits him like a ton of bricks. He walks toward the sink and then turns to her, "You were the only one who knew where I kept the pistol and that means you were the only one that could have taken it and then put it back." She backs up as he steps closer and closer. He suddenly grabs her by the throat, "You killed Willie, that's why you never told the jury I was with you."

She struggles to reply, "Listen to yourself; I was with you, how could it have been me?"

"I passed out for hours from drinking all that moonshine, then the next thing I knew the law was dragging me to a police unit. What did you do after I passed out? Huh!"

"That's insane Josh; you're not making any sense at all. It wasn't me."

He tightens his grip, "If not you then who else had access to my pistol?"

"I don't know."…. (He squeezes even tighter)… He made me take the pistol and then he shot Willie, not me."

"He who?" Josh tightens his grip even more as she struggles to get free and then he suddenly jerks his hand away. "You helped McNally kill Willie for his ranch and then you let me take the fall for it."

Susan, with an apprehensive look on her face, turns and looks the other way. Josh suddenly realized something.

"Wait a minute; McNally always had someone else do his dirty work." Josh turns and goes into deep thought. Suddenly he turns and gives her an obvious stare, "It wasn't McNally; it was Clint, wasn't it? Now everything is falling in place. You were seeing Clint the whole time we were together, but you couldn't figure out how to get the best of both worlds. If you married Clint, you would have had to wait for the old man to die to collect. So, you married McNally and kept on seeing Clint behind his back."

Susan starts crying, "I didn't know he would really shoot him. I thought he was just trying to scare the old man into signing the deed over to Walter."

"Why didn't you two keep the deed and the money from the cigar box?"

"After Clint killed him, he had to leave you a motive for murder. Walter knew Willie had no other living relative except a brother who he hated. That left only you in the way. With you in prison, he could buy the ranch when it came up at auction. I swear I had no ideal Clint would go through with it."

Jill and Bubba walked back into the room. Josh shakes his head, "Go back to where you belong, Susan. I'm sure your conscience won't interfere with your life. I feel nothing but contempt and scorn for you. You are one pathetic human being."

"You gonna just let her walk away huh?"

He gives Jill a glance and answers, "There's nothing she can say that will change a thing."

Jill bites her lower lip, "Can I hit the murdering bitch with the pan now!? We can call it justice."

Josh replies, "No, what I need for you and Bubba to do is get my things together, I'm leaving now."

Jill asks, "What about her?"

"What do you mean, what about her?"

"Walter sent her over here to find out where you were at and how you plan on getting out of the county."

He turns to Susan, "Go back and tell the bastard, that if he wants me, I'll be crossing the Flats."

Bubba jumps in, "That's suicide. I say we keep her right here until you've crossed those damn Flats and then let her go once, you're in the mountains."

Susan shakes her head and then says, "Maybe I can go with you, and we can start over."

Jill gets really steamed and is shocked at what she's hearing, "If there's gonna be an ass sitting on Elvira behind Josh, it's going to be mine bitch!!"

Susan steps closer and places her hand on Josh's arm, "I promise I won't tell a soul."

Jill shakes her head, "Your promises don't mean shit around here; you have a bad track record, whore."

Josh tells Susan, "Go back and tell 'em and make sure you tell 'em I'll be waiting for him. Tell him to bring Clint too; I have a little score to settle with him."

"I won't do it; they'll kill you for sure."

Jill jumps in, "I wouldn't underestimate Josh you bitch, and what has that got to do with you anyway?"

Susan looks over at him, "I do love you; can you believe me?"

Jill grits her teeth, "Why you low life desert rat! All you care about is living up there in that mansion bleeding McNally for all he's worth until he dies. Then you and asshole Clint get all that money and the house. Hell, I would lay two to one odds you two will even beat stupid Pete out of his share."

"You're wrong, I love him. You just want him for yourself."

Jill jumps toward her as she yells out again, "Bingo!!" Bubba grabs her and holds her back.

Josh turns back to Susan, "If you really care for me, go back and tell McNally what I said. If they kill me, then so be it. You have nothing to lose. You get the money and the house. And if I kill them, you still get everything."

Jill jerks loose from Bubba and walks over next to Josh and says to Susan, "You win either way, but if you ever come around Josh again, I'll shove a cactus so far up your ..."

Josh interrupts, "Go Susan!! Go tell 'em what I said."

She walks toward the door and then stops, slowly turns back around and asks, "Can I have a goodbye kiss?"

Jill can't believe she just ask that, "You kiss him, and I'll bust your ass with that pan for sure."

Josh gives her a smile, "Goodbye, Sue."

She stomps out the door. Josh starts laughing, "She'll go tell him alright and he knows that we wouldn't tell her the truth, so he won't check the Flats until he's looked everywhere else."

Bubba says, "And you knew that all along. What if Walter's smarter than that and the Flats is the first place he looks?"

Josh shrugs his shoulders, "Doesn't really matter now anyway."

They hear Susan's car spin out into the night. Jill gives him a look, "I don't understand, she might as well have pulled the trigger herself. She just cleared you and we are your witnesses."

"I'm not giving McNally a reason to come after you two so drop it."

Thirty minutes later Bubba walks over with two small cylinders of compressed air and says to Josh as he loaded Elvira down with a few supplies. "I decided to use these instead of those store-bought cans because the chemicals will eat the tubes up when it sets."

Josh places them in the left saddle bag. "Good thinking, I never thought of that, and you know why Bubba?"

Bubba, "Why?"

Because I use tubeless tires and what's funny about that is you put the tires on."

Bubba, "Oh, and a bitch those tires were."

Jill comes walking from the kitchen with some sandwiches wrapped in aluminum foil. Hanging over her shoulder were three leather covered canteens of water. Josh places the rest in the right saddle bag then knowing it was time to go, walks over to her and says in a low soft voice, "Well, I guess this is it, Little Bit."

He grabs her by the hands as she responds, "All that weight; a hundred and ten pounds of flesh wouldn't have made a difference."

He smiles, "I wish I could Little Bit, I really do." He gives her a long passionate kiss and then slowly turns to Bubba, "If you don't mind, I'll pass on your kiss and take a handshake."

Bubba, being funny replies, "Damn you, I was so looking forward to a sloppy ass kiss with some tongue action or, or maybe you and I can take bath."

They shake hands as Josh continues, "You take good care of my woman and yourself. I'll see you two in a few days after I cross the border. If that storm you say moves in, it will be nightfall before I get to the highway."

Bubba nods his head, "I will. What else do I have to live for? My best friend is leaving again. I can't read or write. I have no business per say, and I have no idea what this rash I have on my fat ass is. Now let's see what I have going for me…oh yes, I don't have herpes because you need to be with a woman to get them."

Josh laughs and gives him a big bear hug, "You're going to be alright my friend." He turns back to Jill who was in tears by now, "I want you to keep something for me until we meet up across the border." He hands her a small chrome logo medallion. "It belonged to my father, and it means the world to me. I wish I had bought a ring of some kind, but I've been so caught up with everything. This will have to do. I gave Bubba the rest of my money for you and him to pay bills and fix things up."

She starts crying and grabs him tight. "This medallion means more to me than any ole ring could. I know that it's part of you. Why don't I just bring the money with me to Mexico? We'll need it for a new start."

Josh, "That money will keep Bubba's station, your café and you and your father's place."

He nods for Bubba to take her. Bubba walks over and pulls her from his arms as he turns and mounts Elvira, firing her off with one powerful kick. The sound of the roaring pipes filled the room. He glances back at her, gives her a wink and takes off like a rocket out to the road and across the Flats.

CHAPTER 25

An hour later Josh with his lights off and his ribs in inculcating pain is having a lot of trouble with the soft mounds of dirt blown up by the frequent windstorms that race across the desert floor. He attempts to dodge scattered cacti and stray boulders that appeared only as shadows in the dark and prove to be more difficult than he had anticipated. He was straining his eyes to see through the darkness hoping a washout wouldn't abruptly appear from out of nowhere. The shadows of the rolling tumbling weeds took on a whole new meaning and the wind gusts began to gain momentum. The currents swept under Elvira and scattered the dust blown up behind her as she made her way. Consider it like rolling wind tunnels on the Sahara Desert. He kept making his way, as his journey became more treacherous.

Back at Bubba's place, Jill was standing about a hundred yards from the front porch freezing from the cold night air that was taking over where the heat had left off. Bubba walks up behind her and gently places a homemade quilted blanket over her shoulders.

"I have ice sickles hanging off my nuts. How long are you going to stand out here in the cold?"

"As long as it takes. You know, occasionally, I think I can see the movement of his rear taillight."

Bubba glances into the darkness and says in an easy tone, "Impossible; I removed the bulb before he left." He places his right hand on her left shoulder, "He'll be alright. By daybreak he'll be almost to the foothills and then the mountains and just a few miles from Highway 64 and then another thousand feet to the border."

She turns to him, "He left late. Morning will catch him on the Flats and if he docs make it through, he needs to deal with the mountains. He's never going to get to the border, and you know it. Elvira is too big and too heavy. And I think you were right for once about the weather. I saw lightning flashes from the southeast."

Bubba glances around into the darkness, shakes his head back and forth then lets out a few deep grunts, "I haven't been right in while. Maybe it will be just a brief drizzle."

She quickly turns and sees a funny expression on his face, "Okay, you know something; I can see those little gears rolling around inside that empty head of yours, and you've been acting uptight for the last hour. I can always tell when you're keeping something from me because of the absence of nose picking and ass scratching."

He gets a lump in his throat, "I've been meaning to tell you something, but didn't want you to go off the deep end on me."

"What did I tell you about keeping secrets from me? Especially when it came to Josh. Now spit it out!"

"You're not gonna slap me, are you?"

"I'm going to slap you if you make me wait any longer."

"Getting to Mexico won't help him, he knows his days are numbered."

"What the hell are you talking about!?"

"Henry told me Josh has a brain tumor and he doesn't think he'll last but a few more days anyway. That's why he passes out all the time."

She slaps him and yells, "Damn you; get the tow truck fired up!!"

"It's not going to do us any good; they have roadblocks set up everywhere."

She snaps back, "They're looking for him stupid, not us."

"Oh, sorry, I guess I wasn't thinking straight."

"That's because you always have your head in your ass."

"Now wait a cotton-picking minute, I care about him too. He's my best friend."

"You love him enough to have sex with him?"

"Okay, you got me there, but I care more about him than you give me credit for. He's like a brother to me."

She turns and walks in the front door but stops and turns to Bubba, and yells again, "Why is he crossing the Flats if he's dying! I mean what's the whole purpose of running for the border?"

"I don't know; maybe it's the thrill of the chase or some other macho things like that. Josh always was an adventurer at heart and this way he goes out like a man."

She starts crying, stomps her feet, "Damn you men, always trying to piss me off!" She turns and runs back inside.

He shakes his head, turns and stares into the desert and says to Josh, "You better die before she gets to you dude. My alligator mouth has overloaded my hummingbird ass again. That sounded stupid, 'my hummingbird ass,'...right!!"

McNally stands in his den pouring himself a glass of expensive Scotch whiskey. He turns and casually walks over to where Pete and the Robinson brothers were sitting on the sofa. Pete just sat there with a stupid look on his face, wondering what purpose his father had called them together.

"What's up, Pop?"

McNally just shakes his head, "You call me Pop one more time and I'll knock your damn teeth out of that ugly ass face of yours. The way you act sometimes; I think you belong to some damn drifter that passed through town."

"Sorry."

"You let that bastard paint those new bikes yellow and then drag yours down the road. Do you know what that makes me look like? I'm the laughingstock of the whole town."

"Look, we were inside the club; we had no idea what was going on until it was all over. Is that why you called us here?"

McNally answers sarcastically. "You were inside the club when you should have been out looking for the bastard, but you are right, I didn't call you over here for that, I just felt like having a drink with you boys." They all laugh when suddenly he throws his glass across the room shattering it against the wall. They are all startled, but not surprised by his raging anger.

He steps closer, "In a few minutes Susan will be back, and I'll have Josh's route out of this county. Then I want you boys to stage a little surprise reunion for him."

Pete asks, "Why would they tell her?"

"They won't, they'll give us the wrong way and that will narrow down the search grid." No sooner did he finish saying that she came walking through the front door.

He turns with an angry grin stretched across his aged face, "Speak of the little devil and she pops right in."

She throws her fur on a chair and walks over to fix herself a drink. He chuckles and asks, "Well, you gonna tell me what they said?"

She takes a sip of her drink and answers, "The Flats, he's crossing the Flats."

They all start laughing when Pete blurts out, "If that's not the biggest pile of crap I've ever heard; nobody in their right mind would attempt to cross the Flats!"

She turns to him and gives him a smirk, "You don't know Joshua Harley James too well."

Pete raises his voice, "Yeah and you don't know the Flats too well either. That place is hotter than Death Valley when the sun rises and dryer than fresh picked cotton. The Flats will have him for lunch. Problem solved."

She blurts out, "He's crossed it before, you smartass little shit!"

McNally turns and walks over to the bar, fixes another stiff drink and then turns and starts laughing. "Pete may not be too far off here. I believe Josh will take that beat up road just off old Highway 28. It's a tough route but can be made if he catches it before a rainstorm. Then on the other hand, he knows this country better than anyone and he knows the Flats, the one place we'll never suspect him of taking. We got him boys. I'll keep the roads blocked just in case I'm wrong. You idiots get your bikes and take Flaming Gap to the south mining road. Trailer your trail bikes as far as Feather Pass then use them to get into the mountains just in case, he does make it that far."

Pete interrupts, "Feather Pass is impossible to travel this time of the year; everything is washed out."

McNally frowns, "That's why I said take the trail bikes stupid ass; we didn't have a lot of rain this year so you and your ignorant friends here should have it easy. All that riding you little shits do; you should be able to handle a little rough terrain, or would you like me to have the girl scouts go up there for you?"

Pete stands, "I overheard some Indians saying something about some murky clouds coming in between Twin Peaks and a wind coming from the west."

McNally nods, "So, what the hell does that crap mean?"

"They said that it means a storm is moving in and not just any storm but a bad storm. Those Indians say it's going to be the mother storm of all storms."

"First of all, that's just a bunch of drunken Indians talking out their ass."

"They know their shit when it comes to the weather. Their lives depend on it."

"Is that a fact?"

"That's a fact."

"What a coincidence; your lives depend on it also. You stupid jackass, there's no way you can have any of my blood running through your veins. The news said light rain, nothing about a storm and even if it were true, you boys will be in those mountains long before it sets in. Now get your shit ready and get plenty of rest. You'll be moving at first light." They stand and start to leave when McNally yells, "When you boys catch up to him, I want it to look like he fell off a cliff. He's on horseback, so take a lunch and plenty of water. You can be there waiting for his ass the whole day before he makes it."

Pete snaps back, "What if we can't catch up to him?"

McNally gets frustrated, "Then I'll make it look like you boys fell off a cliff. Like I said he will be on horseback. You can catch him easy."

Susan, "He's not taking a horse this time, he's riding the Harley."

"Nobody in their right mind would attempt the Flats or the mountains with a bike that size; now move it." He then turns his attention to Susan, "And you can get your ass to the bedroom and put on something sexy; the thrill before a good chase always makes me feel rough and horny."

She smiles, walks over and rubs his shoulders, "I have a better idea, why don't you sit in the recliner and watch the news. I'll go put on my nightgown and garter belts and then fix you a drink. Then I'll let you spank me real hard."

He turns with a menacing grin, "I don't need your permission to slap your ass, bitch."

She takes a hard swallow, turns and disappears up the staircase. She enters the room, steps into the walk-in closet and removes a sexy see through nightgown. She starts changing when suddenly a small crack appears in the door leading to the bathroom. Clint steps out with a large white bandage wrapped around his head, sneaks up behind her and grabs her around the waist causing her to jump.

"Damn!! You scared the crap out of me!" She takes a gander of the white bandage wrapped tightly around his head and says, "Wow, he really did a number on you."

"If he hadn't come up behind me, I would have cleaned his plow. What took you so long? I've been waiting up here for two hours."

"Well, you're just gonna have to wait a little longer. Your father is downstairs waiting for another night of sexual abuse."

"It shouldn't take long for a knockout like you to hurry him up a little."

"Are you kidding; he slaps me around for an hour before he can even get a hard-on."

Clint holds a small capsule between two fingers and dangles it up in the air, "Not if you put three of these in his drink. Then he'll tell you anything you wanna hear and I mean anything."

She asks, "Like what?"

"Like the combination to that damn safe downstairs. I'll take the money and see to it he doesn't come back from our little hunting trip."

"What are those?"

"It's some pink wonder pills I got from a nurse in the E.R. to help me sleep. You open the capsules up and dump three of these in his drink and he'll be out in about ten minutes. He won't remember a thing."

She takes the pills from his hand as he turns her around and bends her over. She asks, "What the hell do you think you're doing now?"

He takes out his penis and quickly shoves it inside her. She lets out a grunt, "Not now. He'll know something is wrong."

"He'll just think you're turned on or something." He strokes her hard and fast. So hard she needed to place her hands on the corner bedpost to keep from being shoved on the floor. He forces her to arch her back into a curve to gain more penetration.

She stutters, "Hurry up, he's gonna catch us or think…something." He lets out a chuckle and grabs her by the hair pulling her head back so far, she says with pain, "You're hurting me."

"Tough shit, it runs in the family. You don't mind that fat sorry ass father of mine when he's shoving all kinds of stuff up in there, you kinky blonde whore." He talks himself into a sexual frenzy and strokes her so hard she falls over the bed. He grabs her ass and pulls her back up.

"Hold still, I'm almost there." He lets out a moan and grunts loudly. She falls back to the bed, and he flops on top of her.

He flips over on his back sweating like crazy. She lays there trying to catch her breath. He slaps her on the rear end and says, "Now go downstairs and get that combination."

"I need to clean myself up a little." She replied.

He snaps back, "No you don't!" She struggles to stand and as she walks to the door he says, "Hey, are you forgetting something?"

"What now?"

"You're forgetting the pills on the dresser." She slowly walks over to the dresser, still feeling uncomfortable between the legs after the rough ride and takes the pills in hand.

He laughs, "Don't take too long with the old goat. I feel the need to crawl back between those fine ass thighs again. One thing that old bastard did pass down in those genes and that's the desire to screw like a wild animal."

CHAPTER 26

The moonlight is casting long shadows across the desert as Josh rides fast over the Flats, dodging rocks and washouts. He could see that taking a straight shot was going to be impossible for him, except for a few occasional soft spots, the desert sand seemed more packed than normal. The Flats must be getting more rain than the rest of the county. A funny thing about the Flats, it can take on a personality of its own sometimes causing the warm air traveling north to suddenly turn to the west and climb the mountain range so fast that it would mix quickly with the cold air coming off the peaks. Brief storms are common and could cause serious problems even if they didn't last very long. He's glad he decided to leave at dark. It's cold as a witch's tit, but the good thing is, there's no warm current to create problems. He knows that during the day sand can get so heated, and the hot air will rise slowly a few feet from the ground and cause Elvira's air-cooled engine to overheat in minutes.

Suddenly, twenty miles into the Flats, he strikes a sand bed causing the front tire to bury so deep that he took a spill flipping sideways, throwing him twenty feet. He quickly recovers from the spill and slowly crawls back to Elvira and lets a small amount of air from the tires before straining to stand her up straight. His ribs were giving him more trouble. He speaks to her as if she had ears to hear him with, "I sure got us in a mess this time… the sun will be coming up in about six hours sweetie and we better be off these Flats. He takes the pain pills out and pops one."

Back at the station Jill was getting some things together when Bubba asks, "What are you doing?"

"I'm getting us some food and water together; then I'm going back to my house and explain things to Pop, pack a few things and then you can pick me up."

"Why, are we going someplace?"

"We're going to use your tow truck and meet Josh at the border."

"Do you know how many miles it is around that mountain range? We'll have to go all the way to Crows Junction, then travel west for four hours and that's if Bear Tooth Road isn't washed out. Then we turn south for another four or five hours before getting to the border and that's if we can determine exactly where he will be coming out of the mountains."

"You don't have one positive thing to say about finding him, so shut the hell up and help me get some things together."

"Okay, whatever you say."

About this time Jim comes pulling around back. Bubba peeks out the window and turns back to Jill, "Oh shit, Jim's back."

"Damn; what the hell can he want now?" She walks out onto the back porch and meets him with a smile on her face.

"Hey, back so soon?"

"I was just making sure everything has been taken care of."

Bubba walks out behind her, "Oh hey Jim, what brings you back?"

Jim steps up on the porch, "I saw Susan driving in the other direction a few hours ago. Was she leaving here?"

Bubba quickly replies, "Yep."

Jill, at the same time yells, "Nope!"

Jim smiles, "Why don't you two walk back inside the house, pour me a cup of fresh brewed coffee and get your stories straight." She gives Bubba a look and waves for Jim to come inside. As they all walked in, he could see some supplies lying out across the table.

"You two going somewhere?"

She steps in front of the table, "Okay Jim, he's dying and Bubba's taking me to the border to meet him."

"Did you two tell Susan anything?"

"Josh told her he was using the Flats to get to the mountains." Jill replied.

He shakes his head, "That was stupid! Now he has doubled his chances of not making it. This evening, I notified the District Attorney and he's looking into Clint's arrest. I think we can clear this thing up."

She turns to Bubba and then back to Big Jim, "Susan all but confessed to helping murder Willie. She's the one that took Josh's pistol from the barn and Clint shot him."

Jim takes a careful sip of hot coffee, "I figured that, but wasn't much I could say at the time. Out of three daughters, she was always on the wild side."

She pulls up a chair next to him, "I bet that if you were to put a little pressure on her you'll have enough to arrest Clint."

"Yeah, and McNally will have me, you, Bubba and Susan killed."

"Look, Josh is innocent of any wrongdoing; you can't just sit back and let them kill him."

He gives her a look, "I contacted Josh's warden and I know about his condition. This is the way he would want it. He always wandered on the wild side himself and I'm not going to be the one to take that away from him. Now if you're going after him, I can get you past the roadblock on 61 by sending those two cars on a wild goose chase. You still have the state roadblock on 84 to get past…I have no pull with those state boys." Jim stands: places his hat on his head and slowly walks to the door, then hesitates and thinking hard before saying, "I bet that if we use my police unit, we can slip right past those state boys."

Bubba breaks in, "You'll never get the car past those washouts near Crow's Junction."

"Okay, that nips the patrol car in the bud, but I bet Jill's Jeep can."

A big smile comes across her face, "I never even thought about the Jeep; it's four-wheel drive. I'll get a few more things together."

Jim and Bubba walk over to where the yard stops and the desert begins. Jim places his arm over Bubba's shoulder, "I'm freezing my ass off. That's one hardheaded woman."

Bubba, with a shake of the head, "I'm freezing my ass off too. He doesn't have a chance, does he?"

"I think an ice sickle just fell from my ass and run down my leg. Nope, he won't make it thirty miles with that big Harley."

"Okay, I just lost all feelings in my left nut. Where were we, oh yeah, then why are we going anywhere?"

"My toes Bubba."

"What about them?"

"They just went numb. You ask, 'why are we going then?'"

"I think that's what I ask."

"Because it's the only way that wildcat inside the house is going to be satisfied."

Bubba went silent for a minute or two and then says, "I remember the first time he made it across the Flats. He was riding on the Old Iron side. That horse was sixteen years old and was the toughest buckskin I'd ever seen. Elvira won't do anything but slow him down or fall on top of his ass in a gully."

Jim looks into the sky at the many stars and the bright full moon casting its glow across the Flats.

"He has a few things in his favor."

Bubba, "Being cold isn't one of them. That Josh must be freezing his ass off right about now."

"Let's entertain ourselves and head that way. I sure would like to see him make it, just to show everyone it can be done." Jim replies.

Jim gets no rebuttal from Bubba. He stares into the night, "You too cold to comment?" There's still no reply. Jim turns around and sees Bubba heading for the door, "Are you leaving right in the middle of a conversation?"

Bubba yells back, "Screw the conversation! I think a nipple just fell off! We can talk that same shit inside!"

CHAPTER 27

McNally paces back and forth in front of the fireplace when the phone suddenly rings. Susan, slowly working her way back down the staircase in a sexy nightgown listens from the lower step.

He takes the phone in hand and in a heated conversation, "I don't give a shit how bad the weather will get, I said I want that chopper before daybreak." He listens and then responds, "I don't give a damn what your captain says. Listen up Earl; every year I donate a small fortune to those charity drives you guardsmen are always doing for that stinking Indian orphanage up in Las Cruces. Now you can pick me up in the morning before light or you can forget anymore donations."

He slams the phone down at the same time she walks into the den and asks, "What are you going to do?"

"We're going to check the Flats just before light and see if the desert has already solved our problem for us. Then if we fail to find a body, I'm going to have the chopper set us down near Deer Lake Gorge. Then I'm going to wait for him to show and kill that bastard like it should have been done sixteen years ago."

She hesitates before saying, "You said 'we' and 'us.'"

"That's right, you're going with Clint and me and you're going to watch as I blow Josh's brains all over those canyon walls."

"I don't understand why you need to kill him at all. He can't hurt you, just let him go."

"I'm not taking any chance of him coming back and causing any more problems."

"What kind of problems?"

"Like screwing around with my wife or looking deeper into Willie's death." She starts to say something, but he interrupts before she could open her mouth, "Not another word. I know you still have feelings for him, but let me tell you something bitch, you don't clean house, you're not standing on your feet all day waiting tables or working behind some cash register. You get waited on hand and foot and you get to spend every day at that damn mall you love so much. All you need to do is lie around and spread those legs when I tell you to. Now get your ass up those stairs. We have a long day ahead of us tomorrow."

"I'll fix you another drink and we can do it in the recliner."

Turned on by the fact she wants to do it at all, he agrees. She walks over to the bar and pours a drink, then as he flips the channels with the remote, she breaks open one capsule after another sprinkling the fine powder into his drink and stirs it with her finger. She returns to the chair and hands him the drink. She takes the remote and turns the TV off. Slowly she makes her way between his legs unzipping his pants as she takes to her knees. At the top of the stairway Clint was watching her performed oral sex on the old bastard and he's steaming with anger.

An hour later she climbs the stairway and into the bedroom. Clint quickly walks over and asks, "Well?"

"He's out cold."

"Good. Did you get the combination?"

She hands him a small piece of paper. "It wasn't easy."

"Well, clean yourself up while I'll give it a try." He walks back downstairs, takes a glimpse at his father sleeping in the leather recliner, then removes the large picture from the dining room wall, placing it down on the floor before slowly turning the black knob.

Another hour passes, she walks from the shower and there lying on the bed was Clint rolling around in a large pile of money.

"Crap, how much is that?"

"About two million dollars, just like I said there would be."

"What if he checks the safe in the morning?"

"He has no reason to. We are rich and it's all ours."

"What about Pete?" She asks. "He might have something to say about all this."

"Screw him; we can live here, and I'll run this county for a change. He can get only half of what comes from the mines. Who says Pete and his bunch of cronies will make it out of those mountains alive anyway? I'll leave their bodies to rot right next to that old bastard downstairs. I saw you going down on that wrinkled old pecker. It made me sick to my stomach."

"How else was I supposed to get that damn combination?"

He starts laughing as he throws some cash up into the air, "To hell with that; bring those lips over here and take care of me while I count the moola……

Josh was still having great difficulty in the softer sand. The deflated tires helped, but the handlebars are playing havoc in his tight firm grips. The night covered desert begins to play tricks on his eyes. No sooner did the soft sand give way to harder ground, a sharp pain begin throbbing in his head. Things started to get blurry, and the darkness began to produce images he could not identify. He felt himself losing control of all his surroundings. He slows down and falls over and loses consciousness ……..

Hours pass as he slowly opens his eyes trying to bring things into focus. He crawls a hundred feet and climbs up on a boulder to get a better look at the foothills when he suddenly stares out across the desert at the distant rock formations. There in front of him were two dark figures sitting on horseback coming his way. He could see one man's long hair flowing in the breeze. Minutes later the two figures stop and one dismounted and walked over. The man leans over and says in a strong broken Indian dialect, "You okay young foolish white man who's very stupid to take on desert gods as if they were some cheap Mexican whores?"

Josh struggles to make out the man's face then asks, "Are you an angel?"

"Hell no, me great Indian warrior."

"Well, if you're gonna scalp me, get it over with, your breath ripens with three-day old pizza, but if you're angels you're way too early."

"Your scalp not worth trouble crazy white man."

Josh, with blurred vision, "Who are you?"

"Me great and powerful warrior from Comanche tribe; guardsman of the desert. Caretaker of the great mountains."

Josh tries to clear his vision as he rubs his eyes with his left hand. "I can't see your face, but the voice I know. You're a little too far south for a Comanche and I thought the Apache were the guardsman of the desert."

The deep voice speaks out, "We know; we heap big'um lost also, white man."

Josh starts laughing, "I thought so. Are you sure you're not Apache?"

"Could be, Mama got a round. I'm Eagle Claw and my friend is Lone Wolf, also guardian of desert, just less committed."

Josh struggles to get a better look and then the faces become all too familiar, "Is that right?"

"That right white man with arms bigger than brain."

Josh smiles, "I don't know anyone by the name Eagle Claw or Lone Wolf, but I do know two guys from school. One is hair lipped and the other had the odor of a mangy dog; now what were their names…?" He thinks for a second and then blurts out, "Now I remember, you're Buzzard Lip and he's Lonely Dog because he couldn't get a date in high school!!"

The deep voice hesitates and then responds, "Damn you Josh, how can we ever grow out of that shit with asshole friends reminding us of the past all the time?"

He laughs as the man helps him to his feet. Josh brushes himself off and walks over to the horses and then shakes his head, "How in the hell can you two be real Indians if you're riding around with dried-out saddles under your asses? Real Indians don't have saddles."

Lonely Dog replies, "Obvious you haven't seen enough John Wayne movies. We have learned the white man's ways plus riding bareback causes great pain in ass if you have hemorrhoids." They all laugh and take a seat on some rocks.

Buzzard Lip, "I was going to ask what would make a man come out on the Flats, but I've already heard."

Josh nods, "What did you hear old great warrior who pissed in pants in fourth grade?"

He leans closer, "I heard you whopped Clint McNally over the head and damn near killed his ass. They say he was found with his penis in his hand, which will be remembered around these parts for many moons. We also heard you dragged Little Pete's new bike down the highway busting up pavement as you went. That also will be remembered for many moons."

Lonely Dog interrupts, "The cops say there was nothing left but a foot peg when you got through with it. Way to go Josh. Pete and that gang of gutless asses had it coming. That 'high and mighty' attitude of theirs sucks the life out of folks around this area."

Buzzard Lip smiles, "Do you know what all this means Josh?"

"No; what?"

"It means you're still our freaking hero." They give each other a high five.

Josh laughs, "Actually, it was Jill who hit Clint, but I'll take full credit for it."

"You do know there's a bad storm coming around noon maybe sooner tomorrow, that's going to turn this place into hell. Where's your horse?"

Josh chuckles, "This place is already hell. Let me guess, you can tell the weather by the way a desert toad pisses on a rock. I hope you're better at it than Bubba. And I'm not on a horse, I'm riding that!" He points at a short distance at Elvira leaning over near a bolder.

They start laughing when Buzzard Lip says, "You will never make it on iron horse and about that weather, not even close white man. The desert toad pisses on a rock because he has to piss. I know about the rain because the great Chief Crooked Back left us his television before he left on his journey to the happy hunting ground."

They all start laughing again when a serious look came over Josh's face and he asks, "Crooked Back's dead?"

"Yep."

Josh, with a sad expression on his face continues, "I liked him a lot, but it sure is good to see you boys. I was wondering if you guys still lived in that old house trailer."

Lonely Dog laughs, "Yep; that bastard McNally won't give an Indian a job in the mines, so we make a living showing stupid tourist sand and rock. Not much money in it, but it will buy beer, groceries and condoms for heap big Indian special needs."

Buzzard Lip gives Josh a look, "You will never make it in those mountains with that hunk of steel."

"I made it this far."

They both glance back over at Elvira and start laughing. "You're one crazy white boy. What in the hell made you think you could make it across these treacherous Flats on that big ass bike?"

Josh grins, "Like I just said, I made it this far, didn't I?"

Lonely Dog shakes his head and then stops laughing when he sees the serious look on Josh's face.

"Hey man; you're not kidding, are you?"

"Nope."

"Let me get this right; you're crossing the Flats and then you're gonna take on the mountains and make it to Mexico on that hog?"

"Yep."

"What would make a man try some stupid shit like that?"

Josh stretches his large arms over his head and answers, "About 200 pissed off law enforcement officers and others that we have already mentioned."

Lonely Dog turns to Buzzard Lip, "That would make me try it." He turns back to Josh, "Wow! You must have really pissed some white folks off to try this shit? You are one desperate crazy fool! Do you know how many white men and Indians have left their bones out here?"

"Yep! Plenty!"

"And that doesn't scare you?"

"Nope, me and Elvira are gonna ride right over that mountain range and into a quiet little cantina in Samaro Mexico and get drunk."

Buzzard Lip glances over at Lonely Dog again with an awkward stare and then back, "You'll never make it, unless a big ass eagle flies down and grabs your ass up and drops you off in that cantina."

Josh with a grin, "Wanna bet?"

"I make it a point to never bet with you again. Last time I did, I lost fifty bucks to a dude who jumped a Harley over Russell's Gorge."

Josh laughs, "I broke my wrist on that jump and wrecked Randall's Harley."

"Yeah, but you did make it to the other side. Randall was not happy with that."

Buzzard Lip stands and places his hand on Josh's shoulder, "Well, we need to go if we gonna beat that storm. Is there anything we can do for you before we go?"

Josh thinks for a second and then answers, "It would be nice if you two would look in on Bubba and Jill once in a while."

"We can do that. That Jill has a nice ass."

Josh responds with a stern look; "You two Indian scavengers might wanna leave that alone; she can use a sawed-off double barrel shotgun as well as most men and she's not too shabby with a frying skillet."

He walks with them over to the horses, "That's some fine mounts you two have there."

"They ain't stolen if that's what you're getting at."

"Thought never crossed my mind."

They mount their horses and turn to ride off. Buzzard Lip stops and glances back, "Good luck, maybe we'll see you at that cantina later and you can buy us some firewater!"

Lonely Dog scans the sky in all directions, "May the desert gods look after you Josh!"

Josh yells, "I don't believe in the desert gods. I believe in Jesus!"

Buzzard Lip yells back, "Jesus is smart enough not to be out here on the Flats!"

Josh waves and yells, "Take it easy Eagle Claw and you too, Lone Wolf!"

They trot off into the darkness and disappear....

Josh, after standing Elvira up, throws his leg over, kick starts her and takes off into the night, hoping he wouldn't have to take another spill, but knowing there were many more to come…..

Time passes and he starts to make some headway, dodging rocks and struggling through the numerous sand beds. Every so often, he would bump into a small cactus or run over a wandering tumbleweed or two. He was getting tired. He could hardly keep his eyes open and the pain vibrating through his ribcage and the kickstarting was making it worse by the minute. To add to all this the night cold is chilling him to the bone. All the rough riding was taking a toll on him. He knew he had to stop for just a few minutes. He stared into the darkness and could barely make out a small gorge about four or five feet deep. It will make a good place to rest, and the cool clay walls should hide any heat signatures from his engine. A chopper equipped with a thermal imaging camera wouldn't have any trouble in this cold if he left her out in the open.

CHAPTER 28

Back at the mansion, Walter is getting dressed as Clint's driving up in his police unit with the white bandage still wrapped around his head. Susan was dressing in the bathroom, when Walter bangs on the door and yells, "Get a move on it; that chopper will be here any minute."

She yells back, "I'm working on it. I don't see why we need to start so early. It's still dark outside."

Clint comes barging in the front door as Walter is walking down the staircase. With an angry expression on his face, "They're late."

Walter pours himself a small drink and in a casual tone, "Calm down asshole; Susan is still trying to get her damn makeup on."

Clint with the shake of his head, "Makeup for a ride in the desert; doesn't make any sense to me."

"A damn old mountain goat knows more about women than you do."

"Why does she even need to go? She'll just be in the way."

Walter replies, "Because I want her to get a good look when you put that bullet through Josh's head. That'll take the fire out of her ass. God, my head hurts. That Scotch worth every penny it cost me. I slept like a baby last night."

A few minutes later Susan comes walking down the staircase wearing a light brown blouse and tight-fitting jeans and carrying a fur coat in her hands. The sound of a chopper could be heard coming across the valley.

Clint smiles, "I do believe that's our ride I hear coming."

They step out on the long porch and watch as the army green Huey makes its way up the valley and into a landing position with a spotlight lighting the large front yard, kicking up freshly cut grass. Clint walks over to his car and pulls a leather rifle case and a large duffle bag from the backseat. The old man and Susan walk out and start to load up. Walter turns to the pilot, "You familiar with the Flats?"

"To some degree. I know enough to know it's not the friendliest place on earth."

"Good, because I'm gonna need a pilot that can work his way around and not get caught in those crosswinds."

"It shouldn't be too much of a problem if the weather holds out." After Clint jumps in the pilot increases the R.P.M.s with a twist of his wrist and the chopper blades speed up and take a pitch forward causing it to slowly lift off and fade into the early morning darkness…..

An hour later Josh was still sleeping when the bopping sound of chopper blades beating the air into submission in the distance awoke him. What was more disturbing than that was the fact that the sun's far-reaching rays of light are rising over the flats from the east. This meant that he had overslept and was now running, not minutes, but hours behind. Its bright rays struck the tips of the jagged peaks to the west giving off a blinding reflection of what is to come. He glances down at his watch and can see that this was not going as well as expected. He had slept too long, and Elvira was having a hard time of it.

With the sound of the chopper getting ever so close, he peeked over the embankment, but it was still too dark. Then from a distance a light could be seen flashing across the desert floor searching for any sign of life other than a jackrabbit frozen in the blinding spotlight. He shakes his head and thinks, "There's no sense in cranking up right now, the heat from his engine will just give his position away and he wasn't about to give those bastards an easy shot.

There were two ways to look at this situation. If he was traveling, the chopper would peg him, but he could take that chance and get to the mountains before sunrise or he could sit here until they leave and get caught by the scorching sun. So, the best thing to do right now is just sit tight and let the thing pass over.

Back in the chopper, Clint was looking through a small thermal imaging camera lens protruding through the center between the front seats. Mounted on the bottom of the aircraft was a small oval shaped camera that swiveled in a complete 360 degrees. Walter screams over the sound of the blades cutting into the cold, dark morning air, "The sun will be up in about thirty minutes, and you still haven't spotted him yet!"

Clint lifts his head up and rubs his eyes, then turns to him, "This is funny Pop, you should look through this thing. I can see every rabbit and coyote for miles. Looks like a Christmas tree all lit up."

"I'm just about three seconds from burying my foot up your ass! I'm looking for a man on a horse, not rabbits and coyotes! You get that, boy?!"

"I don't believe he took the Flats and if he did, he must be sitting it out somewhere. If he was moving, I would have picked him up by now. I'm telling you right now, we're wasting our time. No one can cross the Flats."

Walter responds, "Maybe you're right or maybe he has made it to the mountains already."

Clint fires back, "Maybe he didn't. Maybe he's sitting in a gulley just waiting us out. That's if he even made it this far."

"You should be able to pick a horse out through that damn thing." He turns to Susan and gives her a look, "You sure he said the Flats?"

"Yes, I'm sure. He will be on his Harley."

Clint shakes his head, "That's bullshit! If he's made it to the mountains, we're just killing valuable time running up and down these flats."

Josh laid down in the gulley as the chopper; with its blinking red landing light flashing away as the spotlight combs the desert into the early morning darkness. He watches as the spotlight rakes across the walls of the gorge. The chopper flips around and makes another pass. As it flies off into the west, he quickly fires Elvira up and takes off in the same direction, heading in a straight line for the foothills, hoping there was enough desert pine to make him invisible as he made his way into the mountains. There was no slowing down now. He throttles up with his wrist and throws sand into the air as he increases his speed.

Clint goes back to looking through the optical viewfinder when Walter yells at the pilot, "Take us to Sunrise Gorge and then turn around and make another pass."

"Yes sir."

Josh could feel the ground getting harder as the desert gave way to the rocky foothills. He was enjoying the heat flowing up from the engine breaking the chill of early morning. Even the leather chaps was no protection in this cold. He knew that in a few hours the heat from the sun would be cooking the sand to a harsh 140 degrees. He slowed and then, realizing that the sand beds were disappearing, stops and decides this was as good a time as any to put the air back in his tires. Taking one small canister of air, he brings his tires back to the proper air pressure.

Minutes later he takes off again keeping the mountains in sight. One could actually see the sunlight traveling down the east face of the Rockies causing a rainbow of colors to appear.

Walter yells again as they pass over Sunrise Gorge, "Now turn around and check the Flats again, this time get closer to the foothills."

Clint over the loud batting noise of the chopper blades, "He will be hours if not another day making it to the foothills on horseback. I say he and the horse is dead miles east of here."

The pilot turns to him with a frighten look on his face, "If we get caught in those strong crosswinds coming off those mountains, this trip will be over quick, and our blood and guts will be splattered all over this God forsaken place."

Walter pats the pilot on the shoulder and with a pissed look, "You don't get closer to those foothills; I'll splatter your blood and guts all over that glass canopy. Now turn this damn thing around. That's why I asked for a pilot who knew the Flats."

"I didn't realize you wanted me to get that close to the mountain range."

Walter places the barrel of a Colt 45 to the back of the man's head, "Turn around like I said."

Clint leans over, "Maybe he's right; that wind can drive us straight into the ground."

Walter turns and places the gun in Clint's face, "One more word from your mouth and I'll throw you out of this damn noise maker! Now go back to looking through that 'whatever you call it' and the next words you say better be, 'I found him'." The chopper swings around and heads back across the flats.

Josh could just make out the pine thicket but couldn't hear the sound of the chopper making its way toward him over his own engine's loud rumble.

Clint, still checking the thermal imaging camera, suddenly picks up a green and red heat signature cutting across the flats and toward the mountains.

He yells, "I got something here!"

Walter, with a grin yells, "I knew it, only Josh could have pulled off a crazy stunt like this!! Are you sure it's him?"

"You are damn right I'm sure and the crazy bastard is on that big Harley just as Susan said. He's moving west southwest about thirty miles an hour."

Walter yells back to the pilot, "Get in behind him." He turns to Clint and continues, "Get your rifle and let's end this bastard's adventure right now. We can finish what the desert started to do."

The pilot gently moves the craft in behind Josh and slows to match the bike's speed. Josh still hasn't notice them coming up behind him. Clint pulls his rifle from the case and makes an adjustment to the scope, "This is not going to be easy, it's still too dark."

"Don't give me any of your excuses, just take the shot."

Clint slides the side door open allowing cold air to send an ice-cold chill through the inside of the chopper. He moves toward the edge.

Walter taps the pilot on the shoulder, "Put the spotlight on him." As the light tries to catch Josh, Clint takes aim and as he squeezes off a shot the chopper jolted hard to the right and then to the left.

Josh watches as his rearview mirror is shattered. He then turns to see the spotlight bearing down on him. He starts to swerve from side to side, being very careful not to take the hard ground for granted. Clint tried to take another shot, but the wind was playing havoc with them. He yells back at the pilot, "Stop all the jerking around, I have enough problem with the light conditions!!"

The pilot in return yells back, "I told you that we're too close to the foothills! If we get too much closer a downdraft will catch us and drive us into the ground, ending this mission quickly and killing all of us to boot."

Walter interrupts, "Just do your best." He turns back to Clint, "Now kill that son-of-a-bitch."

Clint takes a few more shots and then grazes Josh's shoulder tearing through the leather jacket like paper-mâché, not far from where he was shot a few days before. He loses control and flips the bike.

Clint yells, "I think I got him!" He smiles and tells the pilot, "Put me right on top of him and I'll make sure." The chopper levels out and hovers about a hundred feet over the bike lying over on its side. Suddenly Josh runs over and picks up the bike.

Clint yells, "I got his ass now." He takes careful aim and before he can take a shot, a crosswind throws them into a spin. The pilot fights to control the craft when he figures it's time to bug out. He tilts the joystick and rapidly takes them further away from the foothills and toward the Flats.

Clint yells, "You stupid son-of-a-bitch, I had him in my crosshairs!"

"I don't care how much money or pull you have; I'm not putting my ass and a two-million-dollar Huey in the side of a mountain. Shoot me now if you must."

Back on the ground Josh heads into the thicket. By now the sun was beating down on the pines and slowly making its way across the Flats.

Walter is so mad that he kicks the front seat with his boot. He leans forward toward the pilot, "Drop us off near Twin Sister Peaks and we'll take it from there. We'll call you on the radio to pick us up in a few hours."

Clint interrupts, "We can let Susan go back with the chopper."

Walter slaps him across the face, "She's my wife and I say she stays with us."

"You didn't have to slap me."

"Then stop concerning yourself with my woman." He glances at a large duffle bag and asks, "What's in that bag?"

Clint and Susan give each other a look knowing that two million dollars in cash was at their fingertips. He wasn't about to leave it, just lying around. "It's a jacket and some more ammo." McNally not being to the wiser nods as the chopper heads for Twin Sister Peaks…

CHAPTER 29

Jill, Bubba, and Jim are driving the back roads like a bat out of hell in her Jeep when suddenly they come upon a deep washout. Jim shakes his head, "I told you guys that this road was a bad idea, but no; you had to try the shortcut."

She bangs the steering wheel and yells, "Damn you, Bubba!!"

Bubba turns to her with a surprised look on his face, "I agreed with Jim about not taking this way, but you're too hardheaded…I need a beer to help me think straight."

Tears start rolling down her face and with great disappointment she responds, "I was just trying to find the shortest route; we're running out of time and now we have to go all the way back to Route 31; that will set us back three hours."

Bubba places his hand on her shoulder, "It's going to be okay; I have a plan. Stick this baby in four-wheel drive and get us down in the wash-out then make a hard left."

Jim breaks in, "Whatta ya have up your sleeve?"

"About a mile down this washout is an old goat trail that me and Josh would take when we were going across the border to see some Mexican gals."

She gives him one of her angry glares, "How many years ago was that?"

"I don't remember, about seventeen, I guess. My God, the man had a life before you came along!"

Jim lets out a chuckle and responds with, "These old trails change every time it rains hard. We could end up back tracking ourselves."

Bubba snaps back, "It's better than going back to Route 31."

Jill yells, "I'll take that chance!" She pours the throttle to it throwing dirt everywhere. After getting to the bottom of the slop, she makes a hard left.

Back near Twin Sisters, Walter, Clint, and Susan are dropped off with their supplies. Clint could see dust flying in the distance, "I see dust being kicked up north into the mountains, Pop. It's got to be him."

Walter walks over and watches for a few seconds before saying, "Hand me those binoculars." Clint passes the binoculars to him. He scans the pass as the sunlight makes its way down the ridge. "That's our backup plan and they're right on time for a change. Pete and his group are going to cut the bastard off near Deer Lake and if they miss him, we'll catch him as he tops Hell's Pass."

Jill is trying to work her way through the soft dirt while Bubba was yelling, "You're gonna get us stuck, stay in the middle of the ditch!!"

"Shut your pie hole, I'm driving this damn thing! Did you just say, 'stay in the middle bitch'?"

"No, I said, 'stay in the middle of the ditch. But you won't be driving long if you get too close to the bank. The dirt is always harder in the center."

Jim interrupts, "He's right, you're too close to the bank."

She turns and gives them an evil glance, "A damn woman can drive just as good as a man." No sooner did the words leave her mouth, the Jeep hits a soft spot and buries itself a foot deep in the sand throwing Bubba into the windshield.

He grabs his nose and yells, "Thanks, you just broke my freaking nose!!"

Jim pulls on Bubba's shoulder, "Let me have a look at that you big-ass crybaby." He examines the nose, "Yep, it's broken alright and getting bigger. Too bad you didn't shove your pecker into the dash."

Bubba nods, "Well if this isn't just great; now I'll look like an overweight anteater." He slowly turns to Jill with a fake grin, "What were you saying?" She just lays her head over on the steering wheel and starts crying. Jim gives Bubba a nasty look and shakes his head.

Bubba yells, "What!! I know what I'm talking about. I pull people out of this shit with my tow truck all the damn time."

"Can't you see she's all upset?" Jim snaps back.

Bubba, "I'm the one with a broken nose. Like I was saying, you gotta stay in the middle. Now I need to get out and take the winch and wrap it around that rock over there and pull us out. Then I'm going to take over driving for a while." He jumps from the Jeep holding his bloody nose and unhooks the winch pulling it out a good sixty feet as he struggles in the deep sand.

Pete and his bunch make their way up a steep incline for several hundred feet until it levels out. They take to a narrow overhang, but one bike loses its traction and slides over the edge. Ray, the rider, manages to get a grip on the jagged rock and yells as he watches his motor bike plummet down the cliff tumbling end over end.

"Shit! I'm falling!"

Pete looks back and seeing him about to fall to his death, throws his bike down, runs over and grabs him by the wrist, "Hold on buddy, I gotcha." The other guys lean their bikes against the rock face and rushed over to help. They grab Pete by the feet to prevent him from falling as he pulls Ray back up over the edge, placing him against a large boulder. Breathing hard, he looks over at Pete who was also catching his breath.

"That did it for me; I almost fell and became buzzard food. Your dad can keep his damn money."

Pete gives him an irritated look and responds, "It ain't about the money; that son-of-a-bitch dragged my new bike down the highway."

"That's just it, it was your bike he dragged; not ours! Now I'm all for having a little fun, but this dude ain't worth getting killed over."

"What about him cutting the tires on your bikes and painting them yellow?"

Mike laughs, "My bike was already yellow."

Ray continues, "We started that shit, Pete and you know it. We didn't have to paint his Harley and piss in the tank; now that was low down even for us and you know it."

Mike jumps in again, "He's right. We brought all that on ourselves."

Pete gets really pissed, "What the hell has gotten into you boys. You're losing your love for the hunt. It's all about the adventure."

Ray fires back, "No! Josh is all about adventure, we just burn time following you around screwing with people."

Mike shakes his head, "I personally think he never made it across the Flats and if he is using the Harley instead of a horse, he'll never get that big bike through the mountain passes and if he does that, he's the best damn rider in the world. I can respect that."

Pete stands and looks to the others, "That bastards on horseback. Now what about the rest of you? I know you guys can use the money. None of us wanna work those mines."

The other two look at each other and Jeff says, "I'm game, how about you Steve?"

Steve nods and answers, "I'm game for now."

Pete turns back to Ray and Mike, "Look, we're just gonna rough him up a little, that's all."

Ray, with a chuckle responds, "The last time we tried that, we didn't do so good. What did I hear your dad say about throwing him off a cliff?"

Mike interrupts, "That's right, he whipped our asses at Bubba's and then he whipped it again at the Cactus Rose, but that ain't worth killing anyone over. He's one tough bastard and I personally hope he makes it."

Ray shakes his head in agreement.

Pete, with a smirk says, "Well… get your candy asses back down the mountain. The three of us can handle him because I have an edge this time." Pete lifts his jacket up and shows the grip of a 38 snub nose revolver."

Ray stands, "You know something, this thing has gotten way outta hand and me and Mike ain't gonna be around when the Feds start investigating all this shit. I never thought Josh killed old Willie anyway. Your old man needed that right-of-way and when Willie refused to sell, he killed him or had him killed."

Pete yells, "If you think that, you two can ride your asses back down on the back of Mike's bike. Now get the hell outta here." Mike jumps on his bike and backs it up until he can turn around. Ray jumps on the back and they take off……

CHAPTER 30

Josh stops at the top of a bluff, pats Elvira on the fuel tank and says out loud, "We beat the Flats girl, just you and me. All excited he yells with an echo, "Screw you, you man-eating pile of sand!!"

He smiles and takes off through the pine thicket and then stops at the foot of a narrow passage leading into the mountains. The incline was very steep but that wasn't going to stop him now, so he shot the juice at Elvira and started up the hill. The rear tire was kicking up rooster tails of rocks and dirt ten feet in the air. The large tire on the back of Elvira danced from side to side trying to get a solid grip in the loose dirt. Just another ten feet and the ground would level a little but that was not to be. The rear tire caught a small piece of sandstone and jolted sideways causing him to lose control of the climb. Elvira lands on her side and before he could get a grip on the crash bar, she starts sliding down the slope. He latches onto the crash bar, but the momentum was just too much for him. Elvira drags him all the way down to the pine thicket. The slide tore into his chaps.

He struggled to right her and then fires the big twin up, never hesitating to start. He gets angry and was even more determined to do this. He had tackled far steeper inclines and wasn't about to let this one beat him. Elvira takes off again, but this time she makes it stopping at the top to crest for a minute or two.

Sitting there, Josh could see through the openings in the mountains. Slow moving, dark, storm clouds were forming at the distance.

Looking down at Elvira he says, "Bubba was right for once; that looks like a bad one for sure. Whatta, ya think ole girl?" He nods; "I thought so. I'm not scared either." With a hard kick, he starts her back up and pushes off taking advantage of the smooth trail ahead of him.

An hour later he stops to take in a little water and food. He reaches into the saddlebag and removes a canteen, then some sandwiches wrapped in aluminum foil Jill had fixed for him before he left. He took a swig from the canteen and sat back against a rock and took a few bites. He just sat there not having a real appetite and watched the storm clouds slowly drift toward the mountains wondering when he would have his next seizure and stumble to his death. Was it going to be painful, or would he slip into a coma and go into a painless death? Never in his life could he remember ever harming anyone, so why the whole wide world is coming down on his shoulders, was anyone's guess. He's thinking this is as good a time as any to make peace with his maker, so he drops his head on his knees and just prays to the Lord to make his death a quick one, without pain. He also prays for Bubba and Jill as he would only be able to watch them from the afterlife. He hoped Bubba would find a woman who can contend with his farting, eating and drinking and Jill to find a good, caring man to take care of her.

Henry was not gonna be around much longer. He shed a tear for his misery and hoped that things would work out soon. He gave a little confession to the Lord and then raised his head feeling the tension lift from his tired shoulders.

He places his free hand on his shoulder where Clint's rifle bullet grazed him. He scans his surroundings and then stares down below at the Flats and thinks aloud, "It must already be 120 degrees down there." He turns to Elvira, "I'm sure glad we're not still down in that oven." He hesitates for a second or two and then thinks, "Deer Lake is just a few hundred yards higher up, so the ground should level a little and make it easier to travel." As he undoes his leather chap, he starts coughing up blood. He throws the chaps to the ground, then wipes the sweat from his brow and mounts Elvira.....

Jill and her companions were bouncing over the rough trail when Jim asks, "How much further Bubba, you're tearing my ass a new hole. You must have hit every hole and rock in this damn gorge. How much longer do we have to ride on this pig trail?"

Bubba answers, "We should be seeing the highway in about five minutes or less."

Jill jumps into the conversation, "I think we're lost; this trail is taking us nowhere. I say we missed it back there a ways."

Bubba yells, "Have I ever let you down before!?"

Jill, with a frown asks, "Are you sure you want me to answer that?"

Minutes pass when Bubba drives through some underbrush and over several large tumble weeds and out on the pavement. He comes to a stop, "Well, I told you so! Damn it's getting hot."

Jill gives him a hug and says to Bubba's surprise, "I knew you could do it."

Bubba responds, "But you just said…"

She interrupts again, "I know what I said, I'm just trying to keep you on your toes."

Jim breaks in, "Don't look now but we're in trouble again."

She looks up and sees a roadblock several hundred feet down the road.

Bubba turns to Jim, "Too late, they've seen us already. I could have sworn that trail would have put us on the other side of them."

Jill was speechless and then turns to Jim, "What now?"

"I might know those guys."

Bubba shakes his head and blurts out, "Hell, they can't stop us, we haven't done anything. It's Josh they're after."

Jill agrees, "That's right, we can go anywhere we want." She turns to Bubba, "Let's go, we're losing time, and we have a storm to beat."

Bubba slowly pulls up to the roadblock when an officer walks up to him and asks, "How's it going?"

Bubba replies, "Not too shabby."

The officer asks, "What brings you good people out here in the middle of nowhere with a bad storm brewing? By the looks of your jeep, you guys have been doing some dirt riding."

Bubba replies, "We're just out enjoying the sunshine while it lasts."

The officer lets out a chuckle, "You're kidding me right, it's hot as hell out here."

Jim speaks up, "Rodger, is that you?"

The officer takes a closer look and sees Jim in the back seat, "Big Jim Davis, well I be damned. I haven't seen you in years, hardly recognized you."

Jim laughs, "I wasn't always this fat."

Bubba interrupts, "You've been that fat as long as I've known you."

The officer glancing over Bubba's shoulder says, "I heard you made sheriff."

"Yeah, they were hard up."

Jill, giving the officer one of her famous smiles asks, "Can we leave now, we're kind of in a hurry."

The officer asks, "Why the hurry?"

Jim replies, "We just need to get to Crows Junction before the storm sets in."

The officer nods, "No problem…Look, if you see a muscled-up guy in his late thirties to early forties, wearing jeans, a black t-shirt, black boots, a black belt with shinny conchos and riding a big ass maroon Harley, give us a call."

"Why, what did he do; wear too much black?"

"Seems he hurt Pete and his bunch over at the Cactus Rose and then resisted an arrest before busting Clint McNally over the head. They say he damn near killed him. Found him lying over your desk, Jim, with his pecker in his hand. But you should know that."

"I'm on vacation for a week. Try to stay away from work when I'm relaxing."

Rodger nods, "Well now you know why the roadblock."

Jim just shakes his head, "Yeah, too bad about Clint, I love him like a brother."

The man laughs, "Well you're the only one that does."

Bubba nods, "If I see anyone fitting that description, you will be the first I notify."

They drive through the roadblock with Bubba wiping the sweat from his brow. He turns to Jill than looks over the seat at Jim and starts laughing…

Jim, "What so funny Bubba?"

"Everyone we have met up with knows about Clint playing with his little man tool. That was the funniest joke. I got to give it to you Jill, I would have never even thought of doing that. I bet long after Josh's story disappears, that story will still be funny and being told for five hundred miles in every direction."

Jim starts laughing, "I can't even think about Clint without laughing at that story.

Chapter 31

Josh is riding over bluffs and through some small rock formations and narrow corridors making good time when he suddenly stops for a moment to take in the view of the valley below and could see he is well over 7500 feet above sea level. He noticed the smell of cool, clean moisture in the air and knew that in a few hours he would be feeling the cool fierce wind being pushed by the approaching storm.

He takes off again, but after turning a sharp curve in the trail he comes across a clearing. There sitting at the other end on their bikes is Little Pete and two out of the original four friends.

Josh stops and with a smile, "Well howdy boys, didn't expect to see you this soon."

Pete just snickers, "Only Joshua Harley James could have made it across the Flats on a bike. I would have never believed it. I'm shocked and impressed that you made it up Silver Dome Pass."

Josh shakes his head, "I would say it almost killed me, but it was a walk in the park. You know how determine these American machines can be at times. You boys waiting for me or just out for a bike ride?"

"We're waiting for you, mister smart guy." Pete quickly replies.

Josh shakes his head, "Why don't you three go back home and leave me alone? We don't have to do this."

"Can't do that, but if it makes you feel any better, we'll make it really quick."

Josh laughs, "Good, there's a storm coming, and I do not wanna be caught up here when it hits."

Pete turns to Jeff and Steve and then back to Josh, "I don't give a rat's ass what you did to Clint, but you shouldn't have done what you did to my bike. That just wasn't right."

"Well, you should have thought of that before you did what you did to Elvira. You see, I ride an American machine and I just can't stand back and watch someone do that to an American."

Pete pulls out his snub nose revolver, smiles and says as he spins the cylinder, "I've been waiting to do this for the last twenty years."

"Now, are you still angry about all those pranks Bubba and I pulled on you in school?"

"I was little for my age, but that didn't give you two the right to play games with me. And it wasn't fair telling Margaret Riches that I was gay. I loved her and after that she wouldn't give me the time of day."

Josh, "Times has changed, I didn't know at the time she was so homophobic. Funny, after all those years in school she ended up moving in with Sherry Miles. Uh, I guess it was you after all she didn't like. We didn't pull those pranks because of your size or being gay; it was because you were a sneaky little shit. I shouldn't have done it, but I can't go back in time and make that right. We were just teenagers looking for a good time. I hardly see it's worth killing me over."

"Well, it's payback time."

Josh glances at the other two, "I'll spare you two if you stay out of this." Jeff hesitates and looks over at Steve, then back at Josh, "I think you may have something there. We bow to you Josh. Anyone who can cross the flats and these mountains on a big ass Harley gets our respects... sorry for the trouble dude."

"I forgive you boys as I hope the Lord will forgive me for all the things I have done in the past."

Pete yells, "Why you yellow belly cowards!"

Josh interrupts, "Let's do this the way they used to do it in the old days, Pete."

Pete thinks hard for a second or two, "And how's that?"

Josh, with a grin, answers, "We joust, using the bikes as our preferred weapons."

Pete, getting a little worried, asks, "You think I'm scared of you?"

"Yes, I believe you are. If you weren't, you wouldn't have brought a pistol with ya. Yeah...fear is written all over your face."

Pete shoves the pistol down in his waistband, reaches behind him and removes a short piece of chain from a canvas bag strapped to the rear part of the seat.

He smiles, "You know what this is?"

Josh, a little puzzled at the site of the four-foot chain answers, "I give up, what is it?"

"It's a of piece of the chain that you used to drag my bike down the highway."

"What now?"

"I'm going to wrap this around your neck, then I'm gonna drag your ass all over this mountain until there's nothing left of you. Just like what you did to my bike."

"Can I tell you something before we do this?"

"Please, entertain me."

"You know why we started calling you Little Pete? We called you that because Linda Marcel saw you taking a piss behind the portable one day and she said you had the smallest Mexican bean she has ever seen. Now I'm saying your balls aren't much bigger."

"I'm going to make you suffer like you've never suffered before." Pete fires up his bike. The screeching irritating noise coming from his bike sounded like a chain saw ribbing up just before cutting into an old oak tree. Josh fires off Elvira and the roar coming from her two pipes echoed through the entire mountain chain drowning out any and every other sound. They both take off heading right for each other. Pete starts swinging the chain over his head, but as Josh passes, he lowers his head and catches the side of Pete's fuel tank with his foot causing him to lose control. It throws him several feet. Josh locks up the rear brakes and slides around facing him handling Elvira as if she's a bicycle. "Have you had enough, Pete?"

Pete staggers to his feet and yells, "That's it!" He pulls the pistol from his waistband.

Josh looks up at the Heavens and says, "Forgive me Lord for what I'm about to do."

As Pete starts to pull the trigger, Josh takes off heading straight for him. The fender of Elvira's front tire struck Pete so hard it threw him over the edge and down the cliff. He plunges more than four hundred feet. As Pete is still screaming, Josh notices the blood slowly oozing from his lower thigh. Pete had managed to get a shot off and no one even heard it over the sound of Elvira. He slowly turns to the other two, "Go back and tell the people of Sun Valley what happened here and then go to church on Sunday and thank God, I decided to show mercy on you two."

"We will Josh. We will tell everyone what happen, and you take care, and we hope you make it." Without hesitation they quickly take off down the mountain. Josh could tell the bullet went all the way through, exiting into Elvira's hot leather seat.

Bubba is speeding down the road when Jill yells over the noisy wind gusts, which were whipping through the Jeep's canvas top like crazy, "How much further!?"

Jim answers in a loud voice, "We must be getting close to old 29!!"

Bubba, "He's right, we should be coming up on 29 any second, but we'll never make it to 81 before dark. Damn anyone have any idea why we're not using the air-conditioning?"

Jill asks as she flips the air-conditioning on, "How come you think we can't make 81 before dark?'

Bubba answers, "Old 29 will take the better part of the day. That road is in bad shape and curves in and out of that canyon pass for miles."

She just shakes her head back and forth, "That's what's wrong with this freakin county; the roads are always in bad shape."

Hours later drops of rain started to strike the windshield when she sees the highway marker and screams, "There it is!" Bubba takes a quick left almost losing control. The tires of her jeep are screaming with agony as the vehicle cut the turns ever so sharply.

Jill turns to Jim and asks, "How far is it to where you think he will exit the mountains?"

"When we reach 81, I would say about two or three miles. That's if he makes it that far."

Jill quickly snaps back, "Don't talk that way, he'll be there, I just feel it."

Josh travels a little further and stops for another break in the trail, this time overlooking the west side of the mountain range. He could see the highway a few miles away and the blue sky instantly giving way to the dark gray thundering clouds rolling in and they appeared angrier than he had ever seen them. There's a nice breeze flowing over the mountains now. It struck his face, and he could smell the moisture traveling with it. Lightning was dancing across the sky and thunder rumbled across the valley like canon fire in a war zone. The distant rain gave the appearance of a gunmetal colored curtain draped across the landscape.

It took the better part of the day to get this far, but it's downhill from here and if the rain would just hold off for another thirty minutes, night will take over in two hours, and it would be easy riding.

As he kicks started Elvira, a shot from a hi-powered rifle was heard and then a sharp pain struck him in the calf of his leg, this time shattering bone. He laid Elvira over using it for cover.

Up on a high ridge Clint was ejecting an empty casing and throwing another round in the chamber of his bolt action 30/06. Walter leans over trying to get a better look, "Did you get him?"

"I think so."

"Think my ass. You said the same damn thing over the Flats. I don't want that bastard to make it another foot. We need a confirmed kill this time."

Clint looks through the scope trying to find Josh. The bike is there, but his body is nowhere in sight. He gets pissed, "I know I hit him; I seen him fall." Susan couldn't take it anymore and tries to grab Clint's rifle. Walter pulls her away and throws her to the ground.

"What the hell do you think you're doing?"

"I've had enough, this is insane. He can't do you any harm now and you know it."

"I don't need him showing up and running around the country every few years digging up old news and causing trouble. I want him dead."

Clint interrupts, "He's right Susan, if we kill him now the buzzards will eat the evidence for us."

Walter snatches Clint's rifle from his hands and yells, "Let's get down there and see if he's alive!"

Josh is lying behind a boulder. He drags himself over to Elvira and opens his saddle bag. He takes out a roll of duct tape and an old tire iron. He tapes the tire iron tightly around his leg so he could walk with a limp.

They were now caught in a blinding rainstorm. Bubba could not drive any faster than 15 or 20 miles an hour. Darkness was setting in. Jill, getting impatient, yells "You're driving too slow!"

"I can't drive any faster, visibility is down to nothing."

Jim shakes his head, "We can't do Josh any good if we kill ourselves Jill. He will be in the same storm in another thirty minutes, and he has no road. It will slow him down and give us plenty of time."

She fires back, "It's getting dark!"

Clint, Walter, and Susan made it down to where Elvira was laying over on her side. Walter slaps Clint in the back of the head and at the top of his lungs, "You missed him again asshole!!"

Clint grabs the back of his head and gives Susan an embarrassing stare, "Damn you Pop, that hurt." He walks over to the bike, leans down and sees blood on the chrome primary cover.

"Missed my ass, he's hurt. He couldn't have gone far."

Walter walks over to the edge and glances across the canyon floor when suddenly he comes across Pete's broken body lying on the rocks in the distance below. He looks through the binoculars and drops to his knees and starts to weep. Clint, not understanding asks, "What's wrong Pop?"

He slowly turns to him with tears in his eyes, "He's killed my baby boy."

Clint and Susan walk over and peek over the edge. Susan turns and covers her face when she sees Pete lying there limp as a ragdoll with every bone in his body broken up and blood spattered on the surrounding rocks.

Clint gets angry and yells out across the canyon, "I'm gonna make you suffer for this Josh!!"

A voice can be heard as Josh limps from behind a small bluff, "I guess we've all suffered enough. Pete was just another bad seed this valley didn't need."

Clint stands as Walter climbs to his feet and raises the rifle to mid-level.

"Now's your chance Pop, shoot the bastard." Walter, with a smile, points the rifle at Josh's midsection.

Josh, with a grin, says, "Before you pull the trigger, I have some information that may surprise even you old man."

Walter responds, "Nothing you can say will help you now, boy."

"Let me try. I watched something the other night at your place that might come as a shock to you. It seems that your son here has been stuffing your wife on the kitchen table and anywhere else he can find. In between him humping like a dog, they were planning on killing you and make it look like an accident."

Clint interrupts, "That's a lie Pop! He's stalling. You know I wouldn't do anything like that. Shoot him now!!"

Walter turns to her then to Clint and then back at Josh, "You're just trying to save your hide."

Josh turns to Susan, "Tell him; tell him how every Friday night after your beloved husband leaves to go out on the town, you and Clint get it on like two horny buffalo."

Susan shakes her head and turns to Walter with a strange empty look on her face.

Clint yells, "He's just trying to save his ass! I'm your son; who you gonna believe, me or him?"

Josh lets out a chuckle, "That's right, who you gonna believe. I stood there at that window and watched your son take your wife, his stepmother and my ex-girlfriend on the same table you eat three square meals a day on. He was sucking on her breast, and she was squeezing his skinny ass with every stroke."

Walter shakes his head, "Clint would not do that to me. You're stalling."

"I see Clint brought his duffle bag. Why don't you check the contents out? I'm gonna take a wild guess and say that thing is stuffed full of your money."

Clint yells, "He's lying, it's just a coat and ammo like I said."

Josh with a chuckle, "Right, I know you all too well. You and Susan were planning on killing him as soon as I was out of the picture. Now I'm not sure how much money is in that bag, but I going to say it's whatever old Pop here kept in his safe."

Walter turns the rifle to Clint and in an angry tone, "Let's have a look in that bag boy." Clint, with fear in his eyes hesitates. Walter walks over and unties the top on the bag keeping his eyes on everyone else. Reaching inside he pulls a handful of cash out. He slowly turns to Clint, "You little bastard; you've been screwing your stepmother behind my back and now you cleaned my safe out. How did you get the combination?"

Josh laughs, "The same way he got his hands on my gun the night Willie was killed."

Walter turns to Susan, "So you two were planning on killing me out here and setting up housekeeping in my home."

Clint holds his hand up and replies, "That's not true Pop. I'm on your side. Didn't I kill Willie like you told me too?"

Walter turns to Susan standing next to him and then turns back toward Clint, "I can tell by the expression on my wife's face, that Josh is telling the truth." He pulls the bolt back ejecting an empty casing and continues, "Well, I'll tell you right now Clint, you and Josh ain't gonna make out of these mountains alive."

Susan blurts out, "Don't do it, I'm in love with him."

The old man quickly snaps his head around and gives her a puzzling look, "And which one are you in love with old loyal and faithful wife?"

"Clint! I have been for many years."

Josh snickers, "I would have saved that one for a little later, but then again your timing was always a little off."

Walter takes aim at Clint, but before he could pull the trigger Susan picks up a large rock and slams it over his skull. He falls to the ground with blood pouring from the wound, dropping the rifle at his side.

Clint smiles, "That's a good girl, now we can have it all." Josh suddenly jumps for the rifle at the same time Clint dives for it. They struggle on the ground as Clint yells for her to get the rifle. She stands there hesitating, not knowing what to do. She had just killed her husband and now two men who she cared about or at least pretended to care about were struggling on the ground. Josh easily overpowers Clint, stands him up and strikes him so hard in the jaw that it sounded like a firecracker going off.

Clint falls to the dirt as Josh turns to Susan, "Go home and tell no one the truth. Nothing is going to change the past, present or future."

She steps even closer, placing her hand in his, "We can be together now. I'll tell everyone how Clint killed Willie and his own father. We can have the life I always wanted."

"The life 'you' always wanted. That was your problem; it was always about you, you, and you." Josh continues, "That's the difference between you and Jill, she wanted me anyway she could get me, just as I am. When this weather passes, you can radio the chopper and it will return for you."

As Josh was standing there talking, Clint struggled to his feet and runs for him. Josh sidesteps him and he goes over the edge and falls to his death landing hundreds of yards, not far from Pete's body. Susan stood there for a second looking over the bluff and then turns to Josh, "Now what will I do with all that money and no one to share it with?"

Josh could not believe what he was hearing, thinking this heartless woman had just killed her husband and saw her lover fall to his death, "Damn woman, do you care about anyone but yourself?"

"I care about you."

"Yeah, right, at least until you hit me over the head with a boulder or I stumble over the edge of a cliff." He picks up the money, "If I know Jill and my best friend and I think I do; they will be racing to meet me near the border. I'll have them divide this money among the town's people who Walter has robbed all these years. You have the mansion and all the land, plus the mines. You'll never be in need. Take the trail down the south slope to a good pick-up point."

He turns, picks up the duffle bag full of money and limps off with her yelling, "We can be together now, just you and me!! Please take me with you." The rain starts to fall as she just stood there screaming. He struggles to right Elvira and then hooks the duffle bag to the back part of the seat, and with a grin rides off.

Later he comes to a stop as the rain begins to fall heavy and the roaring wind was whipping faster and faster. He turns and looks over the valley as the rain turned the desert into tiny rivers traveling down away from the mountains. It would be night in twenty minutes, and he knew between the night and this vicious storm, he wasn't going to make it, but he had to try. He took off down the western slope kicking sand in the air.......

CHAPTER 32

Hours later, Jill was trying to make out the road through the blinding rainstorm. Bubba is driving like a mad man and trying to dodge the large puddles of standing water. Jim was holding on to the crash bar for dear life as the Jeep swerved back and forth. She turns to Bubba and then to Jim, "You think he's made it yet?"

"He can take care of himself; you need to start worrying about us." Jim replies.

Jill snaps back, "What if he has one of those attacks?'

"Think positive, he's going to make it."

Bubba wipes the windshield with his hand, "This rain must be beating him to death."

Jim shakes his head, "It's going to get worse before it gets better."

"Faster Bubba!! I gotta see him before anything happens!" Jill yells.

Bubba fires back, "Jim's right, we'll be lucky if we make it!"

Back on the mountain Josh was sitting on Elvira in the heavy downpour looking to the west at the two tall rock formations called the Dragon's Teeth. They stand on each side of a gorge called the Dragon's Mouth. Another mile and he would meet Highway 81 and then cross the border and into Mexico. He looks down the long muddy slope with the rain beating in his face. It felt like thousands of sharp needles being rammed into his cheek bones. His calf had stopped bleeding and the throbbing pain had turned numb. He raises the R.P.M.s, pops the clutch and takes off down the slope. Halfway down Elvira's front tire loses its grip in the mud and slides out from under him. The big bike lying on her side races down the trail with Josh sliding not far behind her. The money bag was still strapped to her seat. The rain and mud were turning into a dirty stream as the hot pipes grinded against the ground and steam bellowed from the pipes surface.

At the bottom was a small ravine, Elvira tumbled over the side with Josh right behind her. Both landed in a small stream that was flowing rapidly as the rain filled the trench with a never-ending run off from the mountains. He slowly looks up in all directions. He struggled over to Elvira as the lightning reflected off the mud-covered chrome and the one bent mirror left after Clint had taken the other out. He rested for a second or two before standing. His calf was numb but the pain from his ribs were giving him some real trouble. Blood is caught in his throat, and he tries to clear it. The fall in the ravine only compounded matters. The fall had also torn open one saddle bag losing its contents. The big bike is getting harder to stand now. Every muscle in his body is aching. He knew that this was the last time he would be able to stand Elvira up straight, although the crash bars kept her at a tilted angle. Even a man in good shape, not wounded and rested up, had to know the trick to standing one. He learned early on to turn the front forks up and roll the bike over using your legs, which Josh, because of the bullet wounds, is having trouble doing.

Back in the Jeep, Jill yells, "How much farther!?"

Bubba quickly makes a turn onto 81, shakes his head and replies, "Longer than you think if you keep asking the same damn question over and over. Now shut up and let me drive this damn thing!!"

Jim is getting worried now, "Pull over."

She just gives him a look before asking, "What for? We're almost there."

"There are a dozen places he could come out and that's if he's still alive."

"I have already told you not to say that. He's not dead, I can feel it."

Bubba interrupts, "You're both right. We're not sure where he's coming out at, and I feel what she's feeling. He's alive, now what do we do from here?"

"I'm going to take a wild guess and say he'll be coming out near Dragon's Mouth." Jim says.

Jill asks, "How can, you be sure?"

"I'm not; there are five different ways he can get to the highway. I chose Dragon's Mouth because it's the closest to the border and it's where he came out twenty years ago."

"How far is that?"

"About five miles."

About this time a large semi-tractor rigs passes them. Bubba turns to Jim, "That's funny; a few minutes ago, there wasn't any traffic at all on this road."

Jim quickly responds, "That's because all the trucks are taking advantage of the storm. They can pass right by the weight scales, and no one will stop them with it raining like hell."

Jill yells, "Enough talk, start moving, we're wasting time!"

Jim leans forward, "Go slow, I want you two to keep an eye open for two rock formations known as the Dragon's Teeth. It will be two jagged needle rocks standing a hundred feet high."

Bubba, "I know what the Dragon's Teeth looks like; I'm not that stupid."

Josh stands the bike in an upright position with his last bit of strength and kick starts her with his right leg and with great difficulty. To his surprise she started right up. After all the slides, spills and water, she hadn't failed to start once.

"That's a girl. We can do this." Josh looks down at the fuel gauge. It was almost empty. He wipes the water and mud from his eyes and then does the same to the gauge. His jacket is torn to shreds. He looks up into the deep, dark foreboding black sky and says in a gentle voice, "I need help Lord. Just give me the strength and the gas to go a little further."

Jill and Bubba are looking to the left, but don't see the rock formations Jim had referred to. Jim is trying to look through the faded plastic windows of the ragtop. "Wait until the lightning strikes to the east. That's the only way you're gonna see them."

Josh takes off digging into the soft ground with the bike lurching forward every time the back tire strikes a hard spot. Elvira's rear tire was sliding from side to side as he worked the throttle to keep power to the rear wheel.

A few minutes later, he sees headlights on the highway. The traffic is heavier than normal, but he's made it. He did the impossible. He stops near the edge of the road as the big rigs pass by throwing up water in his face. No matter, he made it. He turns and sees the lightning as it flashes behind the Dragon's Teeth.

"Well girl… a few hundred yards down this road and we can cross the border and not a minute too soon. He works the throttle banging out a smooth roar of the big stroked out V-twin. With a smile he watches as he sees a break in the long line of trucks. He takes off entering the highway. Elvira's rear tire slips a little before gaining a grip. Suddenly a sharp pain shot through his head as if he had been struck by a bolt of lightning. He throttles down barely able to stay up straight. Water running from his soaked bandana ran down his face and into his eyes. His gets dizzy and yells, "Not now, I need more time!!"

He stops in the center of the highway and leans over the wide fuel tank, laying his forehead on the handlebars with his chin resting on the speedometer. A loud air horn screams over and over in short bursts. He struggles to lift his head only to see the two blinding headlights of a large freight liner. He smiles, "Wind and Steel, is that too much to ask?" Airbrakes lock up and the smell of wet burning rubber filled the air. The horns sounded as if it was coming from all directions. The horrific impact sent him flying fifty feet landing near a crop of desert grass near the side of the road. Elvira was shattered into a thousand pieces. Chrome is spread out for a hundred feet or more. A small, silver-plated fuel tank cape spins on the yellow line for what seems like forever, but only seconds. The money is scattered in with the pieces of motorcycle…

Jill is getting frustrated and yells, "I can't take this anymore! We will never see the Dragon's Teeth unless we get out! Stop this damn Jeep!" She jumps from the vehicle and stares over the hood into the mountains.

Bubba and Jim step out also. Jim yells over the rain, "No sense in standing in the rain, we're just going to have to wait for daybreak!!" Suddenly the sky lights up and she sees the two rock formations casting awry shadows in front of the lit-up background.

Jill, "I see something! I think I see the Dragon's Teeth."

"It's just the rain and wind playing tricks on your eyes!"

 Bubba wipes his eyes as another lightning bolt lights up the horizon silhouetting the mountains. "Wait!! She's right, I think I see something!"

"I can't see a thing, Bubba. It's just the weather!" Jim replied.

Lightning lights the sky again and Bubba sees it clearly.

"There it is, the Dragon's Teeth!!" Jim looks closer and he sees it too.

"Damn, you're right, this is it!"

Jill yell's, "But where is he!?" Bubba starts to walk closer when he barely sees flashing amber emergency lights down the road.

"What's that!?" Jill takes a hard look and takes off running. Bubba and Jim fell in behind her but could not keep up. Hundreds of yards from where they parked the Jeep, she sees the large tractor trailer rig parked at an angle to the highway with its emergency lights flashing. She gets a nauseating feeling and slows to a walk raking her hand down the side of the long-wet metal trailer. She stops near the front bumper and freezes in time as men ran to the roadside and surround Josh's mangled body. Vehicles were pulling off the road with one man taking it upon himself to flag the traffic as it started to back up. Others were placing small amber emergency flashing lights in the road. Jill runs over to the crowd and starts pulling men back struggling to get to Josh only to find his broken-up body stretched out in the grass. There on the ground he grasps for air.

A stranger yells, "Somebody get on a CB and call an ambulance!!"

Another man yells over the rain, "I have them on their way!!"

Jill slowly staggers through the crowd and takes a knee next him. Her mine was frozen in time. She slowly leans over and chokes on the lump forming in her throat.

An old man looks up at her, "I couldn't see him until it was too late. He just sat there and watched me slam into him. When my lights came up on him, I could tell he was saying something with his lips, but I'm not sure. I couldn't stop on the wet pavement!"

Another man shakes his head, "I think every bone in his body's broken. Does anyone know him?"

Jill places her hand on his forehead, then picks his head up and she places her knee under it. "I do, he's..... my man and soul mate."

About this time Bubba make it to the scene. Jim just stands there not wanting to say anything to Jill. Bubba fell to his knees and wept like a baby.

Josh struggles to open one eye with blood streaming from his wet lips and ears. He manages to grab her hand and squeezes it tight.

"Hello girl...told you I would see you...on the ...(gasp)...other side."

She leans closer, "I love you Joshua Harley James."

"I love you too Little Bit." He struggles to take a breath, "I made it. I asks the Lord, and I made it."

"You sure did."

He tries to look toward the highway, "How's Elvira?"

Jill turns and sees pieces of Elvira and money scattered across the highway.

She slowly turns back to him, "She's okay Josh, just wet and a little muddy; nothing that old Bubba can't clean up."

He smiles, "The old girl was something else, wasn't she? You should… have…seen her work that desert like she was born there. Reminded me of old Iron side…and…the mountains Jill; she never batted an eye. I'm proud of her. Only an American machine can do stuff like that."

Jill choking on every word, "She's something else Josh."

With a faint grin he says, "You and her…would have gotten along… well." He gasps for another breath of air and then continues, "Both of you are pretty as a desert rose and tough as… I can't feel my legs…Where's my Mama?"

"She'll be her soon.

"Don't you cry Little Bit; we had some good times you and me."

"We sure did. I wouldn't trade it for anything in the world."

"Will you ask Jim to help Bubba push Elvira from the road?"

"It's been done baby, it's been done."

"Tell Bubba, she takes the good gas, not that cheap…"

"You just hold on, Josh, the ambulance is on its way."

He tried to pick his head up, but he did not have the energy. Jill leans closer and kisses him on his bloody lips, "I love you Joshua Harley James."

He smiles, "Your lips are as sweet as honey…I love you, Jill! You take good care of Bubba. Remember, he likes his chicken…..I…I." He closes his eyes as his head flops to the side and passes on to a world where he could ride forever. Jill leans over and gently kisses him again on his lips again. No one could tell tears from rain drops as they ran down her face. She slowly stands and scans the crowd of people who had stopped and gathered around, then walks over to Bubba and hugs him tight. Jim walks over as a New Mexico State Trooper walks up.

"Is this the man you've been looking for?"

Jim with tears in his eyes, steps closer and stares into Josh's face, then answers, "No, this is not the man we're looking for. Looks like just another unfortunate motorcycle victim. Keep your guys looking until morning and if we don't find him by then, I'll call off the search. Tell them not to look to hard." Jim starts to walk off when he suddenly stops and turns to the trooper, "I could use a little help from some of your men picking up the money. It belongs to the town of Sun Valley."

"Sure, thing Sheriff."

Nine months later

The sound of shoes tapping out a rhythm on the freshly waxed floors could be heard throughout the corridors of the Albuquerque General Hospital. The strong odor of lemon disinfectant fills the air. Bubba, Henry, and Jim, hands filled with stuff animals and assorted baby toys with Bubba carrying a small metal casting of a Harley. They stop at the nurse's station on the third-floor maternity ward.

The nurse smiles, "What can I do for you three fine gentlemen today?"

Bubba, with grin, "How about dinner tonight, say around eightish?"

Henry bumps him in the side with his elbow and says to the nurse, "We're looking for room 324 please. I'm a damn grand pappy by God."

"Third room on the right." She points down the hallway.

They walk down the hallway and step into the room and there's Jill lying in bed smiling and holding a small baby boy in her arms. Bubba slowly and with great apprehension walks over, with Jim and Henry walking behind him like they were defusing some kind of explosive device.

Jill, with a giggle, "He won't bite."

Bubba, with a grin, "Did you say he?"

"It's a boy, Bubba."

Jim gets choked up, "So much for buying the pink stuffed bear. Look at the arms on that boy."

Henry smiles, "Finally, I'm a grandpa. I wanna be called Pappy after my great grand Pappy."

Bubba, after swallowing the lump in his throat, "Can I hold him?"

Jill grins, "You're his godfather, I guess you can if you don't drop and break him. Just remember Bubba, he's not a piece of chicken."

Bubba reaches over and gently takes the baby in his arms. "I've never dropped a piece of chicken in my life. What did you name him Jill?"

"Joshua Harley James Jr."

"Wow!! I wish Josh could see this."

Jill, with her eyes tearing up, "Oh don't worry about that, Josh will find a way. Somewhere up there in Heaven he's sitting on Elvira, looking down on us smiling with that big smile he always had."

Henry steps forward, "We planted three cactus roses between Josh's grave and his mother's, just like you told us too. And that headstone you ordered finally came in and it looks fantastic. That's if you think those things can look good."

All around the room was flowers from everyone at the Albuquerque prison facility, and the town of Sun Valley.

Jill smiles, "Was the little silver-plated Harley logo placed in the center of the head stone like I wanted?"

"They sure did."

"Good, you three go find something to do for about twenty minutes."

Bubba, as he gently hands the baby boy back to her asks, "Why? We just got here."

The nurse walks in, "Okay, it's feeding time. Everyone leaves the room except the mother and baby."

Jill says, "That's why."

Bubba is surprised by being asked to leave, "Why can't we watch?"

"Because she breast feeds him." The nurse replied.

Bubba, with a grin, "And your point is?"

"Move it Uncle Bubba." The nurse belted out in a loud tone.

Bubba snaps back, "Speaking of breast feeding; you busy tonight?"

The nurse pushes them out the door with Bubba saying, "I need to see this if I'm the godfather. I never know when I'll have to keep the little rebel while Jill cooking."

Jim shakes his head, "With those sagging breast you have there, I bet you could."

"Is that right, you look like you could feed a few yourself."

"What did you just say to me!?

"You heard me, you old Billy goat!"

"Is that right!?........

"That's right!!"

Epilogue

Jill never married and closed the café so she could spend all her time raising Little Josh. She lives her life in Sun Valley and visits Josh's Grave site on his birthday every October the 4th and every Father's Day.

Henry bought a lot of horses and business was booming again. He and Jill took Josh's money and fixed the ranch up real nice. Bubba sold the station and stays in the extra bedroom behind the ranch house with his new wife Martha. He works for Henry during the day and raises chickens behind the barn on his time off. His wife keeps him so busy he never has time to visit old lady Crenshaw's nanny goat.

Jim stayed Sheriff for a few more years, then retired and went back to selling cowboy hats and belt buckles. Cancer took his life three years later.

Susan was picked up by the National Guard chopper the next morning. Years later she married a male stripper one month after losing her new husband. He got her hooked-on drugs and cleaned her out. The mines were stripped out and she lost the mansion due to back taxes. She now lives alone in a rundown mobile home living off child support she receives for three children she birthed from failed relationships with men passing through town.

The town council voted six to zero to change the name 'Platteville' back to 'Sun Valley' and divided the two million dollars between all the people McNally screwed over except for a small portion that they used to erect a small five-foot bronze statue of Josh and his Harley and placed it in the center of the town square in honor of his passing. At the bottom of the marble stand is a small bronze plague with a dedication written on it….

Uncle Bubba closes the thick booklet and with a smile asks, "Well, what did you think Little Josh?"

"It's a great story Uncle Bubba. What does the writing say about my Daddy and Elvira?" They stand and walk over to the bronze statue.

Bubba takes a knee and leans closer, "It says, ***This plaque is dedicated to all the men who believe in Wind and Steel, the iron horse of the last***

American cowboy. Underneath this statue of Joshua Harley James and Elvira are the remains of that very bike that became a legend in Sun Valley after doing the impossible by being the only machine on wheels to cross the Flats of No Man's Land. To this day a steel cross rest out on Highway 81, on the very spot where Joshua Harley James lost his life, exactly one hundred yards from the Mexican Border. For all who reads this, we hope you find freedom and enjoyment in the simple things in life and know by these words, that money is here today and gone tomorrow, but life will always flow on."

Little Josh looks up with a big smile, "Wow, all this for my Daddy?"

Bubba stretches his arms back over his head, "Yep, now let's get home before grand Pappy eats all the food. Your Mama is frying chicken as we speak." Suddenly five F-16s fly over with the roar of thunder. Bubba looks up and says, "They sound good, but not as good as Elvira. Now that was a roar!" They start to walk off when suddenly the bottom falls out and a downpour soaks them to the bone before they can make it to the truck. They quickly open the doors and jump inside. Little Josh wipes his face with his hands and says, "So you're a weather expert huh?"

"Well, I haven't gotten it down to a science yet, but I'm working on it. And with all that being said, let me tell you another story. This one is about the greatest gas pumper of them all. This story isn't gonna take long…"

The End